MURRAY KRIEGER
AND CONTEMPORARY
CRITICAL THEORY

IRVINE STUDIES IN THE HUMANITIES
Robert Folkenflik, General Editor

MURRAY KRIEGER
AND CONTEMPORARY
CRITICAL THEORY

Edited by Bruce Henricksen

COLUMBIA UNIVERSITY PRESS

New York   1986

Columbia University Press
New York   Guildford, Surrey
Copyright © 1986 Columbia University Press

Printed in the United States of America

Library of Congress Cataloging-in-Publication Data
Main entry under title:

Murray Krieger and contemporary critical theory.

Includes bibliographies and index.
1. Krieger, Murray, 1923–   —Addresses, essays,
lectures.   2. Criticism—Addresses, essays, lectures.
I. Henricksen, Bruce.
PN75.K68M87   1986   801'.95'0924   85-19064
ISBN 0-231-06118-8

A NOTE ON THIS SERIES

This is the first in a series of volumes to be published by Columbia University Press on topics in the humanities. The series is sponsored by the School of Humanities at the University of California, Irvine. I am grateful to Dean Kendall E. Bailes and Vice-Chancellor William J. Lillyman for their support. For help with a broad range of problems, I am indebted to the Board of Directors of Irvine Studies in the Humanities. Jean Symonds gave our group secretarial support. These volumes are published in conjunction with the Wellek Lectures, given annually at the University.

Robert Folkenflik, General Editor

THE CONTRIBUTORS

HAZARD ADAMS is a Professor of English at the University of Washington, Seattle. Recently he has published *Philosophy of the Literary Symbolic* (Tallahassee: University of Florida Press, 1983) and *Joyce Cary's Trilogy* (Tallahassee: University of Florida Press, 1983).

RICHARD BERG is an Assistant Professor at Occidental College in Los Angeles and has his doctorate from the University of California, Irvine, where he studied with Professor Krieger.

MICHAEL CLARK is an Associate Professor of English at the University of California, Irvine. He published an annotated bibliography of Michel Foucault with Garland Publishing, Inc. (New York, 1983) and has an annotated bibliography of Lacan forthcoming from the same publisher. His book *Language in Colonial America* is forthcoming from the University of Wisconsin Press.

SANDOR GOODHART is an Assistant Professor of English at the University of Michigan.

BRUCE HENRICKSEN is an Associate Professor of English at Loyola University in New Orleans and is the Criticism and Theory Editor of *New Orleans Review*.

JAMES HUFFMAN is a Professor of English and Coordinator of American Studies at the State University of New York College at Fredonia. He has published essays in the fields of literature, psychology, American studies, and popular culture, and is currently working on a book on psychological approaches to American literature. His essay for the present volume was aided by a research grant from the Research Foundation of the State University of New York.

WOLFGANG ISER is a Professor at both the Universtät Konstanz and the University of California at Irvine. His books include *The Implied Reader: Patterns of Communication in Prose Fiction from Bunyan to Beckett* (Baltimore: Johns Hopkins University Press, 1974) and *The Act of Reading: A Theory of Aesthetic Response* (Baltimore: Johns Hopkins University Press, 1978). The other participants in the Konstanz Colloquy who are affiliated with Universität Konstanz are: Ulrich Gaier and Anselm Haverkamp, Professors of German; Hans Robert Jauss, Professor of French; Jürgen Schlaeger, professor of English. Gabriele Schwab has recently moved from Universität Konstanz to an Associate Professorship in Comparative Literature at the University of Wisconsin, Milwaukee.

MURRAY KRIEGER is a University Professor and Professor of English at the University of California, Irvine. He has received many fellowships and will be awarded the Humboldt Prize by the West German government in 1986. A checklist of his writings appears at the end of this volume.

VINCENT LEITCH is an Associate Professor of English at Mercer University, Macon, Georgia. He is the author of *Deconstructive Criticism* (New York: Columbia University Press, 1983).

WESLEY MORRIS is a Professor of English at Rice University. His most recent book is *Friday's Footprint: Structuralism and the Articulated Text* (Columbus: Ohio University Press, 1979).

HERMAN RAPAPORT is an Associate Professor of English and Comparative Literature at the University of Iowa. He is the author of *Milton and the Post-Modern* (Lincoln: University of Nebraska Press, 1983).

MARK ROSE is a Professor of English at the University of California, Santa Barbara. He is the author of *Aliens: Anatomy of Science Fiction* (Cambridge: Harvard University Press, 1981).

ADENA ROSMARIN is an Associate Professor at the University of Miami and was a Fellow at the Stanford Humanities Center during 1984–85. Her articles have appeared in such journals as *ELH*, *PMLA*, and *Critical Inquiry*, and her book *The Power of Genre* is scheduled for publication in 1985 with the University of Minnesota Press.

EDDIE YEGHIAYAN is an Associate Librarian at the University of California, Irvine.

CONTENTS

PREFACE

MURRAY Krieger's career as a theorist and practicing critic has traversed what seems, although we may lack perspective as of yet, an unprecedented series of tremors, shiftings, and outright ruptures in the epistemological terrain. Krieger's own texts, as though picking up sympathetic vibrations from these tremors, constitute a structure that is constantly moving and recentering itself. If one wanted to choose the most representative American theorist of, say, the past twenty-five years, the theorist within whose texts one could best study recent developments in American theory as a whole, Murray Krieger would be the most likely candidate. Any study of Krieger's work is also a study in microcosm of recent theoretical history; his early attempts to correct formalism along more philosophically rigorous lines, his existentialism, his attempts to account for history within the framework of contextualism, his increasing interest in phenomenology, his more recent acceptance of an anthropological/reader-response perspective, and finally, his encounter with Derridean deconstruction, are just some of the ways his theorizing has responded to contemporary theoretical history as a whole.

However, it would do scant justice to Krieger's texts to claim for them simply a mimetic or responsive function. For one thing, changes in the theoretical terrain have themselves been initiated by these texts, as *The New Apologists for Poetry* was a powerful force compelling the reevaluation of New Criticism; primary vibrations also occur in Krieger's work. Secondly, his responses inevitably harmonize with the evolving structure of his own work, each new response or appropriation revealing another aspect of an increasingly sophisticated structural development. It might be proper to see this development as an enactment within theory of the very claims he makes for poetry under the nomination "contextualism." If the poem creates an all embracing context which includes the outside within its own structure—if its walls are at once windows and mirrors—this is also true of Krieger's own theoretical discourse and its relation to an outside discourse of contemporary theory that is also its inside. Thus his own text, like the poem, is an organic structure of paradoxes, and there is always an element of self-reference in his poetics, which is also always, one might say, a "theoretics."

But Krieger's acceptance of paradox—of a theoretical language bearing the traces of poetic language—is one of the reasons he is a controversial figure, as the essays in this volume demonstrate. The Kriegerean persona who remains responsive to the centered word, the closed poem, and the humanistic tradition is unacceptable to the deconstructionist, no matter how much the other Krieger of the open poem and the absent signified may claim an equal "presence." The opposition between these two Kriegers, the deconstructionist might say, is dialectical, failing to deconstruct and thus enact a post-structural analytic. And both Kriegers are identical twins from the point of view of the Marxist, who sees them as conspiring to depoliticize theoretical language.

The foregoing is to suggest some, but by no means all, of the issues dealt with by the essays in this volume, essays chosen to constitute an appreciation, which is nonetheless analytical and critical, of Krieger's achievement. No one would expect or even desire that Krieger satisfy every theorist on the scene, and, on the other hand, it is respectable intellectual work for other theorists to remain unsatisfied.

Yet his syntheses have suggested a sophisticated sort of *bricolage* even to theorists who do not accept his specific propositions or conclusions. One thinks, for instance, of recent attempts to synthesize Marxism and deconstruction, or Marxism and psychoanalysis. If theorists are again beginning to seek ways to meet upon some common ground, Krieger's career of open and responsive discussion argues for the value and presents a model of such a quest.

B.H.

ACKNOWLEDGMENTS

THIS volume originated with the inspiration of Richard Berg, who communicated to *New Orleans Review*, early in 1982, the idea of publishing papers on Murray Krieger that had been delivered at the 1981 MLA convention. The journal was receptive, and Mr. Berg contacted the authors of those papers (Mark Rose, Vincent Leitch, and Murray Krieger), contacted Michael Clark and Wesley Morris about writing additional papers, and conducted his own interview with Professor Krieger. These papers, and an extensive bibliography by Eddie Yeghiayan, were published in NOR, vol. 10, no.1, and are reprinted with permission. Hazard Adams, who chaired the MLA session and wrote an introduction to the NOR issue, generously retains the role of moderator by introducing this volume.

In addition to the invaluable initial efforts of Richard Berg, others have helped shape this volume with their suggestions or through their own work on Krieger. I am particularly grateful for suggestions offered by Gregory S. Jay, David Miller, and Robert Folkenflik, and for the assistance of William Germano and the Columbia University Press editorial staff and referee readers. Richard Johnson, my departmental chairman, has been patiently supportive in his awareness of the time consuming nature of editorial work.

Two institutional debts are to the Mellon Foundation

for sponsoring a workshop at Rice University, where I met Wesley Morris and Frank Lentricchia, and to Loyola University of New Orleans for funding my attendance at the School of Criticism and Theory, where I met Professor Krieger, Adena Rosmarin, and Herman Rapaport. That summer at Northwestern University was another of the beginnings of this volume.

Thanks to John Mosier for introducing me and the secretarial staff here at Loyola to the mysteries of the disk, the console, and the screen. Lisa Carter, Bobbie Porter, and Mary Metoyer helped in preparing the manuscript—a very special thanks to Mary for her cheerful, energetic, and skillful assistance during what must have seemed like an eternal twilight of typing and retyping.

Abbreviations of Frequently Cited Works
by Murray Krieger

AL   *Arts on the Level: The Fall of the Elite Object*. Knoxville: University of Tennessee Press, 1981.

AP   "An Apology for Poetics." *American Criticism in the Post-structuralist Age*, Ira Konigsberg, ed. Ann Arbor: University of Michigan Press, 1981.

CV   *The Classic Vision: The Retreat from Extremity in Modern Literature*. Baltimore and London: Johns Hopkins University Press, 1971.

NAP   *The New Apologists for Poetry*. Minneapolis: University of Minnesota Press, 1956.

PPC   *The Play and Place of Criticism*. Baltimore: Johns Hopkins University Press, 1967.

PPI   *Poetic Presence and Illusion: Essays in Critical History and Theory*. Baltimore: Johns Hopkins University Press, 1979.

TC   *Theory of Criticism: A Tradition and Its System*. Baltimore: Johns Hopkins University Press, 1976.

TV   *The Tragic Vision: The Confrontation of Extremity*. Baltimore and London: Johns Hopkins University Press, 1973. Reprint of *The Tragic Vision: Variations on a Theme in Literary Interpretation*. New York: Holt, Rhinehart & Winston, 1960.

WC   *A Window to Criticism: Shakespeare's Sonnets and Modern Poetics*. Princeton: Princeton University Press, 1964.

Additional Abbreviation

ANC   Lentricchia, Frank. *After the New Criticism*. Chicago: University of Chicago Press, 1980.

MURRAY KRIEGER
AND CONTEMPORARY
CRITICAL THEORY

INTRODUCTION: THE GENTLE BEHEMOTH

Hazard Adams

THIS collection of essays has in its making a complicated history, beginning with the session on literary criticism of the Modern Language Association meetings in December 1981, arranged and chaired by myself and entitled, "The Criticism of Murray Krieger: The Question of Presence." The true source, of course, is Murray Krieger's long, pioneering service to the enterprise of literary criticism and theory in America. Author of eight books and numerous shorter works, Krieger has developed over thirty years a subtle literary theory in the venerable tradition of the apology for poetry, extending it to an apology for poetics; and he has been at the forefront of pedagogy in a field he himself has pioneered. At the Modern Language Association session, Mark Rose and Vincent B. Leitch presented their papers just as we have them here. (In order to maintain the flavor of the original event both have been constrained from extending them.) Krieger responded with the engaging remarks entitled "Both Sides Now," also unrevised. Shortly thereafter, Richard Berg recorded his interview with Krieger.

Then Bruce Henricksen entered the picture, commissioning essays by two former students of Krieger, Wesley Morris and Michael Clark, and publishing all six in the March 1983 issue of the *New Orleans Review*. Now, Henricksen has collected several more essays and a transcription of Krieger's colloquium at the University of Konstanz to compose the present volume. I am honored to have been asked to write the introduction to this collection of writings about the work of a brilliant theorist, respected colleague, and valued friend.

Let me return for a moment to the original scene (if I may indulge in unfashionable nostalgia; for some theory-minded readers these texts are radically free of their original spoken events). The Modern Language Association session honored an active theorist whose writings from the time of his first book *The New Apologists for Poetry* (1956) constitute a major body of critical theory that has gradually and surely become well known in Europe and Asia as well as in America. I say *active* theorist because this collection certainly does not mark a culmination of Krieger's career, which has continued to develop in subtlety and scope. It is by no means, then, a festschrift, but rather an examination of Krieger's theoretical accomplishment to date. The essayists here show that Krieger's work is capable of generating a variety of responses, sometimes in conflict, sometimes emphasizing special aspects. At the same time, many of the commentators return to certain themes in Krieger's recent work that address current fashions in literary theory, influenced as it has been so profoundly by Post-Structuralism and now by an upsurge of historico-political concerns. Krieger's recent work, of course, attempts to offer an alternative to deconstruction as it is usually presented and perceived. I shall take the liberty of calling him a "constructionist," admitting at the same time that his constructions have a considerable irony about them.

Issues surrounding Krieger's brand of construction are central to the early essays in this volume. The question that seems first to have to be settled is whether there is, after all, any sense (as Krieger wants there to be) in which we can claim that in poetry (providing there is such a thing) the linguistic signifier can have a relation to a signified other than that of difference. For Krieger, with important reservations it can contain its signified; this miraculous situation (which is also for Krieger *not* a miracle) can only be expressed in paradoxes such as have always been present in theories of the symbol since the eighteenth century, but which are given a subtle and unique formulation in Krieger's concept of an illusion that we know as illusion, and actually constitute as illusion, even as we submit (almost) to its power.

In the essays which follow there are generally three responses to Krieger's position on this matter: a) profound skepticism about any theory that must have recourse to paradox (Vincent B. Leitch); b) efforts to unravel the paradox and complete the system by naming a place between or transcending Krieger's polar opposites (Michael Clark, who cunningly attempts to provide the solution via Jacques Lacan's theory of desire, and James R. Huffman, who has recourse to recent logical analysis); c) willingness to accept paradox as an ending (never ending) place for theory (Adena Rosmarin, and, I might add, were I to have submitted an essay, myself). Woven into these central concerns are questions rather more peculiar to Krieger's own work—for example, *ekphrasis*, the central term of perhaps Krieger's most striking essay, discussed here critically by Herman Rapaport, who finds it inadequate to a reading of Spenser and outlines an alternative phenomenologico-Lacanian approach. Another question involves to what extent Krieger's theory is a theory of fictions and connected to the Vaihingerian notion of "as if" and, perhaps, the poetry of Wallace Stevens. Adena Rosmarin addresses this question in a provocative essay that would see Krieger's work in the neo-Kantian tradition of fiction theory.

There are also questions of how much remains of Krieger's early existentialism and what role the historical has in his theory today. This is Wesley Morris' concern in a subtle essay that considers Krieger's whole career, and it is also that of Bruce Henricksen, who finds that Krieger's poetics isolate him from history and thus politics but sees the possibility of opening up channels to those things by working outward or expanding from Krieger's theory.

The two papers in at the origin, written for oral presentation, set forth the central issues that these other matters circle around. Of the two, that of Mark Rose is more nearly a piece of direct explication. For him, Krieger puts equal weight on the presence of the signified in the signifier and on its absence, though of course Krieger claims that the presence is a special sort of illusion, not the "transcendental signified" denied to be possible by Jacques Derrida. Rose sees Krieger as a paradoxist and notes that his presence/illusion paradox has its parallels in his treatment of space/time and closure/openness. He sees Krieger viewing man as a heroic creator of forms; his Krieger quests for an absolute authority, but is always returned (always returns) to the quarrel of existence with forms. Thus Krieger's early existentialism, most evident in The Tragic Vision, is organized into one half of an opposition, the other pole of which is a celebration of cultural possibility and not merely the repression of bourgeois culture that concerns Wesley Morris in his essay. Rose's Krieger, like the good natured Behemoth of Thurber's cartoon, who is asked "What have you done with Dr. Millmoss?" by someone whom we can for a moment imagine to be an anxiety-ridden academic, swallows all theory preceding him, finding a place, if sometimes only a secondary place, for all of it worth attention.

Vincent B. Leitch sees Krieger differently. Coming from his own deconstructionist commitment, he characterizes Krieger as a "believer," with which appellation he quaintly associates quaintness. There is an element of this also in Wesley Morris' attitude toward aspects of Krieger's earlier theory, which he identifies with a just post-World War

II sensibility, issues of survival being now no longer individual, as Krieger then saw them, but collective. This theme of obsolescence appears here and there in recent books where writers critical of Krieger take him up. (Some of these writers are discussed in James R. Huffman and Sandor Goodhart's essays; in the interview with Richard Berg, Krieger comments wryly but I think fairly on one attack against him.) Leitch regards Krieger's "formalist way of writing" as passé and a "rhetorical trick," merely figurative at the critical points and, therefore, in his view suspect. However, a good Post-Structuralist of Derridean stamp, which Leitch certainly is, ought to acknowledge that his own discourse is caught up in the same deceptive behavior and that it is unavoidable, there being either no "mere figures," or there being nothing but "mere figures." Leitch, nevertheless, raises the central question on which so many of these essays turn: Does Krieger really have it both ways, which is to say, can Krieger really have it both ways, or is the opposition of presence (as illusion) and absence, alleged to be in equal balance by Rose, still weighted nostalgically toward presence, formalism, contextualism, closure, and the like? For Leitch the answer is clear. It is so weighted. Krieger, therefore, becomes a theologian of humanism, an especially anxious one seeking "security and self-protection."

Others, like Adena Rosmarin, acknowledge the anxiety in Krieger's work. (A critic once observed to me that Krieger's writing always wore a belt and suspenders.) Rosmarin sees it especially when he first had to confront post-structural absence, but she sees Krieger also as having worked through this crisis to a greater confidence. I think it fair to say that the anxiety to save critical tradition and the canon of great works remains and that, in fact, Krieger's work was given new life by the confrontation with Post-Structuralism. For Leitch, on the other hand, Krieger is a "stoical figure" who "worries the hedonism of his times." This remark must be somewhat amusing to Krieger, given the recent charge of hedonism leveled against him by the anti-deconstructionist Frank Lentricchia. Together, these responses put him somewhere between two extremes: just where I am sure he desires to be. For Leitch, Krieger's alleged emphasis on presence at the expense of absence makes him produce only the illusion of truth, not, as the paradoxical Krieger might put it, the truth of illusion. So we have Rose explicating Krieger as Krieger would more or less have it, and Leitch saying, wait a minute, don't be taken in, as Krieger has perhaps been taken in, by his own rhetoric of paradox: Krieger's claim for balance only disguises the anxiety of an old-style formalist.

Krieger's lively answer, with its allusion to Joni Mitchell's popular song, holds out against Leitch for semiotic doubleness and the truth of paradox, declaring that "we are less than satisfied when we do not find it." (I might add that this is hardly a hedonistic satisfaction.) Krieger holds out for what I would call the necessity of "as if" *as* "as if." Yet it is understandable that Leitch sees Krieger privileging presence. In recent years the pendulum has swung so violently toward a privileging of absence that it has become the harbor for a belief itself, whereas the original impulse was one of skepticism. Many today cannot imagine an idea of presence without connecting it with an allegedly outmoded religiosity, political reaction, and nostalgia for a day of repressive order—before the appearance of the new trinity of Marx, Nietzsche, and Freud and the eventual making of absence the only conceivable object (non-object) of worship. The history of this development will one day be written from beyond it, and its writer is likely to marvel over how Saussure's linguistic theory, designed to delimit linguistics as a special form of study and coming down to us in the distorting notes of some students, spread abroad and engendered belief beyond its intended boundaries.

One need not assume with Leitch that Krieger's rhetorical emphasis on presence jeopardizes his theory of opposites. (One could, incidentally, very well argue that Krieger has so hedged around his concept of presence that the terror of absence still rules.) Krieger's desire to save presence in some form stands out partly because the present situation demands a restoration of the conflict or balance (one can't make a choice between these two terms) that the theory requires. Krieger's emphasis is a social act based on a theory, but unlike and superior to many such acts, it *does* bring in the opposite. This is exactly what so many acts by lesser theorists fail to do: distinguish their own emphasis from their theory, allowing emphasis to rule entirely in the form of a crude polemic. Krieger speaks to this matter of "both sides now" when he responds to Leitch's complaint of irrationality, by which Leitch means that Krieger is absurdly content with paradox.

Krieger once remarked to me that he finds the greatest critical theorists to be those whose writings contain some great unresolved contradiction or incompatibility. Is it not true that there is always unresolvable contradiction in critical theory? Whatever the answer to that may be, it seems that Krieger has sought to tame the contradiction in his own work by constructing a theory paradoxical at its very base, thus preserving the contradiction, but on his terms and in his language. It is this, of course, that some of his commentators see as an evasion or breach of reason that renders his position untenable or only a beginning. To others, it means an unwarranted closure or repression.

Adena Rosmarin sympathizes with Kriegerian paradoxicality. She divides us all not into Coleridge's Platonists and Aristotelians but instead into Platonists and Kantians. For her, Krieger is one of the latter; he is also both a radical innovator and a traditionalist. For her, Krieger's radicalism is his insistence that the critic appropriate the poet's language of paradox. This she sees as the thing about Krieger's work that most irritates his critics, and she hastens to introduce the element that, when it does not irritate them, most baffles them. This is, in her Vaihingerian words, the "as if" implicit in Krieger's critical categories, critical fictions chosen purposively for their explanatory power. The poem is presented to us by Krieger as a normative category, and his goal is to create a hypothesis for the form of a poem, not a right reading. He is explicitly deductive; there is no poem-in-itself in Krieger's poem. So Krieger moves from a traditional correspondence theory and induction through to coherence and deduction, unfolding what can be known within his own schemata.

Here Rosmarin sets forth her sense of what I call critical irony. Any piece of criticism, were it to be a perfect correspondence, "would lack conceptual or aesthetic value of its own as well as heuristic power." It would have no power to interest us or to discover anything. She points out that if we begin with this assumption—that our access to the poem is biased—we shall be paradoxically more "accurate" about it. This she sees as the way of Krieger's paradoxes. His definition of the poem is, then, not as disinterested as the poem he defines, and it ought never to be. Criticism is an activity that must define its own ground. All this brings Rosmarin to stating a connection between Krieger's constitution of the poem and the making of fictions as Vaihinger describes them. If she is correct about this, and we should remember that Krieger disavows the connection Lentricchia makes between him and the fiction-making of Stevens, we must hasten to say that Krieger's fictions are far more sophisticated than Vaihinger's. The latter stood helpless before literary fictions, which he dismissed in a footnote as "figments" (a point those who have canonized him overlook). Rosmarin returns in the end to Krieger's paradox and her belief in the almost universal misunderstanding his critics have had of it. They have not recognized the role of fiction-making that Krieger, she says, finds necessary to criticism, the process inevitable to critical discourse.

James R. Huffman would dispel all paradox. Krieger's paradoxes he sees as signs of "logical impasse in contextualism," and he sets out on a quest to discover a logic that will resolve them, claiming that Krieger's logic is old fashioned. At the same time, he attacks those who consider Krieger's work obsolete, rejecting the view of Grant Webster on this point. Webster steals from Thomas Kuhn's theory of paradigm shifts in the history of science and vulgarizes it, Huffman claims, to argue that radical shifts render theories suddenly obsolete, as in Kuhn's notion of science. (Anyone with a passing acquaintance with the history of critical theory should have a hard time swallowing this idea, considering the astonishing persistence of certain theories and issues.)

Huffman sees Krieger as trying to be empirical *and* systematic, though he is interested primarily in Krieger's system. He sees Krieger's early work as concerned with the paradoxes and oppositions that Krieger found in New Critical practice; in the later work he sees Krieger working paradoxes into system. He wants to find a transcendent term, certain that there is a logic that will resolve paradox, thus satisfactorily completing Krieger's theory. This sort of event he believes to have occurred in science. He faults Krieger not for the imagination of his theory but for returning endlessly to the law of contradiction, which he believes is a superseded law in logic, and not forging ahead with the help of more advanced logics. It is an interesting question whether the successful logics that Huffman points to can successfully be transferred to literary theory. From Krieger's point of view, I should think, there is no logic that can fully cope with poetry, and paradox is a form of ironic resort in critical performance. It is on this point, after all, that Krieger diverges from the most fashionable contemporary theories. (It is also possible that new logics only hold for a while in the realm of science before paradox again appears.)

Critics have from time to time sought to banish the matter of history, like the matter of Troy, but never successfully. The New Criticism was, of course, vigorously opposed by various historical schools, including the old-style philologists, so-called literary historians, and sociologists of various stripes. Krieger has claimed always to have given attention to history—as a practicing critic he has been interested espe-

cially in the Renaissance and the eighteenth century—but
before we can understand the extent or limitation of that
attention, we must understand what "history" means to
him—and to his critics.

One of Krieger's former students who has paid close
attention to history or, in contemporary parlance, the diachronic is Wesley Morris. In his essay, he quickly recognizes
that the term "history" itself is problematical, noting
Krieger's dual usage of the term and questioning whether this
dual usage is proper. In fact, it might be best—particularly in
the light of Bruce Henricksen's essay that follows—to sort out
various notions of the term alluded to or implicit in these
essays or in Krieger's own work: 1) There is history as pure
flux, in Kantian terms unknowable in itself. 2) There is, in
Kriegerian terms, the "living, felt, pulsating history of breathing man" that separately exists but comes only into know-
ability in the poem. This is, for Morris, in the early Krieger an
existential world from which art constitutes a "Manichaean"
density of experience. 3) There is the Marxist "objective"
notion of history, as in Henricksen's essay, which refuses the
name of history or reality to the Kantian thing-in-itself of
definition 1. 4) There is history as *constituted* by historians, a
neo-Kantian notion. 5) There is history written *objectively*,
which inevitably displays a Marxist development. Indeed, in
the Marxist view, no history can fail to produce a picture of
that truth, for bourgeois history inevitably expresses contradictions interpretable plausibly only in Marxist terms.

In a far-reaching essay, Morris charts, with the economy
and subtlety of one who has closely studied Krieger's early
work, the history of Krieger's existentialism, his adoption of
the idea of "Manichaean" disorder, his revising of the theory
of his teacher Eliseo Vivas, and his constant concern with
historical tradition and the social role of criticism (a point
about which some of Krieger's critics are skeptical). Morris
sees the departure from Vivas as Krieger's calling into question the first term of Vivas' triad "subsistence, insistence, and
existence," holding that Vivas' notion of subsistence of mean-

ings and values on the threshold of society is reactionary and "politically vicious." He notes Krieger's muting of this idea in his later work. In his view, it always conflicted with Krieger's existential Manichaeanism. But in observing this, Morris would turn Krieger's views toward a notion of history that is very close to a Marxist one, and he tends to suppress Krieger's continued curious mixture of neo-Kantianism and the existential: "Have I departed too far from Krieger, employing much of his terminology to distort his theory?"

Bruce Henricksen would say "yes" to the extent that he believes Krieger does not reach a notion of history consistent with definition 3 above. This failure Henricksen sees as an incapacity to reconcile historical constitution in literature with the history objectively outside and affecting literature. Henricksen calls for greater appropriation of a "hermeneutics of suspicion" to get beyond the closure of the poem and into the social and historical field. In order to accomplish this, Krieger must escape from his early poetics.

At this point, one is tempted to rewrite Adena Rosmarin's rewriting of Coleridge and claim that apparently everyone is either a Kantian or a Marxist. What Krieger seems stubbornly to hold to, and what worries both Morris and Henricksen, is the neo-Kantian idea that history is constituted. This would mean that Krieger's existential realm is always already constituted, that his Manichaeanism is a constitution of poetic imagination, and that the Marxist version of history, which is Henricksen's "reality," is also a constitution and would be, to use Henricksen's own term, a flight from a deeper reality. Henricksen moves at the end of his essay to recognize that to speak with any confidence of history is to court the charge of naive realism that Krieger might well make against him. Henricksen's solution to this Kantian/Marxist impasse is twofold—to suggest that we recognize history as extra-literary but still constituted within textuality, and to adopt a fictive notion of the extra-textual that is social and political rather than existential. This does not, I think, relax the opposition of the Kantian to the Marxist, for it

merely displaces the issue of the activity of constitution. In-
vocation of the shadowy Lacanian symbolic will not erase
but only exacerbate this fundamental question. The essays of
Morris and Henricksen clearly reveal the question at the bottom of much contemporary critical quarreling. What is prior?
Which can swallow which?

Lacan figures also in Michael Clark's essay, as does
phenomenology, which Clark sees Krieger attempting to join
to formalism. Clark remarks of Krieger's "tautological logic,"
which Leitch believes is no logic at all, but merely rhetoric.
However, accepting the illogic that Krieger holds to in order
to respect the experience of the poem, he attempts to go beyond it to discover the missing term that he believes stands
between or bridges the gap between the poles of Krieger's
paradoxes. By claiming to find a relation between Lacan's
theory of the "psychoanalytic properties of the trope" and
Krieger's "aesthetic theory of metaphor," he attempts to supply Krieger with an unparadoxical concept that will replace
the mystery or miracle that, in his view, has remained resistant to Krieger's aesthetic.

Krieger's own career at one time embraced the notion
of miracle and then qualified it severely by invoking perilous
balance in the critical act, insisting on paradox not only in
the poem but also in its reading. Krieger would not care for
the Lacanian solution for the simple reason that he deeply
distrusts the use of any vocabulary from another discipline
trailing its epistemological assumptions into the critical act.
He knows all too well the problems this raised earlier in the
century in both politically and psychoanalytically oriented
criticism of the thirties and forties. The recent critical world
has been insistently interdisciplinary, and the danger he sees
in this (along with some virtues, perhaps) is the capturing of
the poem for naive (vulgar?) ideological purposes. In this he
may be, as Morris claims, somewhat out of date, but if that is
the case now, perhaps we should wait awhile before pro-
nouncing him dead. This concern has a way of rising up
periodically in criticism as a necessary response to ideologi-

cal crassness, of which we have seen quite a bit in recent years, to say nothing of faddishness.

One of the those problems that does not go away Krieger addressed in his essay of 1965 "The Ekphrastic Principle and the Still Movement of Poetry, or *Laocoön* Revisited." It is proper that one of the essays here treat the matter of *ekphrasis*, the literary imitation of plastic form, because it continues to be one of Krieger's main interests. Herman Rapaport's essay, which in its own right is a piece of literary analysis, studies a passage from Spenser's *Faerie Queene* in order to claim an instance where *ekphrasis* resists the model advanced by Krieger, which he regards as oversimplified. At the base of Rapaport's difference with Krieger is Rapaport's theory of perception, borrowed from Merleau-Ponty. Rapaport also invokes Lacan's psychoanalytic theory to argue that *ekphrasis* is a manifold of perceptual styles that can only be temporarily unified as a particular conception of a work and not as a definitive model for art. Rapaport argues that Krieger's formalist assumption requires that he translate art into a "logically continuous and stable model," while phenomenological analysis is less reductive and considers phenomena by way of how consciousness constitutes them. (We should remember here Rosmarin's analysis of Krieger as having a system of theoretical fictions, implying that a constitution must be quite aware of its reductiveness.) Rapaport's own analysis of the *Faerie Queene* passage, it seems to me, stabilizes by way of allegorization what he gazes on.

The most violent lengthy attack on Krieger's work has come from Frank Lentricchia's *After the New Criticism*, the title of which apes the title of an essay written by Krieger in the sixties. Sandor Goodhart points this out in his analysis of Lentricchia's analysis and speculates on the relation between the two former colleagues. Goodhart is sympathetic to Krieger and discusses Lentricchia's criticism as one that does not escape from the clutches of its own object of attack. It is *The*

Tragic Vision, according to Goodhart, that Lentricchia ignores and cannot encompass. In its implication of Manichaean conflict and monstrosity, still in his view present in the later work, Krieger's theory escapes reducing "the discourse of literature to just another form of institutional practice," while Lentricchia's analysis fails to escape.

It is clear from the interview with Richard Berg which follows that Krieger does not identify himself with either of the most fashionable forces—deconstructionists and (roughly) Foucaultians—on the scene today, being doggedly committed to his paradoxes and ever willing to explain their necessity once again under the various forms he has given them or borrowed for them—systematic duplicity, covert containment of the anti-poem, unmetaphoring (from Rosalie Colie), counterlogic, and so on. He freely admits holding on to "a notion of argument that is clearly pre-deconstructionist," while at the same time driving that argument to an antinomial conclusion. Indeed, he goes so far as to speculate that this element may be the only one that appears consistently from his early to his later work.

Much of the interview is devoted to Krieger's observations, teased out by Berg, of Lentricchia's discussion of his work. It is on the matter of the counterlogical that Lentricchia focuses an attack that is nearly an outright dismissal or at least an assertion that Krieger is an old fashioned formalist who trivializes literature by cutting it off from life. In this view, Krieger represents the last gasp of a Kantian aestheticism that must now be viewed with contempt. Krieger believes that Lentricchia has made him an object of misplaced anxiety and that in reducing him to a hedonistic theorist of fictions he has turned him into Wallace Stevens, one of the favored subjects of Lentricchia's first book.

The interview ends with speculation about the fashionability of theory today, the dangers to established academic processes in some forms of it, and what is very nearly a confession of nostalgia for "the days when criticism assumed for itself the crucial roles of mediating between literary works and the culture and of ruling as the arbiter of taste." Krieger sees us quite possibly approaching an academic crisis generated by the recent turns of theory in a number of areas. No one among his commentators addresses this interesting observation, which Krieger makes sound almost apocalyptic. Will the new theoretical fashions break the boundaries between academic disciplines, restructuring universities? Certainly some restructuring may occur, but academic organization has never—witness English departments—corresponded to disciplines very rigidly; and many departments are collections of disciplines—witness English departments again—rather than being definable in terms of a single one. So though disciplines may change radically, organization and behavior may not change as radically. Why have not these remarks of Krieger's interested his commentators? Perhaps because he, by virtue of longer professional experience and more attention to history, can see the issue more clearly as perpetrating a possible crisis, and because he has seen some of it before. He fears that the discourses of the social sciences threaten the critical activity, which in his view must call their capacities for mastery into question. This to him is an ethical issue. One senses that the questions I mentioned as having been raised by Morris' and Henricksen's essays may have to be answered in the realm of ethics.

In the summer of 1982, Krieger traveled to the University of Konstanz in Germany, where his colleague at Irvine, Wolfgang Iser, spends part of every academic year. The transcription of the Konstanz colloquium that ends this book is not a faithful transcription of what actually went on there, because the questioners later reformulated their questions, improving them perhaps by hindsight, and this required Krieger to revise some of his answers. The point of departure for the colloquium was Krieger's essay "An Apology for Poetics" (1981), an essay of considerable importance in the Krieger canon. Krieger's position seems to have been received in a friendly way by the members of the colloquium at Konstanz, where concern for the role of readers, rather than deconstruction, holds sway. Wolfgang Iser presents a brief, shrewd introduction emphasizing the oppositions closure/openness and metaphor/metonymy, arguing that in his use of these concepts, Krieger stands between the New Critics and the Post-Structuralists.

That Krieger should have a sympathetic hearing at Konstanz is explained by his own statement at the outset, where he allies himself with the reader-response theorist Iser to the extent that he is not interested in the ontological status of the work but instead in the phenomenological. This statement, while certainly correct, does not, however, cement the alliance at more than a very abstract level. Nor because Krieger speaks here with interest about the reception-theory of Hans Robert Jauss, one of his Konstanz inquisitors, does this really identify him with those methods in any significant way. Krieger sees that Jauss' historical study of reception may connect to his own desire to preserve the notion of an historical literary canon which calls upon every age for interpretation.

Here we observe Krieger confronting a group of critics schooled in a different critical language, extending his position and encompassing others. (The activity is particularly noticeable in his response to Gabriele Schwab.) This is why I have succumbed to the temptation to characterize Krieger as the Gentle Behemoth of critical theory, the swallower of others. Here I leave the matter of these essays and colloquia only to remark that Krieger accepts a poetics based upon a concept of poetic value which comes from experience and refuses any theory that does not, or at least he chews it up very thoroughly.

But now I invoke the privilege of long colleagueship and friendship and turn to an aspect of Krieger's work mentioned only in passing by a few of our commentators. This is his pioneering commitment to the teaching of the history of criticism and literary theory. When I first met Krieger sometime in the mid- to late fifties, I felt a sense of colleagueship with him in an enterprise—need I call it a conspiracy? At the time, I was not sure how many of us there were, but I was certain not many. We shared the notion of criticism and theory as a discipline, understanding of the history of which was a necessary ground.

None of this seems unusual today (although the emphasis on history is quaint to some). The situation has much changed. By the mid-seventies Krieger and I had founded the School of Criticism and Theory to give voice not to theory so much as to provide a place for discussion of the immense variety of it that had become of interest to academic critics. In the forties and fifties, both the New Criticism and the old historical scholarship with which it struggled in English departments were atheoretical. On the one hand Krieger was theoretical and on the other historical and critical, though his notion of the history of critical theory was not that of the leading belletristic anthologies. Nor was critical theory itself identified in his mind with the phrase as it emerged from the German sociologists. Rather it meant *literary* theory. Krieger paid attention to aestheticians and philosophers. What I shall call "practical Kriegerism," which is ethical in the Kantian sense of practical as well as practical in Richards' sense, has never abandoned the principle that the theorists of the past are important to us and that each deserves to be considered initially in terms of the situation he has found, the language bequeathed to him, and the critical issues as his age has seen them.

Krieger has had as much to do as anyone—probably more—with making the history of criticism and theory a subject regularly taught and debated in our universities, fighting single-mindedly for it as a whole, rather than for some narrow version of it. He has always required that his students become *informed*. I am not sure that anyone before him insisted, in the face of academic convention, that he was a professor of *criticism*, not of some literary period. Today that seems not unusual, and it is a measure of his success that it is not. I suspect, however, that like many stubborn pioneers he may look with a certain irritation on the spread of theory among the ahistorically trained and those with marginal interests in literary texts. Perhaps, however, he views such people merely as innocents who have unfortunately missed the rigors of his course in the history of critical theory, initiation into the mysteries of *ekphrasis,* and the famous casebook assignment that has daunted so many graduate students over the years at Minnesota, Illinois, Iowa, and Irvine.

Whatever he thinks about all of this, while holding staunchly to his own always developing apology for poetry *and* poetics, he meets competing systems, historical or ahistorical, as if they were part of a collegial enterprise—with open arms, and jaws. He professes "both sides now," but in fact he is a man of many sides and by now, as we see here, many interpretations.

PART I: PRESENCE AND PARADOX/
FICTIONS AND LOGIC

1.

CRITICISM AS QUEST: MURRAY KRIEGER AND THE PURSUIT OF PRESENCE

Mark Rose

POETIC presence, as Murray Krieger conceives it, is, to say the least, a subtle and elusive matter. On the one hand Krieger proclaims the poem to be "utterly and ultimately present" and on the other he proclaims with equal intensity that poetic presence is merely an illusion (*TC*, 207). Thus the title of his latest collection of essays, *Poetic Presence and Illusion*, which gives equal weight to both halves of the crucial equation, plenitude and poverty, fullness and emptiness.

This studied duplicity should come as no surprise to those familiar with Krieger's work, for from the start of his career he has been a paradoxist, formulating his understanding of art in terms of polarities and contradictions. Nor should the centrality of the concept of presence in his recent work come as a surprise, for, as Krieger conceives it, the relationship between presence and absence, identity and difference, incorporates many of his favorite and most longstanding themes. Thus for him the dialogue of presence and absence is a version of the dialogue of space and time in art, the continuous struggle of poetry to escape the temporality of its medium, to "freeze its dynamics of movement into a fixed presence—and a permanent present" (*TC*, 208). The relationship between presence and absence is also, for him, a version of the struggle between closure and openness. As Krieger understands it, the poem in the process of creation is a nearly alive creature, a "growing monster," as he calls it, that struggles to separate itself from the rest of the linguistic world, becoming an organic and self-contained form that must be understood as a special linguistic system unto itself.

Presence versus absence, spatiality versus temporality, closure versus openness—all of these oppositions can be understood as versions of the basic struggle between form and chaos that has long been prominent in Krieger's thought. The ubiquity of human form-making is, as Krieger says in the preface to *Theory of Criticism*, the foundation on which he rests his intellectual machine. His conception is of man as the creator of forms, the appropriator of chaos, shaping the unthinkable world that is outside him into symbolic orders "susceptible of human manipulation and human meaning" (*TC*, xiii), and it is this heroic figure that his work explicitly celebrates.

But "celebrates," with its heartily optimistic overtones, is a poor word to capture the complex and frequently elegiac tonality of *Theory of Criticism*. For the dialogue of presence and absence, spatiality and temporality, is indeed a dialogue, and the claims of poverty are no less powerful than those of plenitude. Thus, although the poem may for a miraculous moment produce the felt sense of presence, nevertheless we ultimately return to the temporal reality that undercuts our "mythic projection of that sacramental moment of aesthetic experience" (*TC*, 209). Poems, as Krieger reminds us, "do not literally achieve self-enclosed perfection": the language of poetry "is not in truth discontinuous with discourse at large." And in the struggle between spatiality and temporality, between the synchronic and the diachronic principles, the diachronic, he says, "never loses" (*TC*, 189) in the end.

And yet to say that time never loses, as Krieger does, is not at all the same as saying that time always wins. Krieger characteristically formulates the relationship between presence and absence in such a way that neither term is allowed to dominate the other; neither is allowed to become a final resting place. Notice, for example, the way the following passage from *Theory of Criticism* enacts the paradoxes of Krieger's conception, asserting simultaneously that the miracle of poetry is believable and unbelievable, a dream and a substantial reality. The poet, Krieger says, performs verbal miracles. But words finally are only words, "so that breath drifts off into air and can have no substance. Verbal miracles dissolve into the illusions in which we can believe only by knowing of their impossibility. But the aesthetic dream of body provides the substance on which human culture as the communal dream depends. It is the dream made into our substance that provides where we live, though it is the reality as an alien substance that kills us" (*TC*, 206).

For Krieger, as this last passage suggests, the "aesthetic dream" is more than illusory because it provides the substance of the world in which we live. And yet beyond the world of forms, beyond the realm of language, is another reality, an alien realm that Krieger has invoked under various names throughout his career. An existential realm of "brawling chaos," as he often refers to it, this messy world of particulars is from one point of view the realm of vitality as opposed to the clean sterility of art. But in Krieger's writing the opposite of art is not usually life but the blank void of "fact" that is sometimes explicitly associated with death. "Art does not undo fact," Krieger remarks in a representative passage, "least of all the fact of death, so that the human mastery art embodies is provisional only. But, though externality and determinateness remain, beyond the myth of a total language and unabsorbable by it, the mastery of the word helps man create for himself where he lives, and for his fellows where they live after he dies" (*TC*, 173). Spatiality versus temporality, closure versus openness, form versus formlessness, life versus death—here, then, is still another version of the struggle between presence and absence as it constructs itself in Krieger's imagination. But now the struggle has become an explicitly moral one, a transformation that perhaps helps to explain the sense of urgency with which he has been drawn to the subject of poetic presence in his recent work.

Krieger's language in the passage that I quoted earlier about faith in verbal miracles is characteristically religious. Krieger frequently speaks of the "sacredness" of the poetic construct in which the word magically becomes flesh. We can note, too, that his conception of the "aesthetic dream" upon which the larger "communal dream" of human culture depends is a form of the traditional religious topos of life as a dream, an insubstantial pageant that must dissolve and fade, leaving, as Prospero says, not a rack behind. For Prospero, as for Shakespeare, the dissolution of the dream reveals the transcendent spiritual substance of God. For Krieger, however, the Manichaean face of reality lying behind the veil of human forms contains, in Matthew Arnold's phrase, neither certitude nor peace nor help for pain. Like Arnold's, Krieger's is an imaginative world presided over by the disappearance of God, a phrase he often invokes. Or perhaps it may be more accurate to say that it is an imaginative world presided over by a nostalgia for the God that has departed—a nostalgia, that is to say, for some final and absolute authority.

Much of Krieger's writing can, I think, be interpreted as a quest for such an authority. Sometimes the existential realm, the pre-linguistic world of inarticulate particularity, seems to function as a kind of guaranteeing authority, a test for human forms. At other times, it is man the creator of forms—another and competing version of the divine—that seems to occupy the central position in his system. The impulse to discover an adequate authority manifests itself in Krieger's concern in *Theory of Criticism* with the illustrious tradition of theorizing from Aristotle to Sigurd Burckhardt that he sees as substantiating his own discourse. And obviously it informs his treatment of the miraculous incarnation of the word that results for him in the real and sacramental presence of the poem for its reader. At once subject to time and superior to time, simultaneously closed off from the world and open to it, the poem is for Krieger a special and absolutely authoritative form of discourse, one that underwrites, so to speak, all of human culture. And yet even as he asserts the idea of an authoritative presence, Krieger acknowledges that any notion of presence is merely a myth, "air after all and not body" (*TC*, 230). There is, as I have suggested, no final resting place in Krieger's system. The quest for authority is an endless pursuit in which the holy chalice is forever gleaming in the distance only to vanish into thin air when approached more closely.

In the final chapter of *Theory of Criticism* Krieger places himself in relation to Jacques Derrida and the Post-Structuralists. Arguing that in his form of presence there is absence and that in Derrida's absence there is presence, Krieger suggests that he and Derrida "represent, respectively, the positive and the negative of a photograph, both seeming to have the same reality (or unreality) but with reverse emphases, the lights of one being the darks of the other" (*TC*, 230). Krieger's metaphor seems to me appropriate, for his project and Derrida's are indeed antithetical. The Derridean drama is the enactment of dissolutions, the dispersal of anything that might prove a barrier to the infinities of discourse. The Kriegerean drama, on the other hand, is the repeated construction of conceptual enclosures, dwelling places for the human spirit, that once inhabited turn out to require reconstruction on a larger and more ample scale.

Largeness or amplitude or myriad-mindedness are important values for Krieger, who speaks feelingly of, for instance, Shakespeare's "capacious verbal center" and Samuel Johnson's "rich, many-directed mind" (*PPI*, 54, 69). At one point, almost in passing, he defines "the proper end of the contemplative life" as the pursuit of "the ultimate catholicity of vision" (*PPI*, 301). One of the interesting things about Krieger's work is the way his poetic theory has grown considerably more ample over the past twenty-five years even as it has remained identifiably the same creature as that which made its first major appearance in *The New Apologists for Poetry*. As Krieger himself has explained, the growth of his theory has been cumulative: rather than rejecting other theories he has sought to "co-opt them, to incorporate them without undoing my own construct (if I may be dangerously candid), to see how much of them I could swallow without giving myself indigestion" (*PPI*, 202). Thus his recent attempt to ingest Derrida, to recast his own thought in terms of the notions of presence and absence and thereby to contain Derrida within a still more ample system. But it is not merely Derrida that Krieger wishes to absorb and enclose: *Theory of Criticism* seeks to become the summation and fulfillment of the entire tradition of literary theory beginning with Aristotle, as well as the summation and fulfillment of Krieger's own quarter of a century of theorizing.

Krieger characteristically speaks of the miracle at the heart of poetry as a version of the incarnation in which the word becomes flesh. He also characteristically speaks of the developing poem's drive to oneness, its will to totalization. I would point out that much the same may be said about his own theory, which is determined both to achieve autonomy, to remain a unified and complete entity, and at the same time to become as capacious, as catholic in vision as possible. What would it mean to achieve that "ultimate catholicity of vision" that Krieger sees as the goal of criticism? Would it not mean a criticism sufficiently ample to be able to see and understand everything at once, a theory as capacious as the infinite universe itself? Would it not mean, in other words, the achievement of the holy grail of absolute authority, the miraculous incarnation of the infinite mind of God in the finitude of a single autonomous theory?

Perhaps criticism always enacts its own subject. In any case, what I am suggesting is that the pursuit of the divine presence, the quest romance enacted in Krieger's theorizing—

writing which is both so charged with religious metaphor and so self-consciously paradoxical in its own simultaneous assertions and withdrawls—may also be understood as the desire of criticism to become poetry. The status of criticism in relation to poetry is of course one of the crucial theoretical questions of the present moment. Is criticism "creative"? Is it outside of literature or part of literature? Many voices today are questioning the conventional distinction between primary and secondary texts, but Krieger's is conspicuously not among them, for the integrity of his theory commits him to maintaining the gap between the magical and authoritative language of poetry and the more prosaic language of criticism. He acknowledges that criticism is an art, but for him it is an inevitably secondary art.

In a recent essay in Paul Hernadi's collection *What is Criticism?* Krieger summarizes his position in an astronomical metaphor: "The satellites that revolve about a major planet may persuade us of their independent brilliance, but satellites they remain."[1] This image at first seems straightforward enough: the poet is primary and authoritative, the critics revolve about him reflecting his light. But, curiously, the central body here is not a sun but a planet, another secondary and reflecting body. Where then is the source of light, given that there is no star present in the image? The problematical, unstable quality of this metaphor epitomizes what seems to me to be the problematical, unstable status of Krieger's writing, which simultaneously aspires to the status of poetry and vigorously disclaims any such authoritative position.

In the same volume in which Krieger's essay "Criticism as a Secondary Art" appears, Cary Nelson, writing under the title "On Whether Criticism is Literature," points out that "no matter how relentlessly critics attempt to purge their writing of its literary character, their subject matter will impart a literary quality to their prose." Nelson sees criticism as a form of writing that is inevitably divided against itself as it struggles to transcend its own metaphorical and literary nature. Rather than considering the question of the boundary

between criticism and literature as a matter of the relationship of one text to another, Nelson proposes that we approach the issue as a problem internal to critical texts. Unstable and indeterminate, the boundary between criticism
and literature is, he suggests, the decisive and constituting
idea of criticism. The relationship between criticism and literature is, he says, both the "informing anxiety" and the subject matter, the "tantalizing object," of critical discourse
(253–67).

I think that Nelson's idea of the drama of criticism as a
continuing enactment of its own unstable status is a notion
that might be fruitfully employed in the discussion of any
literary genre. In a sense, all genres operate in this way, continuously asserting their difference from adjacent genres. But
Nelson's idea seems to me especially relevant to criticism,
particularly at the current anxious moment in critical history.
And it is especially illuminating in connection with Murray
Krieger's criticism, which is at once so artfully poetic in its
strategies and so adamant about being merely a reflection of
an authoritative poetic presence to be found elsewhere. Murray Krieger deals in polarities and paradoxes. His discourse
characteristically presses itself to the extremity of unresolvable contradiction, and in the process it inevitably enacts
another contradiction, one which incorporates the informing
problematic of criticism as a literary genre.

2.

SAVING POETRY: MURRAY KRIEGER'S FAITH IN FORMALISM

Vincent Leitch

IF we share Arnold's loss of faith, we can go either of two ways: we can view poetry as a human triumph made out of darkness, as the creation of verbal meaning in a blank universe to serve as a visionary substitute for a defunct religion; or we can—in our negation—extend our faithlessness, the blankness of our universe, to our poetry. If we choose the latter alternative, then we tend . . . to reject the first, affirmative humanistic claim about poetry's unique power, seeing it as a mystification arising from our nostalgia and our metaphysical deprivation.

Stubbornly humanistic as I am, I must choose that first alternative: I want to remain responsive to the promise of the filled and centered word, a signifier replete with an inseparable signified which it has created within itself. But I am aware also that my demythologizing habit, as modern man, must make me wary of the grounds on which I dare claim verbal presence and fullness. (*PPI*, 173)

WRITING at the close of the seventies, Murray Krieger feels caught between two somber alternatives. Historically speaking, the moment of choice, the unfortunate onset, dates from Matthew Arnold's crisis of faith. The Arnoldian choice, now a century old, still remains a question of faith. In a sense, Krieger's own position, his course of action, hinges on faith. He believes.

The Truth of Poetry and the Heresy of Deconstruction

Murray Krieger believes that poetry is a "human triumph," a "creation of verbal meaning," a "visionary substitute for a defunct religion," a "unique power," a "filled and centered word," a "signifier replete with an inseparable signified," a "verbal presence and fullness." This theory of literature is, as Krieger tells us, "stubbornly humanistic" and "affirmative." It comes into being against a grim cultural background where the universe is blank, religion is defunct, metaphysics is insubstantial and every belief undergoes demythologization. In such a world, affirmation requires wariness and daring. Thus Krieger's words "I want to remain responsive to the promise" exhibit a poised, characteristic care mixed with faith, while his statement "I must choose" accepts the necessity of boldness as it asserts his belief in poetry's visionary power and meaning—poetry's "verbal presence and fullness."

The alternative to Krieger's choice is to extend faithlessness and blankness, to negate poetry and cast it as mystification and nostalgia. This second way separates the signifier from the signified, renounces the belief in poetry as triumph, unique power and vision, decenters the filled and centered word, and demystifies meaning and presence. This other road is, of course, the heretical path of deconstruction—the way of Jacques Derrida and Paul de Man, of Roland Barthes and Harold Bloom, of J. Hillis Miller and Joseph Riddel. Krieger stages his project, from the mid-seventies onward, in opposition to deconstruction; his work emerges as an alternative to the negation and blankness of Derrideanism, a way out of the passing of humanism.[1]

On Tradition, Formalism, and Faith

Krieger labels himself a *humanist*, that is, he self-consciously conceives his work as an extension and preservation of the Western cultural tradition. He also calls himself an *existentialist*, which shows up in his awareness of an anxiety about the death of God, in his perception of the nothingness and blankness of existence, and in his consciousness of death as a nonlinguistic fact (*PPI*, 208). And Murray Krieger presents himself as a *formalist*—an heir and revisionist of American New Criticism, a believer in the unique and superior power of poetic language and in the separate and distinctive status of the literary artifact. Against the dark backdrop of existential reality the great works of Western literature come forth as luminous and visionary creations of verbal meaning, as miraculous and centered signs, offering the fullness and presence of the word.

To keep his formalism dynamic and viable, Krieger constantly refines his theory of literature. In particular, he regularly takes up deconstruction, working to introject and modify its "wisdom" for his own project. In this regard, Krieger represents an important phenomenon, for he is the only well-known American formalist to confront and absorb massively and implacably the Post-Structuralist challenge. This confrontation aims not at undermining Derrideanism, but rather at preserving formalism. Few, if any, current American theorists demonstrate anything comparable to Krieger's sophisticated and wily formalist poetics.

Responding to an essay that champions the Yale school of deconstructive critics, Krieger asserts about the current status of poetry:

If belief in the poet's power to find embodiment in the word is a myth, it has been, for the critical tradition in the West from its beginnings, the necessary fiction that has permitted more than two millennia of our greatest poems to speak to us. Few critical schools in our history have done more than the New Critics did to give them voice. Thanks in large part to these critics—but before them as well—the poems have been *there*, speaking as they do, as if there is a presence in them. They make their own case for presence, and it is out of no mere nostalgia that we continue to value it in them. For presence is present tense, and while we live we must not allow ourselves to be reasoned out of it. (*PPI*, 112)

As he praises the New Critics, Krieger links them with the Western critical tradition. Formalist and humanist, he insists on the need to preserve our greatest poems and to continue our ancient traditions. He urges us "while we live" to oppose the end of humanism and the desacralization of great literature. The odd phrase "while we live" brings death into the argument, reminding us of Krieger's characteristic existential anxiety. When we are warned "we must not allow ourselves to be reasoned out of it," we understand that faith as much as reason motivates Krieger's position. Krieger is a believer.

Murray Krieger believes that the poet possesses the power to discover "embodiment in the word," that great poems "speak to us," that formalist criticism allows poems to have such "voice," that poems are "*there*," that they "speak" and have "presence in them." Krieger's conception of literature here depends on the linkage of voice and presence. The "verbal presence and fullness" of poetry oppose the absence and emptiness of *écriture*—of the isolated, written signifiers declaimed by the deconstructors.

Fictions and Figures

Krieger's formulations about *poetic presence* are more subtle then we have so far allowed. For he everywhere carefully modifies his assertions. He accepts that traditional belief in presence may be a "myth." He concedes that "verbal presence" holds the status of "as if." He tags his incarnational poetics a "necessary fiction"—a belief system that "*permits*" poetry to "speak." Noticeably, Krieger favors "if" (as in our two citations thus far).* Still, he insists that poems "make their own case for presence"—that the poetic signifier is "replete with an inseparable signified which it has created *within itself*" (my italics).

We become curious and wonder how a poem makes its own case for presence. Surely, the language of the reader, the (meta) language of the critic, produces the effect of presence. In its simplest state, the poem seems merely ink marks within margins upon mute pages. When we activate those signs (assuming they are in a recognizable code), we set going a network of linguistic allusions, references, and connections, which make our reading a cultural-personal activity. In effect, we realize the text as the creation of a reader situated within a linguistic-historical matrix of numerous and conflicting layers of signification. In its writing and in its reading, the text is an intertextual production. With connections to the poet, the reader, and various historical-semiotic frames— with links to a stratified psychology and sociology of writing and reading—poems could hardly be said to "make their own case for presence." We cannot conceive poetry as "a signifier replete with an inseparable signified which it has created within itself." The "within itself," a formalist way of writing, is a figure, a rhetorical trick. Installing this "signifier replete with an inseparable signified," Krieger suppresses the *difference* between signifier and signified. Ultimately, he seeks to avoid the absence of the signified from the signifier; he wants to delimit any sliding of the one from the other; thus he turns away from the very possibility of language, which, as Saussure demonstrates, depends precisely on the *difference* between signifiers and signifieds. Trying to save literature, Krieger abandons language.

*See the extended discussion of the Kriegerean "as if" by Adena Rosmarin (essay 4)—Ed.

Of course, Krieger knows all this, but he still reserves for poetry the sacred power to create full presence. Poetry, unlike other language, is special. This formalist notion, as Krieger knows, is an illusion. Poetic presence is an illusion, a necessary fiction, a eucharistic myth for an era of demystification.

Only through tropes and figures, employed consciously and systematically, is Krieger enabled to construct his belief and justify his faith. About one rhetorical device, in particular, he is direct and informative: "So there are several major paradoxes which I find our literary experiences to suggest—paradoxes in which I can see neither side yielding" (*PPI*, 204). For example, the poem for Krieger is through *paradox* both a reader's experience *and* an aesthetic object; both a continuous part of all discourse *and* a discontinuous, separate micro-language; both a closed, totalized, autonomous realm *and* an open network of linguistic elements; both, as Krieger puts it:

the verbal miracle of metaphorical identity *and* the awareness that the miracle depends on our sense of its impossibility, leading to our knowledge that it's only our *illusion.* . . . We both learn to see *and* distrust our seeing, as we view poetic language both as breaking itself off from the normal flow of discourse to become a privileged object, worthy of idolatry, *and* as language self-deconstructed and leveled, joining the march of common *écriture.* (*PPI*, 204–5).

The formalist side of this tropological systematic stages literature, at one moment or another, as object, vision, miracle, identity, and metaphor—all meriting idolatry. The "deconstructive" systematic casts literature as impossible miracle, self-created illusion, untrustworthy vision, leveled language, and common writing. Krieger has it both ways, though he prefers and continuously champions the sacred poetics of formalism, reserving for the "deconstructive" formulation patches of reluctant admiration tempered by painstaking analysis and strategic incorporation. He wants to press the two sides of his tangled, "impossible" paradox together, but his faith insists on hierarchy—on higher and lower or, at least, on better and worse alternatives. He prefers the miraculous over the heretical. *Poetry is metaphor.* (And illusion.)

Strategy in the Service of Saving Poetry

Rather like a theologian trying to explain and justify the Incarnation, Krieger burnishes his expositions with paradoxes wound around a founding metaphor. Just as the theologian's God is in the man, so Krieger's poetic signified is in the signifier. Thus miraculous and material realms meet in a figure. Trying to set the fracture of the sign, the *difference* between the signifier and signified, Krieger does not, like the monk, abandon or renounce language; rather he accelerates its figural powers, producing chains of tropes to minister to a fundamental metaphor (the poem as *identity*). Unlike the older American formalists, Krieger celebrates ambiguity, tension, irony, and particularly paradox, not only in individual poems, but in his overall theory of poetry and in his own work of critical discourse. In its most intense moments, Krieger's criticism is "poetic" and his commentary is "literary": his strongest language is finely figured. A bit like Rome's Tridentine liturgies, his most ornate texts seek to instill faith in an age of reformation and disbelief. In heeding reformers, Krieger ends up compromised—something of an "Anglican" amid a rabble of fundamentalists and other insistent radicals. His seems an "Elizabethan solution" manifested picturesquely in a baroque style studded with strained conceits designed to unify a cracking sensibility. More like a Donne than a Hooker, Krieger sees that all is in doubt. He fashions a particular and special faith in paradox to withstand the splittings of the era of *differance*.

Murray Krieger neither deplores nor rejects deconstruction. He incorporates and contains its "truth." This seems less a neutralization than an appropriation, an impor-

tant purpose of which, we surmise, is to satisfy a pressing
need for security and self-protection. Overcoming the "other"
establishes invulnerability. Below the surface lies a strong
desire to create a durable monument, to build a solid edifice
or "construct"—which drives Krieger to consume and absorb
a host of positions that threaten his undoing. As a theorist,
Krieger is motivated by the desire to erect a master theory
safe from the substance and potency of his rivals. There is an
inevitable connection between saving poetry and salvaging
the formalist system. When Krieger puts his own self-interest
and desire in parentheses, as he does twice in the passage
quoted by Mark Rose, he casts graphic lines of protection
around himself, which he seeks also to set around his theory.
In effect he wants to repress or bury his own longing and to
work as a pure disinterested intellect. The bind he gets into, a
priestly fix requiring a humble self-sacrifice and heroic self-
assertion, makes him a stoical figure, a conservative man of
faith who worries the hedonism of his times while proselytiz-
ing the profits and the pleasures of an old faith.

The paradoxes of Krieger's position assert themselves
almost continuously in his recent theoretical discourse. Not
surprisingly, paradox emerges as his distinguishing stylistic
trait and his main speculative instrument. About this figure
Krieger observes: "Paradox may well be less acceptable in
critical discourse than it is in poetry, but in my defense I can
say only that I can do no better and can do no less if I am to
do justice to what I find our literature requiring of its critic"
(PPI, 203). Though normally limited to poetic discourse,
paradox is here allowed to migrate to the critical text. An
account of literature demands a literary treatment. Paradox
produces paradox. One text touches another. The borderline
between poem and critical work is transgressed. To "defend"
this not quite "acceptable" procedure; Krieger invokes "justice." He is "required," as a faithful servant of "literature," to
borrow the resources of literature. Here we isolate and focus
on the work of paradox because it is the master trope that
powers Krieger's theory, style, and strategy. The general

structure of paradox—of systematic contradiction—underlies his poetics and hermeneutics, serving to found and secure an ambitious theoretical enterprise.

Although he is wary of the grounds on which he dares to claim verbal presence and fullness for poetry, Murray Krieger does forcefully issue this claim. He tempers his fervor and faith by proclaiming his truths to be illusions and fictions. He insists on the necessity of paradoxes and on their strategic value in our present situation. His fictions, figures, illusions, and paradoxes are all marshaled and deployed to save poetry—to keep the play of the signifier in check and to insure the fullness and presence of the word.

Articles of Faith

Heir to the Arnoldian legacy and faced with the challenge of contemporary deconstruction, Krieger, as humanist, constructs a complex theory of literature and criticism out of the rich materials provided by the Western tradition from the Greeks to the present time. Few leading American theorists have been as widely learned and eclectic as Krieger, and only a handful have been so single minded and thorough in building a rich and coherent system. However, no American, as far as I know, has deliberately based an entire theory on a foundation of contradictions turned into a systematics.

Though eclectic, Krieger is not finally interested in grand synthesis. He seeks rather to establish a multifaceted *formalism*. Counterpositions are absorbed as much as possible but short of undoing the work of coherent system-building.[2] While Krieger permits and favors all manner of tension and paradox, he does express preferences for certain contending elements within his system. That poets can create filled and centered words is more important and valuable, even as an illusion, than that their words can be empty and nostalgic mystifications. For Krieger, the idea that the poetic word is actually both full and empty turns out, ultimately, to be less important as an issue of truth and more revealing as a matter of faith. In other words, the truth of the paradox "empty-full" is superseded by the preferences of a faith: the fullness of the word is a stunning miracle worth proclaiming, whereas its emptiness is a dreary reality to account for. While the paradoxical truth is admitted rigorously, the faith in fullness is proclaimed, sometimes lyrically. Thus the assessment of Krieger's poetics forces us beyond questions of truth to analyses of tones. The question—"what does Krieger believe?"—becomes "what does this man of faith value most?" and not "what is true for this theorist?" To seek the truth is to collect paradoxes. To inquire after values is to uncover motivating articles of faith.

For Krieger the poem remains the origin and center of critical activity. Though traditionally a secondary art, criticism in our time threatens to substitute its own text for the central poetic work, but such centrifugal "play," such "criticism," must not re-place the poem (AL, 27–48).[3] The language of literature, superior to critical discourse, should at least moderate the presumption and arrogance of our critical will-to-power over poems. In the role of moralist, Krieger pleads with us to remain servants of the text. The tone grows more urgent in recent works.

Krieger believes that a literary work shapes and orders experience. As such, the work is an artifact or special object possessing potent forms of aesthetic closure. These distinctive features elevate the poem, giving it a place different from and above other types of discourse. With its fundamental and characteristic drive toward closure, the work exhibits an internal purposivenes and coherence, both separating it in kind from ordinary language and justifying its status as sacred object. Despite its connections with an author, a group of readers, a cultural tradition, and an historical language, the poem maintains its essential integrity, refusing to dissolve or erode under any such extrinsic and fragmenting force or entity (AL, 51–71).

The contemporary assaults on formalist articles of faith by reader-response criticism, Marxist hermeneutics, semiotics, and particularly deconstruction, threaten but do not ruin the inherent integrity of the sacred literary artifact. Thus the idolatry of art, a long-standing feature of Western formalism, lives on for Krieger, who, in spite of and by virtue of his compromises and concessions, his paradoxes and illusions, remains steadfastly committed to the old faith. Krieger is a believer—first and last. Ultimately, his faith has little to do with "truth"; he implicitly confers on it the status of "necessary fiction." This modernist strategy aims to counter the undoings and deconstructions of the post-modern era.

The Brotherhood and Critical Reading

Implicit in Krieger's system is a pattern of cultural and social ideas that now and then come into view. The poem is an elite object fit for a few. The role of the critic is to read, explain, and evaluate such works for the culture. The brotherhood of critics, sharing a similar high regard for the stability and integrity of each text, settles disputes by reference to the work. In this way the great tradition undergoes constant sifting and preservation in the present for the future. Only through restraint can the brotherhood persist and high culture continue.

Sensing that this hierophantic economy is coming undone, Krieger in recent books and articles tends toward measured urgency and zeal in keeping with his overall stoicism and sense of existential loss as well as with his commitment to the great tradition and his faith in formalist poetics. Since catastrophe seems imminent, warning and persuasion are called for. Answering the call, Krieger accepts with some reluctance the role of moralist and doomsayer. He joins a whole community composed of distinguished elder statesmen of American literary criticism, but unlike his brothers, often nay-sayers given to blanket condemnations, he works toward absorption and incorporation of the threat. In this endeavor, he broadens and enriches his own system while remaining faithful to the tradition. An obvious and unavoidable irony of this situation is that Krieger rises to the upper ranks of the brotherhood: there is high profit in incorporating contemporary philosophies of loss.

With Krieger the critical reading of literary texts is a controlled practice dependent on a set of articles of faith. When Krieger reads, he "finds" internal purposiveness and cohesion—closure and form. As artifact, the poem appears unique and miraculous, a human triumph. The fullness of the poetic word, its presence, elevates it to a special and sacred place. The reader becomes a worshiper. In our godless age, the text serves as a substitute for religious experience. Poetic language embodies the richness and promise of man's most noble and holy self. The centered word speaks to us. This entire systematic, or poetic-hermeneutic machine, which can produce a certain kind of subtle and scrupulous reading, depends on a complex and uniform dogmatics of formalism, as we have seen. Krieger, we know, is a believer. While he willingly calls his articles of faith necessary fictions and illusions, he avoids conferring upon his actual readings any such dubious status. His readings retain an innocence.

Krieger, following Harold Bloom, admits that critics misread poems on account of their strong self-interest and their inherent will-to-power over texts. Although he accepts the psychology of misreading, he discounts its linguistics. The frail signifier, as differential element, figural substitute, and intertextual nexus, disappears under a weighty incarnational poetics of voice and a ministerial practice of formalist interpretation. Not surprisingly, Krieger's readings by contemporary standards seem relatively blithe and untroubled, neat and symmetrical. In his treatment, poetic texts do not disseminate—unless a critic foregoes restraint and indulges himself. In such a case, human willfulness triumphs—not language as such.

The signifier as linguistic moll and vagrant does not appear for Krieger; it is shy of an ethics of heroic will and wary of a faith in the sacred presence of the poetic voice. Seeking to save the richness of the poetic word, Krieger often ends up reducing it to a linguistic simple—an undifferentiated and eternal here and now, available for use. Yet the signifier shamelessly shows its stuff in Krieger's own writing, as paradoxes go down on metaphors and signifieds slide away in intense moments of slippage. As a theorist and a reader, Krieger appears a most faithful believer in traditional poetics. But as a writer, he emerges as perhaps the most unfaithful member yet of the brotherhood of American formalists.

3.

BOTH SIDES NOW

Murray Krieger

HOWEVER we address "the question of presence" today, there is at least no question about my own presence on this occasion. Indeed, in view of the position I maintain in contemporary theory, it would be inconsistent for me not to present myself, instead of remaining absent, only a ghostly trace inadequately made present (re-presented) in the words we have heard. So here I am, however inadequate myself, but a transcendental signified nonetheless—except that, of course, it is not I but my critical works, my inscribed words, that are at issue; and we know these days that signifieds can consist only of other words and not extra-verbal beings. Still, here I am.[1]

I now understand, from the inside and deep down, Northrop Frye's opening words of lamentation, years ago, when responding to a group of essays I organized about him for the English Institute: "Reading critiques of oneself is normally a distressing pastime, ranking even below the rereading of one's own works." This is true for me now, despite the narcissism induced by the occasion and my feeling flattered by the attention being given my work—so flattered that I'll try to resist whatever crankiness is induced by the distress

Frye spoke of, and not spend this small time with specific complaints or happier reactions to the commentaries we have just heard.

I will content myself with saying what is to be expected: that I prefer Mark Rose's representation of my position to Vincent Leitch's . . . if I were to say Leitch's misrepresentation, how could he—with his deconstructionist view of language—distinguish representation from misrepresentation and claim that his is the one rather than the other? But let be. I was saying that I prefer Rose's version of Krieger over Leitch's because Leitch is less ready to see the continuing doubleness of my claim for an illusionary presence than is Rose, who—I think accurately—suggests that I formulate "the relationship between presence and absence in such a way that neither term is allowed to dominate the other; neither is allowed to become a final resting place." Leitch rather insists that I am less even-handed, that—while I acknowledge the illusionary, "as if" character of poetic presence—I privilege that presence and only grudgingly concede the negative reality that stands outside its pretensions and undercuts them.

So, unlike Rose, who emphasizes an unyielding system of polar tension in my work, Leitch sees only my one-sided fidelity to a hidden god masquerading as a Manichaeism in order to protect itself from the deconstructionist's attack. He sees me fostering one side, secretly suppressing the other, while claiming an unstable duplicity (which seems to have persuaded at least Rose of its authenticity). But I would join Rose in insisting that it is, for me, not a matter of compromise between presence and absence, in which I urge one while being forced to permit the negative participation of the other. It is, rather, a sustained tensional polarity: both sides, each defined by the other, always paradoxically there, at once sustaining and negating one another.

That brings me, by way of answer, to the plea of my title today, "Both Sides Now," as I turn from this brief general response to these two commentaries on my work to make my own statements in their wake.

So, coming out of that plea for readers to resist identifying me with the ontology of a verbal presence uncritically
proclaimed by the New Criticism—the plea to retain my
claim for a doubleness without "resting place"—let me begin
again: "Both Sides Now." This time my text is the dissemina-
tion of another text: my title is taken from the title of a popular song of a number of years ago by the singer-composer Joni
Mitchell. With your indulgence I recall the opening lines to
reinforce my borrowing:

> Rows and flows of angel hair
> And ice cream castles in the air
> And feather canyons everywhere
> I've looked at clouds that way.

> But now they only block the sun
> They rain and snow on everyone
> So many things I would have done
> But clouds got in my way.

> I've looked at clouds from both sides now
> From up and down, and still somehow
> It's cloud illusions I recall.
> I really don't know clouds . . . at all.

What seems to be a choice between the airy freedom of metaphor and the inescapable blockage of earthy reality turns out
to be only a choice between two ways of seeing, two illusions, with reality something other than her language can say
or she can know.

In my work I have persistently emphasized both sides
now, and both at once—both now—as I have pressed my own
notion of illusion. The notion is perhaps best represented in
the emblem, with its companion riddle, created by Joan
Krieger for my recent book, *Poetic Presence and Illusion*. In it
two identical and opposed mythical creatures, in multiple
images, are invariably twinned in their mutual relations: they
look, open-eyed, at one another or are turned, eyes closed,
away; and they are together too in sharing the blackness of
type or the black-enclosed outlines of blank space.

This creature fabricated
multiplies itself, but moves not;
sees itself, or sees not;
exists twice, and is not.

— *Joan Krieger*

In this book I seek to tie this twinned mutuality to the behavior of the participants in the Prisoner's Dilemma game traced in its infinite variations by contemporary social scientists. In the game model, each of two partners in crime, being interrogated separately, is dependent on—but cut off from—the other's testimony. Each must decide either to co-operate with the police by turning against the other out of fear of the other's confession or to remain a faithful confederate in hopes that his partner remains equally true to him. So the choice between plea bargaining or holding out with a claim of innocence is tied to the interpretation by either of the partner's likely choice, which is similarly dependent on a reading of *his*.

Each of the partners, then, must define himself through his speculative interpretation of the other as he moves through a process of at once differentiating his own interest and being forced to identify it with the other's interest. He is both a separate individual and a twin, one that can serve his individuality only by discovering another's precisely like his own. His sense of himself as real is riveted to his illusionary sense of the other, and yet he is aware that in the companion interrogation cell it is all being reversed, that the other turns his back

to convert the first criminal into a similar illusion that con-
founds separateness and identity. Like the creatures in the
above emblem, they see each other, or see not. Or should I
view them as a single, divided creature rather than as two,
doubly bound creatures and say (as the accompanying riddle
does) that it "sees itself, or sees not"? This is just the archetypal duplicity long recorded about what it is to be identical
twins, born of one egg. So, projected out of this model, presence can be defined only by its illusionary double, by its own
vision of its illusionary other, at once absorbed into the self
and rejected as an other.

For the prisoner trapped in his dilemma, in the silence
of his isolated cell confronting himself and his mate (confronting himself as his mate), the question of which is the
signifier and which the signified in his interpretive problem
is one that shifts on him as he ponders it. I press this semiotic doubleness or controlled instability to characterize the
relation between the two elements of poetic metaphor, conceived in the broadest sense; or, indeed, to characterize the
relation between presence and illusion themselves, which I
find similarly twinned. As with the prisoners, or the creatures in the emblem, the signifier and signified—like the tenor and vehicle in metaphor—both look at each other in mutual mimesis, and turn away in separateness—though in this
act too they remain twinned and mimetic.

But I do not believe that the apparent paradox of presence and illusion, as it arises out of the way in which poems
have functioned within our cultural tradition, is as difficult or
obscure or irrational as Vincent Leitch suggests. As we examine the complex of our responses to the literary fiction, we
find in it, I suggest, just such an apparently contradictory combination of presence and the awareness of illusionary emptiness or unsubstantiality, of identity and distinctness, of self-
enclosure and openness. Further, I suggest that we are less
than satisfied when we do not find it.

Far from rare or obscure, this is a rather commonplace
response. It is what happens when, as an audience, we must

come to terms with the actors and their actions on the stage—
or are they to be viewed as dramatic characters? Or as lifelike
(if not real) people and happenings being "imitated"? Our
concern with their fate as if it were real, together with our
role in constituting the illusion that helps it keep its distance
from us, creates the strangely duplicitous terms for our aesthetic contemplation. Given our complicity, once we are in
the theater, with dramatic illusion, surely the "reality" we
bestow upon them is of a radically paradoxical sort: the flesh-
and-blood actor and the actual things we witness him doing,
the character and his doings in the text which we say the
actor represents (or counterfeits), and the supposedly substantial person and deed—in the world, shall we say?—
which the text is presumably telling us *about*. The actor, live
but make-believe, is related to the textual character, and the
textual character related to the presumed lifelike person behind him, in a way that compounds realities and their illusionary would-be equivalents. In either case the first is to be
taken as a representation of the second, as a signifier of a
transcendental signified: we need this mythic assumption to
allow the drama to do its work.

And how can we have any but an ambiguous ontological sense of what is enfolding before us? What is the reality of
a King Lear, who suffers and dies every night (though perhaps played each time by the same actor) and yet is still there
because his make-believe death is not as ours is to be, even
though we must also think of his death as absolute (like ours)
if we are to take the dramatic illusion seriously, as we do. We
suffer for him while knowing our reality must not intrude
upon his. These several simultaneous realities to which we
respond, at once reflective of ours and somehow free of it, at
once tied to the world and locked in a discontinuous realm of
make-believe, obviously have paradoxical relations to one
another. Yet our age-old habit of aesthetic attentiveness on
such occasions has no difficulty sustaining the multiple and
conflicting awarenesses, affirming the presence of what is
before us without altogether succumbing to it, so that it is

also affirming that presence only as illusion, which is to admit that it's not—in another sense—present at all.

There is, among these potential "realities" we sense, no firm ground on which to stand in order to privilege any one of them and from which to deny competing claims since, as in the Prisoner's Dilemma, all claims about relations between reality and illusion can be reversed, and are reversed, as we oscillate between one perspective and its opposite, or somehow, paradoxically, manage to hold both at once. Drama, with its peculiar conjunctions of reality and make-believe, works to remind us of the unstable relation between presence and illusion in all signifier-signified relations—especially within the fictional realm. Drama also leaves us with thematic implications about the illusionary, role playing nature (the "dramatistics") of all symbols of our presumed realities or, conversely, the apparently realistic consequences of our illusionary realms of make-believe.

So, with each stage both affirming and denying its own "real" reality or having it denied by another stage, we move into the infinite regress of illusions within illusions, or presence within presence—as the distinction between presence and illusion blurs before us. And we can move out from drama to discover our similar responses to the other poetic genres, as we observe the power given words to close together *as if* holding a presence within them: indeed, we can observe this about words or any other formal element that is pressed into service as a medium of aesthetic presentation in the struggle to bring to presentation what otherwise seemed to function as no more than self-effacing materials of representation.

It is this tension of polarities that are overlapping or even interchanging which leads me to reject the charge that I privilege one side (the metaphorical) over the other, or that I accept the other, however unhappily, as unavoidable "reality"; which leads me, instead, to insist on "Both Sides Now"—always now. So I argue for an illusion of presence that, because it can refer—if to nothing else—to its own fic-

tional status, can point to its own empty, insubstantial character—in short, to its character *as* illusion.

This affirmation of self-questioning presence can be
made similarly on behalf of an identity (as opposed to difference) and a closure (as opposed to openness) that also question and undercut their own natures. It is self-reference
which permits us to ascribe a self-conscious fictionality to
the poem which can open us to that from which it may be
seen as seeking to cut us off. It is the extra-systematic thrust
that authorizes the system and yet denies it authority. The
poem, as art—mere artifice—betrays, through self-reference, a
consciousness about its fictional self that reminds us of the
illusionary nature of the aesthetic "reality" which seeks to
enclose us. By negative implication, this reminder implicitly
points to the world which the poem explicitly excludes in
order to affirm is own closure. The world outside may be
reduced to the stage in front of us, but so long as we are
aware that it is only the stage in front of us, that world outside threatens to break in.

Thus the work of art, as its own metaphorical substitution for the world of experience beyond, is a metaphor that at
once affirms its own integrity and yet, by negative implication, denies itself, secretly acknowledging that it is but an
artful evasion of the world. This claim to duplicity permits
the work to celebrate its own ways and the ways of its language unencumbered, using the negative residue of its language to point us to the language of the world it self-consciously evades.

Of course, both the affirmation of closure and the self-
reference that leads us to find the opening in it are consequences of our habits of perception as readers trained in the
Western literary canon. The poem is seen as a single entity
created through the complicity of the reader who, sharing the
author's habit of seeking closure, allows the work—even as
he does his share in creating it—to lead him toward the act of
sealing it off within the aesthetic or fictional frame that his
perceptual training leads him to impose. The metaphorical

habits he has learned—from childhood, from religion, from previous traffic with the arts—lead him to seek an eschatology, an end to history, in the work as he seeks in it to bring chronological time to a stop.

Such has been the human use of myth—the quest for the myths we need—in the Western aesthetic since Aristotle formulated the distinction between history and poetry as each relates in its different way to time and to beginnings, middles, and ends. In thus emphasizing the poem as will-o'-the-wisp, I have meant to reintroduce the temporal element, the element of process and of human experience, into our understanding of the literary work as it is created by the poet and created complicitously by us out of what he gives us. While we see the work as functioning within the metaphorical apocalypse we allow it to create for us, it remains also a piece of language running back into the past and forward into the future. And this is all it would be were it *not* for us as aesthetically conscious readers. In serving both sides, I must look for evidence of this self-conscious double awareness in the work as I come upon it and as I, in effect, ask it to function both ways.

On the one side, the pressure for closure is strong enough in the Western tradition. Our propensity to find closure may largely account for the role of the story—like that of the picture frame or the proscenium arch—in the history of our culture. The tendency of our narrative structures reveals a responsiveness to what Frank Kermode has called our "sense of an ending." The satisfying ending is one that fulfills internally aroused expectations, that realizes immanent purposes. From Aristotle's concept of denouement to the formal finality called for by Kant, and in the formalistic tradition that is indebted to both, we find the imposition of a mythic ending, a structural apocalypse, which cuts off fiction from empirical happenings. As we have seen, it acts, in effect, as an intrusion of the spatial imagination on the radical temporality of pure sequence, shaping time into the separateness of fiction. Linear sequence is suspended, transformed into circularity.

But there is something in literature that also keeps it open to the world, to language at large, and to the reader. As we contemplate the verbal object through our culturally imposed habits of perceiving what is presented to us as aesthetic, we must deal with the two-sided nature of its words, now that they have, in spite of their one-dimensional tendencies, been shaped into a poetic medium weighted with body: they try to work their way into self-sufficient presence, and yet they remain transient and empty signifiers. This is the paradoxical nature of language as aesthetic medium, and both sides must be exploited. Language is able to create itself into a self-justified fiction, but, because it is also no more than language—just words after all—it is able to display a self-consciousness about its illusionary character. Language seems in our best poetry to be both full of itself and empty, both totally here as itself and pointing elsewhere, away from itself. It permits its reader at once to cherish its creation as a closed system, one that comes to terms with itself, and to recognize its necessarily incomplete nature in its dependence on us as its readers, on its literary precursors, on the general language system, and on the way of the world.

Not, I remind you, that I am claiming these special characteristics to be in literary works so much as they are products of our aesthetic habits of perception—when dealing with such works—which seek to find them there. And our aesthetic habit of dealing with fiction leads us to respond to its self-consciousness about the occasion that sponsors it. In other words, the literary work persuades us of itself as a special object even as we retain an awareness of the rather extraordinary activity we are performing in contributing to our own persuasion. It is not fetishism when we recognize the tentative conditions that encourage the closure we celebrate, and when we accept the openness that surrounds the moment of our commitment to the closed object—and, in effect, authenticates it.

But I do not suggest that through these workings the aesthetic becomes a game of "now you see it, now you don't." Rather I see the work as touching and unlocking in us the anthropological quest for that which marks and defines every moment of a culture's way of seeing, as well as its inner skepticism that undoes its visionary reality with a supposedly "real" reality which turns out to be no less illusionary. The making and unmaking of our metaphors, our mythic equations, in experience as in art, only reveal the primacy of the operation of the aesthetic in us all—and perhaps explain the extent to which our drive for art is accompanied by a cognitive itch which even the experience of art itself never quite eases, so that the need to experience more art happily remains.

Since the ascendancy of Structuralism more than a decade ago, critics in this country have had to come to terms with the Saussurean notion of verbal signs as arbitrary and as based upon the principle of differentiation. Thus what used to seem to be the simple matter of representation in language—the presence of a fixed signified in the signifier—is converted into a problematic. Signifiers come to be seen as operating in a dynamic field of differentiation and have only arbitrary relations with their presumed signifieds. A culture's confidence in the ontology of verbal meanings, rather than its confrontation with their differentiation and arbitrariness, only testifies to its self-mystifications as its falls prey to the metaphysical habit of logocentrism. Its wistful imposition of identity, accompanied by the ontological claim of presence, upon relations between signifiers and signifieds, is now to be undone by a shrewder philosophy of language that reminds us of the field of absence upon which the system of differences plays. Hence we have the rejection of metaphor for metonymy.

I grant that the conception of metaphor, with its illusion of identity, may well be a secular conversion of the religious myth of transubstantiation, so that we may be quick to reduce it at once to nostalgic mystification. And we may then see it operating whenever we spatialize verbal relations in order to bring linguistic temporality to a stop in an attempt to redeem time. By confessing the illusionary nature of this metaphorical operation we help perform on ourselves, I am suggesting a sophisticated use of a language that knows of its metonymic condition and yet generates among its elements an internal play which appears to create a metaphorical identity existing in the teeth of the principle of difference. It is an identity that knows and has come through the world of difference, a metaphor that has known metonymy, a spatial vision that sustains itself only through the acknowledgement that all may finally be nothing but time. If it functions as what I have elsewhere called a "miracle," it is because it proclaims itself as miracle only while acknowledging that it cannot occur. Yet the differential principle, in its eventual questioning of the representational character of words, reminds us that a world of language founded on difference is not a residual reality, but is only an alternative illusion, however unmiraculous.

Nothing that deconstruction reveals about the mystifications that sponsor claims to verbal presence should distract us altogether from an interest in how poems have functioned and can function within their cultural tradition, whatever the motives buried in nostalgia or political power that we can find beneath that function. And the metaphorical visions enclosed in the poem open us to ways of cultural seeing that have their anthropological validity, whatever the language myths that guided them. So long as poems have served their culture as if they had an objective aesthetic character, their function must be accounted for, though we may find that, through self-reference, the best of them carry their own criticism of the mythic assumptions that sustain that function. The myth of presence, of transcendental signifieds immanent in words, that operates as an assumption in all a culture's language uses, is self-consciously indulged in poetry by a language freely allowed to go on its own.

Mark Rose, subjecting my criticism to a perceptive narratological analysis, finds it to be a version of the quest

romance.[2] In a recent essay I myself suggest a utopian dimension when I admit that the drive for aesthetic closure expresses the dream of a microcosm of satisfied ends.* The
dream of unity, of formal repetitions that are seen as the
temporal equivalent of juxtapositions, that convert the temporal into the spatial through the miracle of simultaneity—
this dream persists, reinforced by every aesthetic illusion
which we help create and to which we succumb. We cultivate the mode of identity, the realm of metaphor, within an
aesthetic frame that acknowledges its character as momentary
construct and thereby its frailty as illusion. But it allows us a
glimpse of our own capacity for vision before the bifurcations
of language have struck. The dream of unity may be enter-
tained tentatively and is hardly to be granted cognitive
power, except for the secret life-without-language or life-
before-language which it suggests, the very life which the
language of difference precludes (as the poem-as-dream
knows and shows us it knows). In poetry we grasp at the
momentary possibility that this can be a life-in-language.
This would be a utopia indeed, one well worth the quest.

Let me suggest that I pursue my quest on horseback—in
Tristram Shandy's sense, on "hobby-horseback." In Sterne's
novel, which is a superb example of my theme of "Both Sides
Now," each character's hobby-horse carries him into his transformed realm, a private world of figuration which encloses his
verbal reality, his hobby-horsical reality. The hobby-horse is
just the creature to carry each of us off into these tropistic
privacies. But in Sterne the hobby-horse is no less a horse than
is an actual horse, whether Uncle Toby's or Trim's or Death's,
which is treated just as metaphorically, as itself a hobby-horse.
Again we have not an illusion set against reality but competing varieties of illusion, of hobby-horses. Mine has been carry-
ing me for more than a couple of decades now, growing—or
aging—and with age spreading, though retaining a firm sense
of its nature. It is a friendly creature, one, like Tristram's,
which I cannot altogether forsake. Let me borrow Tristram's
words:

What a rate have I gone on at, curvetting and frisking it away, two up and two down for four volumes together [actually rather more], without looking once behind, or even on one side of me, to see whom I trod upon!—I'll tread upon no one,—quoth I to myself when I mounted—I'll take a good rattling gallop, but I'll not hurt the poorest jack-ass upon the road—So off I set—up one lane— down another, through this turn-pike—over that, as if the arch-jockey of jockeys had got behind me. (vol. 4, ch. 20)

After such a ride, shall I dismount? What other horse would you have me ride? For there's not a pedestrian among us.

*A reference to "An Apology for Poetics"—Ed.

4.

REREADING CONTEXTUALISM

Adena Rosmarin

> The contextualist will not forfeit the poem's
> chance to transform language—and its capacity to
> transform us.
>
> —Murray Krieger

PLATO, it will be recalled, had two reasons for ousting the poet from his Republic, one conceptual and the other ethical. Having defined poetry as an imitation of a this-worldly reality, itself an imitation of a privileged and other-worldly Reality, Plato deemed the poem not only metaphysically deficient but doubly so. Consequently, "all poetical imitations are ruinous to the understanding of the hearers, unless as an antidote they possess the knowledge of the true nature of the originals."[1] But poetry not only misrepresents, it "feeds and waters the passions instead of drying them up" (R, 482–83). On this count also the poet must depart a "well ordered" state: "he awakens and nourishes this part of the soul, and by strengthening it impairs the reason" (R, 481). Plato readily grants that the poet is a "sacred, marvellous and delightful being" before whom we rightly "fall down and worship" (R, 245). But for "our souls' health" we must learn to prefer "the rougher and severer poet or story-teller, who will imitate the style of the virtuous only" (R, 245).

The poet is doubly faulted, but the difficulty of parrying, let alone returning Plato's opening thrust, is located not only in the doubleness of the fault but in the dexterity with which each fault is made to serve the other. On the one hand, misrepresentation seems to be the lesser evil. The guardians, Plato concedes, "may be allowed to lie for the public good" (R, 234). On the other hand, the well-nourished passion is condemned because it thwarts reason's attempt to discover truth. But this ambidexterity is precisely what makes the charge virtually unanswerable. By refusing to separate fact and value, by assuming that to know the true *is* to know the good, Plato challenged those who would mount a more than merely defensive defense of poetry's "seductions." He concedes its sacred and seductive delights and then dares its defender to show it to be good and true as well.

The history of criticism shows that Plato cannot be effectively rebutted in his own terms, that a convincing defense must begin by refusing these terms or, more precisely, by inverting them. Hence Kant's success. Conceding poetry's usefulness and attending not to what poetry represents but to "the relation of the representative powers to one another," he transforms Plato's concession into poetry's invaluable essence: it is "sacred, marvellous and delightful," or, in Kant's word, "beautiful."[2] It is properly valued disinterestedly rather than pragmatically, for its own sake rather than for what it says about the world or for what it does to its audience. It is at once self-caused and cleansed of causal force.

But therein lies not only the power but also the vulnerability of the Kantian defense. For in the hands of the anti-Kantian, the poem's aesthetic virtues—its powers of self-justification, its unconcern with its origins and effects—all too readily convert to fault: the poem lacks substance, both ethical and metaphysical; its defenders are isolationists, not

virtuously disinterested but guiltily uninterested in matters
human. Moreover, they perpetrate the conceptual sins of
their beloved object: they acquire its liking for express fictionality, self-consciousness, verbal substance, and, worst of
all, paradox. The anti-Kantian, who is invariably a Platonist,
damns the well-wrought poem as simultaneously trivial and
perfidious. He calls its defenders threatened elitists, flaunters
of sophistic skill and useless art, flouters of theoretical rigor
and social responsibility. Even those who write within the
Kantian tradition quail before the severity of its standard: "It
is worth noting that here was a system which conceived
Homer and Shakespeare as less aesthetically pure than
wallpaper."[3]

The Kantian has found his most forceful contemporary
voice in Murray Krieger and the Platonist an incisive voice in
his critics. Krieger's culminating statement, *Theory of Criticism* (1976), has most strongly defined what Krieger himself,
in *The New Apologists for Poetry* (1956), christened the contextualist position. It has also, in effect, defined its own opposition, the critics of *Theory of Criticism* repeatedly finding
therein both metaphysical and ethical sin. The purpose of
mapping these lines of attack and defense is to show the
unrecognized theoretical power of Krieger's radical if seemingly traditional poetics. But it is also to show that this theoretical power is finally a critical power as well. For by recognizing the critic's power of invention, Krieger not only
makes a better theoretical sense of criticism, he also shows
that foregrounding this traditionally denied power is the key
to a stronger criticism.

The most sustained critique is Frank Lentricchia's
After the New Criticism (1980). Like Plato attacking the poet,
Lentricchia attacks Krieger for simultaneously threatening or,
worse yet, discounting the true and the good: "Krieger's contextualism, or aesthetic isolationism as I have called it, represents a consistent (though not always happy and guilt-free)
assault on ancient aesthetic notions of universality and community" (*ANC*, 224). And, again like Plato, Lentricchia de-

fends both notions. He does this primarily by asking a question, the question that haunts all aesthetic defenses of poetry: "How, once having so totally isolated poetry and the poetic consciousness, do we get the unique, intrinsic values of poetry in touch with our human world?" (ANC, 228). Lentricchia's answer is that we can't—unless, of course, we reject the originators of this isolation.

He accordingly faults Krieger for being "elitist," "isolationist," "self-consciously fictive," "anti-populist," and "anti-ethical." The contextualist poem is faulted for being "unique" and enjoying a "privileged status," the contextualist poetics for preferring the "contemplative" or "intransitive" attitude to action, "a tactic which apparently allows one to escape all saying, all stance-taking" (ANC, 234).* The challenge is powerful: has Krieger returned or even parried the Platonic thrust? He has indisputably argued eloquently for the poem as "sacred, marvellous, and delightful," but Plato had already conceded as much. Has Krieger made a case for its metaphysical substance and ethical power? Analysis of his later work reveals that he has, but because his argument does not—indeed cannot—take place in representational terms, his traditionally minded if radical critics have treated it as a deficiency in the old system rather than the beginnings of a new.

Like all powerful poetics, Krieger's is constructed in expressly agonistic terms: "imitation theory," he asserts, "is the enemy" (TC, 67). Both his theory and its authenticating tradition are constructed to justify this assertion, as they indeed do. But we might also consider the process of justification from the other end and say that Krieger—like Eliot, Shelley, Wordsworth, and Sidney—chooses his enemy in order to justify his theory and its tradition, as indeed it does. Either way, the theory has raised and thereby defused its own opposition. Either way, it has acquired the agonistic torque that drives all successful arguments.

*In Richard Berg's interview, Krieger comments on the fallacy of seeing the "privileging" of poetry in political terms—Ed.

Critics of *Theory of Criticism* fault its strategic finesse, but for the moment let us concentrate on how Krieger's definition of an analogous agonistic energy in the poem enables *its* justification. Krieger traces his definition to Sigurd Burckhardt, who in "The Poet as Fool and Priest" argued that the poet uses "poetic devices," particularly rhyme, meter, and tropes, to make his words into a proper poetic medium, one with its own substance or life.[4] These devices work by drawing our attention to the verbal surface and trapping it there, blocking our attempts to refer the words to a meaning beyond the poem. No longer transparent, as is the ideal representational medium, they have become opaque; no longer empty, as is the ideal semiotic signifier, they themselves have acquired the being to which they refer; no longer pointing to *res,* either "naturally" or arbitrarily, *verba* has become *res.* In terms of the archaeological metaphor that informs representational discourse, the poem finesses the problem of grounding by transforming its verbal surface *into* its ground. In terms of the ocular metaphor that alternatively informs such discourse, it invites us not to look *through* its words but, rather, *at* them.

Lentricchia faults Krieger for refusing the Saussurean ideal of an empty and arbitrary signifier. But Krieger does not operate on the naive side of Saussure, whose idea, as Krieger points out, can be traced as far back as Plato's *Cratylus.* Rather, he and Burckhardt *begin* with the empty and arbitrary signifier and "see the poet as torturing his words into fullness" (*TC,* 213). He "violates" his language by *twisting* it, using it "unnaturally" or tropologically, *turning* it to his purpose, which is to create a discourse whose presence depends not upon its power to represent the not-itself but upon its powers of self-substantiation. As Burckhardt observes, the pun is the exemplary instrument of this quintessentially poetic torture. By effecting the sharpest and therefore the most substantiating twist, it most effectively forces multiple meanings into one word, making it self-contradictory or paradoxical.

The pun thus becomes the fundamental paradox of

Krieger's paradoxical poetics—as it does for Derrida's. But as Krieger notes, "It is surely odd that the device of the pun, which for Burckhardt was the dominating, indeed the enabling, act of presence, is for Jacques Derrida the instrument to undo any such notion as presence" (TC, 229). In other words, how can the pun serve both a poetics of presence and a poetics of absence? Krieger answers that

For Derrida verbal ambiguity is seen essentially as Burckhardt claimed Empson saw it: as one word having several meanings (hence for Derrida its presence evaporating into its functions). We recall that Burckhardt, on the other hand, preferred the converse as his definition of ambiguity: as several meanings *having one* word. Hence, for Burckhardt, the word takes on the corporeality that confers substantive presence. (TC, 229)

Krieger uses Burckhardt's insight to define presence as a phenomenon of reverse predication, an incisive definition that bears explicitly on the poet's struggle to substantiate his writing and implicitly on the critic's struggle to substantiate his writing about the poem. Contemporary theoreticians have increasingly conceded the latter struggle, simultaneously accepting and lamenting the incompatibility between literary experience and systematic thought about that experience. "The reasons for this disjunction . . . ," according to Paul de Man, "are inherent in language, in the necessity, which is also an impossibility, to connect the subject with its predicates or the sign with its symbolic manifestations." This "disjunction will always, as it did in Hegel, manifest itself as soon as experience shades into thought, history into theory."[5]

Krieger opens *Theory of Criticism* with a similar lament, phrased as an "inevitable" conflict between "coherence and correspondence," between our philosophic striving for order and our essentially poetic striving to articulate experience in all its fullness (TC, 4). Like de Man, he observes that "if propositional systems in general reveal their inadequacy to the data for which they pretend to account, we find them far more presumptuous when they seek to deal with literature, whose objects are expressly created to capture the complex nuances that make up human existence on the level of its utter singularity, its endless contingencies" (TC, 5). But the difference between the two theorists is all-important. De Man sees no way of repairing the disjunction. He argues that it is a built-in consequence of a built-in desire, one whose fulfillment is endlessly attempted but never accomplished. If to think is to open the gap, to talk is to widen it. Emily Dickinson's prefiguration of this dilemma remains its most concise statement:

> To fill a gap
> Insert the Thing that caused it—
> Block it up
> With Other—and 'twill yawn the more—
> You cannot solder an Abyss
> With Air.
>
> Poem 546

Krieger, however, proposes that we reject the direction of predication, thereby creating the possibility of soldering the Abyss or, more exactly, of canceling its existence. He begins, in short, where the deconstructionist leaves off. He acknowledges the impossibility of fulfilling theory's traditional desire for a perfectly responsive and trace-free medium, for a medium that, in Kenneth Burke's terms, would represent without selecting or deflecting.[6] But he then proceeds to use this acknowledgement as his beginning premise, the paradox that supplies the inventive energy of his argument.

This paradox works conceptually as the pun works verbally, the difference between substantiating and emptying uses of the pun being a particular case of the difference between a poetics of presence and a poetics of absence. Whereas Derrida discovers in the pun a deconstructive instrument that breaks the referential connection, exposing the fictionality of its non-fictional pretensions, Krieger discovers in the articulated paradox of theory's unfulfillable desire a constructive instrument, a way for discourse to place its own fictionality in plain view and, thereby, give its surface the look of substance. The result is neither reference nor its negation but, rather, what might be more properly called strategies of reference. Or, what is in effect the same, of self-substantiation.

Of course, the notion that poetic language is self-referential or paradoxical is not original to *Theory of Criticism*. What is radically revisionary is Krieger's argument that the critic should appropriate the poet's language of paradox. Not surprisingly, it is this thesis that has most antagonized his critics. Thus Joel Weinsheimer:

> it is his paradoxical method itself that I find objectionable. We can briefly reconstruct its history: for Cleanth Brooks the "language of paradox" not only occurred within the poem but defined the nature of poetry itself. So too for Professor Krieger. . . . But in *Theory of Criticism* the critical method employed is itself paradoxical, as it was not in Brooks.[7]

Lentricchia concludes similarly, his attack on Krieger's ethical faults finally diverted by the metaphysical sins of *Theory of Criticism*, in which Krieger's "habit of pushing his thinking to unresolvable contradictions is brought to stark perfection" (*ANC*, 253). Whereas the early Krieger argued laudably if unethically, by *Theory of Criticism* "he has seemed (by intention) to drain the position of all its theoretical vigor," to have given way to "debilitating self-consciousness" and "imaginative play" (*ANC*, 219, 250–51).

As Krieger's critics recognize, the language of paradox thoroughly transforms theory, criticism, and, indeed, the critic himself. Whereas before, he was simply a "person," he now becomes a "persona." He must recognize that his writing, whatever its seeming objectivity, is also a self-writing, that his tradition and theory are as much in the self-justifying service of the self who writes them as vice versa. This "persona," who recalls Wayne Booth's "implied author," which Booth defines as "the sum of his own choices,"[8] also lacks the representationalist's matter-of-fact mind, the *tabula rasa* upon which is inscribed the poem he "sees." Krieger's critic, in other words, discards Locke's epistemology for Kant's and then goes one step further. Whereas Kant conceived of our mental categories as essentially fixed, Krieger's critic exercises his power to choose his categories or conceptual language. Moreover, once having chosen them, he refuses their hypostatization, continually reminding himself and his readers that he is proceeding suppositionally, *as if* the poem, for example, has the objective properties and aesthetic effects he posits.[9]

Far from being "debilitating," then, the self-consciousness of Krieger's critic enables his primary act: the writing of critical arguments. Far from being an elitist do-nothing, he justly presents himself as a "pragmatist," one who chooses his critical fictions not disinterestedly but purposefully, and who justifies his choice not correspondently or inductively but dramatically and deductively. Hence his notion of the "poem" is accordingly presented as "a normative rather than a descriptive category" (*TC*, 20). His announced goal is not to discover the "right" reading but to create "a wholly satisfactory hypothesis for the form of the poem," a "construct" that is "*our fiction*" (*TC*, 41).

We recall that in an essay on the "ambidextrous critic" (1968) Krieger had already acknowledged "the practical impossibility of keeping criticism inductive . . . once we first concede—in post-Kantian manner—the constitutive role of our categories" (*PPI*, 307). And in a yet earlier essay, he used Northrop Frye's *Anatomy of Criticism* to argue the case for "*schematics*" over "*systematics*."[10] Anyone who is trying to read Krieger as a traditional formalist, as proposing to mirror in a category-free or inductive manner the particular and naked formal features of the poem, should be given pause by Krieger's continuing espousal of this explicitly deductive heritage, which includes not only Frye but also Rosalie Colie and E. H. Gombrich. Colie's use of genres and Gombrich's of schemata at once inform and complement Krieger's various fictions, whether poetic or critical, and Gombrich's thesis that making comes before matching prefigures the most significant and radical thesis of *Theory of Criticism:* "The critic must have *his* fictions if he is to gain access to the poet's" (*TC*, 17).[11]

Krieger, then, has not abandoned truth but redefined it. Whereas he previously used the traditionalist's correspondence terminology, he now uses a coherence terminology. Whereas he previously used the procedures and assumptions of an inductive system, he now espouses those of a deductive "schematics." Rather than representing himself as a "person" who literal-mindedly "sees" or "finds" truth, he defines himself as a figuratively minded "persona" who elaborates the truth implicit in his chosen schemata or explanatory fictions. Far from draining his position of theoretical credibility, the change has purchased rigor, which is to say logical consistency.

But how, one might well ask, can such a theory make such a claim? To answer this question, we need first to question the traditional critic's claim to rigor. Validity, as we know, is argued in correspondent terms, in terms of the critical text's consistency not with itself but with its object of knowledge. Criticism is "valid" insofar as it offers a more complete and transparent image, insofar, that is, as it has not used a conceptual medium. But representation requires a medium: not to use a medium is not to represent but to copy, to repeat the literary text word for word.

This *reductio ad absurdum* suggests that insofar as the critical representation is perfect it becomes undesirable, that the theoretical ideal of perfection, if in fact achieved, would be bereft of heuristic power, incapable of "discovering" anything not already self-evident. Only the *imperfect* representation, which is what representations in practice—if not in theory— always are, can make such "discoveries." Its terms select and deflect the poem it explains, thereby articulating implications, emphases, and patterns not previously noticeable. But because theories of representation repudiate these enabling imperfections in order to defend their "validity," the practice of representation is always covertly contradicted by the presence of this theoretical denial. The achieved representation, in other words, is always and ineluctably at odds with its enabling, paradoxical, and denied theoretical premise: that it can body forth the not-itself in terms whose presence is absent.

But if we begin rather than end with paradox, if we acknowledge at the outset that our access to the poet's fictions must be biased and indirect, as is his access to the world, himself, and previous texts, then we may proceed consistently from that beginning acknowledgement. By no accident did Cleanth Brooks appropriate Shakespeare's metaphor of lawnbowls from *Hamlet* to typify the poet's "language of paradox":

> with assays of bias
> By indirections find directions out.

It is the skillful player's recognition and use of the bowl's deliberate distortion (or "bias") which enables him to "bowl a curve," to "win to a fine precision." Science posits a "perfect sphere" and thus the theoretical possibility of a "direct" or medium-free attack on truth. Even in theory, however, "The method of art can . . . ," Brooks tells us, "never be direct—is always indirect. But that does not mean that the master of the game cannot place the bowl where he wants it."[12]

Krieger pushes Brooks' thesis to its logical conclusion by appropriating the poet's language of paradox for his own critical purposes. The result is a criticism that is aware of and consistent with its premises. Put otherwise, it is a theory that is neither apart from nor at odds with our practice. Thus do the features and benefits of paradox, exactly as Brooks has assessed them, transfer as readily as the Platonic antagonism that its use incites. But this result depends upon two beginning assumptions. First, the critic-theorist must recognize that the "perfect sphere," the transparent or absent category, is itself a theoretical fiction and a practical impossibility— much as it is Kant's *Ding an sich*. Even for the non-poet there is no "direct" attack. Second, he must recognize the corollary of this first recognition: that a medium is essential and its distortions ineluctable, that he needs both the "bowl" and its "bias." He knows, in short, that his topic can only be said in terms not its own.

Krieger, then, begins by positing a paradox or self-contradiction or, put otherwise, a contradiction in terms. But from this beginning his reasoning, unlike that of the "inductive" or traditional critic, can proceed rigorously, consistent with its own premises. As it happens, his definition of the poem closely coincides with that of his formalist fathers. The critical (in both senses) difference lies in Krieger's emphasis on the normative nature of the definition and on the explicit pragmatism of its formulation:

I am interested, then, not in whether experiences can occur in accordance with such defined "types" as the poetic nor in whether, if they did, that would be a good thing; only in what they would be like if they did so occur, and this so that we can characterize what the verbal objects would be like that were constructed in order to lead us toward one or another of them. (*TC*, 11)

Krieger's critics characteristically think that Krieger's definition of the "poem" is as disinterested as the poem he defines. Yet in *Theory of Criticism* and elsewhere Krieger emphatically states that his is a "normative definition," one "theoretically rather than experientially derived" (*PPC*, 156). The "disinterested" poem, in other words, is an "interested" definition, one made in order to begin a kind of critical argument: "One must predicate these qualities of the experience if he wishes to make it an experience *of* (which is to say, controlled by) an object of a certain kind, of that kind defined by contextualism" (*PPI*, 156). It is this counter-intuitive predication, the explicitly deductive direction of Krieger's argument, that enables its strength and, moreover, reconciles the poem to its poetics. And this reconciliation, which de Man, reasoning in the more usual or inductive direction, declares impossible, is precisely what motivates Krieger's definition and procedure:

The major advantage to the literary theorist of defining experiences
as if they came in pure, distinct types is that such a definition
enables him, by projection, to read back to a description of the
aesthetic quality of objects, which—in a circular way—he defines
by those which induce us toward (or seduce us into) the kind of
experience dominated by its aesthetic components. Could he not
predict what sort of linguistic entity it would be that seemed to be
constructed expressly to lead us toward such a self-sufficient experience? (TC, 12)

But how, one might now ask, can thinking in terms of
the norm reconcile us to the poem? How can the powerful
type unfold the self-sufficient and ineffably particular poem?
Does it not seem obvious that, as Lentricchia puts it, "The
generic is the enemy, aesthetically and ethically" (ANC,
224)? The answer is simple if counter-intuitive: the generic is
the enemy of the particular only if we begin with the particular and try to reduce it to the general. As Krieger observes in
his analysis of Plato, to begin with the general is to move
"from singleness to multiplicity," a movement in which
"particulars are increasingly proliferated" (TC, 69). This
movement is the opposite of what Plato wants, but it is exactly what the Kantian wants. Analysis that begins with the
particular requires us to generalize whereas analysis that begins with the general empowers us to particularize, to unfold
and value the poem precisely as post-Kantian criticism has
defined it.

But Lentricchia argues that the generic, by which he
means the inductively or intrinsically generic, is the enemy
not only of aesthetics but of ethics: it "would treat the individual as the typical in order to manipulate, use, and dominate him" (ANC, 224). Once again, however, the generic is
culpable only when the argument proceeds inductively:
when the particular is reduced to the typical, when the individual is defined as the empty and passive state upon which
societal or metaphysical norms inscribed themselves. Of
course, this Lockean definition of the individual—he is the
tabula rasa who is written by forces beyond his control and,

usually, beyond his consciousness—has been as philosophically desirable as it is ethically dubious. By making the subject a window on the object, it has seemed to guarantee the objectivity of what is known, whether that be a poem, a class struggle, or whatever.

But if we recognize that the erasure of the subject is no less a discursive strategy than is his glorification—the purposes in either case is justification—then we also recognize that, once again, the critical question is not representational but pragmatic: not whether the individual "really" makes conscious choices, a question that is always ultimately unanswerable, but whether it is desirable and useful to proceed as if he does, a question that is always immediately answerable. For Krieger, the answer is clear: his reader exerts his existential right to proceed *as if* he could write his own self or choose his defining category, the type of person he would like to be, and *as if* by the process of writing he could work that category into fullness. The process is identical to that by which the poet works his words into fullness, substantiating them.

But how exactly does Krieger's reader manage this process of self-definition and self-substantiation? By permitting "himself to be overcome" by the context of the text, by "surrendering his own contexts to it."[13] But does not this answer invoke the opposite of what Krieger wants? Are we not once again being told that the text masters the reader, coercing him into writing himself in its terms rather than his own.?[14] Yes and no. Read carefully, Krieger's answer tells us that the reader *chooses* to be so overcome and that his surrender is not only willing but provisional, repeated with many and various texts. Moreover, he engages in "research" in order to learn how best to perform this act of imaginative supposition, how to treat this other context, however provisionally, *as if* it were his own. Unlike the ideal representational reader, who is passively governed by features of the text, by its "implied author," by some internal ground such as Norman Holland's "identity themes," or by some communal ground such as Jonathan Culler's "conventions" or Stanley Fish's "interpretive strategies," Krieger's reader is active, hermeneutically experienced, and fully capable of defining the grounds or categories that he uses to govern or, more precisely, write his self.

Fish has convincingly argued that we only write within a context or a set of constraints, but Krieger additionally argues that we are free to choose that context and that we read aesthetically *and* ethically when we behave *as if* we can.[15] Krieger's reader, in short, is a critic. And he is a good reader not because he is transparent, a witless inscriber of formal features, conventions, or whatever, but because he knows how to do something well: to read with sophistication and, what is finally the same, to write that reading with self-awareness and reason.

Krieger thus defines his "persona," or ideal reader, much as he has defined his ideal poem: *as if* he were ungrounded and self-sufficient, free to abide by his chosen constraints and work towards his chosen ends. I have been emphasizing the "as if" locution in my analysis, in part because Krieger himself uses it to emphasize the suppositional nature of his hypotheses and procedures, in part to connect Krieger's theory to Hans Vaihinger's *The Philosophy of "As If."* Vaihinger goes unmentioned in *Theory of Criticism,* but Krieger's notion of "fiction" is nevertheless thoroughly Vaihingerian in configuration and function. Wallace Stevens, who, as Lentricchia disapprovingly notes, is the "guiding genius" of *Theory of Criticism* (*ANC,* 247), had pondered Vaihinger's study before writing *Notes toward a Supreme Fiction,* and both there and in *Theory of Criticism* we everywhere find Vaihinger's insistent emphasis on the express fictionality of the fiction, on its essential and enabling self-consciousness.

In his reading of Frank Kermode's *The Sense of An Ending,* itself influenced by Vaihinger through Stevens, Lentricchia classes Vaihinger as a "conservative fictionalist" (*ANC,* 53). This classification is meant to be damning, to connote an "aesthetic" distaste for action in the world. But Vaihinger explicitly resists this reading:

A further essential character of fictions . . . is that they are *means* to a definite end, in other words that they are expedient. . . . This is really the kernel of our position, which distinguishes it fundamentally from previous views. For us the essential element in a fiction is not the fact of its being a conscious deviation from reality, a mere piece of imagination—but we stress the useful nature of this deviation.[16]

But there is, as Vaihinger observes, a problem with deviations, particularly with repeated deviations: if we are not continually reminded of their deviant or fictional nature, they naturalize and become literally matter-of-fact. Like the poet's metaphors, which are kin to the Vaihingerian fiction, they tend either to "die" or to hypostatize, to disappear into the thing described (the consequence we call "realism") or to become themselves the thing described (the consequence we call "idealism"). Vaihinger thus warns against both tendencies: we must neither transfer the fiction's contradictons to the thing itself nor "become attached to these fictions as though they were the essential thing" (*P*, 90). He further warns that the only corrective to these tendencies is to insist on the fictionality of the fiction, thereby disillusioning the very illusion that our fastidious playing out of the "as if" premise is simultaneously enabling. Thus does the *usefulness* of an illusion depend upon our recognizing the illusion as such even as we have it.

But this, as any reader of Gombrich knows, is just what we supposedly cannot do: "though we may be intellectually aware of the fact that any given experience *must* be an illusion, we cannot, strictly speaking, watch ourselves having an illusion" (*AI*, 5–6). We here come to the heart of Krieger's rebuttal to Plato, what Krieger's critics deem his metaphysical sin. Like Vaihinger, Krieger foregrounds his fictions, recognizing that their usefulness is intricately but thoroughly dependent on our recognition of them as fictions, asking his readers to treat them as if they were discovered even when reminded that they are invented. Hence the enabling self-consciousness of his own discourse, particularly *Theory of Criti-*

cism. But, once again, it is just this self-consciousness that
Lentricchia finds "debilitating" and Weinsheimer impossible:

One wonders whether self-conscious illusion is indeed possible as
a simultaneity. E. H. Gombrich, whom Professor Krieger invokes in
support here, in fact asserts just the opposite, namely that we cannot watch ourselves having an illusion. Self-conscious illusion is
an impossibility because self-consciousness is an event, an act in
time, and the moment of self-consciousness marks the terminus of
illusion. We certainly can know that we have been deluded but
only from the viewpoint of disillusionment. Illusion is recognized
only ex post facto. . . . [it] can never be present to itself, that is,
self-conscious. ("On Going Home Again," 577)

Because Weinsheimer assumes that we cannot be of two
minds at once, he concludes that the act of thinking, talking,
or writing "as if"—whether that activity be poetic or critical—
is impossible. The conclusion is Platonic—recall that Plato
damned the poet for, among other things, not abiding by the
Platonic rule that "one man can only do one thing well, and
not many" (R, 241)—and is repeatedly met in arguments
against paradox, particularly those made against theories that
posit readers who are neither simple nor literal-minded.

The conflict between aesthetician and Platonist appears irreconcilable. But if we unpack the implications of
Gombrich's statement we find that he is not saying that we
can't be of two minds at once but that we can't be of two
minds in the same way or on the same "level" at once. Thus
we may be "intellectually aware" of being absorbed in an
illusion, but our absorption and our awareness are not
"strictly speaking" coincident because they happen in different places and ways, the performer of awareness looking
down upon or knowing the performer of absorption but not
vice versa.

Gombrich is here reasoning in a sophisticated but still
representational fashion, separating mental acts into levels
and modes, into those marked by transparent awareness or

knowledge of levels below and those marked by their absorption in belief, by their saturation with schematic error, by their ignorance, in short, of themselves. But Gombrich, unlike Plato, is not arguing against illusion. Rather, he is doubting the possibility of conscious or self-knowing illusion. This doubt follows from his attempt to acknowledge the constitutive power of schemata (his "idealism") *and* to purchase the representational validity conferred by schemata that are powerless (his "realism"). It follows, that is, from his attempt to believe in the illusion and to know the illusion without belief or, to focus the paradox, without illusion. Like all traditional Kantian theorists, Gombrich needs both believer and knower if his theory is to seem both valid and self-aware, but he cannot "strictly speaking" endorse their coincidence in the same person at the same time if he would avoid explicit self-contradiction. His "solution" is to separate the performers perspectively, to have the one look down upon or know the other and to have the other be unaware that he is being "watched" or known. His "solution," in short, is to separate theory and practice.

But this is precisely what Krieger refuses to do. His accomplishment has been to unite theory and practice, to make criticism aware of its opening premises and then to weave that awarness, as a strengthening warp or self-contradiction, into the very fabric of the critical text. By foregrounding the self-contradiction of traditional Kantian theory—its distinctive habit of treating the media described as constitutive or opaque and the media used to describe them as powerless or transparent—Krieger both eschews the always futile attempt to conceal this contradiction and finds a way of defining theory not as an escape from practice but as its inception. The aim and the result is to endow criticism with both assertive energy and defensive immunity.

Weinsheimer reluctantly concedes this last point: "In practice, paradoxical criticism seems the only mode of criticism invulnerable to attack, because . . . we cannot accuse as being contradictory what is intentionally so." He makes this concession, which is itself a kind of self-contradiction, to purchase for his own discourse the very defensive strength condemned in Krieger's. But unlike Krieger he ignores the enabling paradoxes of his practice and faults Krieger for not doing likewise: "In theory, paradox is the signal that both dichotomized antitheses are inadequate and untenable; paradox, except in a religion of art, requires synthesis. For juxtaposing two half-truths will not make a whole one" ("On Going Home Again," 577).

As to Hegel and Plato, Weinsheimer here either misses or strategically ignores the purpose of paradox: to assert a unity that issues not from the synthetic obliteration of opposites or contradictions but from their sustained tension or coexistence.[17] Despite repeated insistence to the contrary, such coexistence is manifestly possible, as all illusionist art and theory, including Plato's own metaphysics, testify. Similarly, being of two minds at once is not only not impossible, it is a quite ordinary mental feat: "What child is there that, coming to a play, and seeing Thebes written in great letters upon an old door, doth believe that it is Thebes?"[18] Sidney is speaking of plays and Krieger of the play of criticism, but the point holds. We readily, it would seem naturally, become adept at making and reading the self-proclaimed trompe l'oeil even as the "trompe" or mistake seduces us into taking what we know is not for what it is. Only the representationalist's decision to argue in unimaginative terms, in terms of an ocular epistemology and an archaeological ontology, requires a reader remarkable for his simple-minded stolidity.[19]

Krieger's choice of an imaginative or "as if" terminology enables him to conceive his reader quite otherwise: as knowledgeable, imaginatively dextrous, and capable of growth. By exercising his capacity to think and feel "as if," to exchange his contexts repeatedly and provisionally for those of many and various texts, he opens himself to change. He thereby achieves a complex freedom. Neither unwillingly constrained (the representationalist's ideal) nor free from all con-

straint (the subjectivist's ideal), he has purposefully chosen
his particular constraints. The "as if" stance, in other words, is
enabling not only aesthetically but ethically. Vaihinger, not
incidentally, argues that this stance "constitutes the real principle of Kantian ethics, namely, that true morality must always rest upon a *fictional* basis":

we must act with the same seriousness and the same scruples *as if*
the duty were imposed by God, *as if* we would be judged therefor,
as if we would be punished for immorality. But as soon as this *as if*
is transformed into a *because*, its purely ethical character vanishes
and it becomes simply a matter of our lower interests, mere egoism.
(*P*, 49)

And it is, of course, the poet who is our best tutor. He
devises dwelling places or contexts that disturb our ordinary
selves; he "wrenches us out of our context and into his"; he
teaches us "patterns that are at variance with our own . . .
and which we did not know we could apprehend until we
have done so under his guidance" (*TC*, 186–87). And, for
Krieger, the scholar-critic works analogously, devising patterns whose variance from those we expect and therefore no
longer "see" teaches us to think anew and differently. Thus
do the critic's fictions, when foregrounded rather than denied, become doubly heuristic: not only do they unfold those
of the poet—"The critic must have *his* fictions if he is to gain
access to the poet's"—they themselves teach and, even,
please.

The self-consciousness of Krieger's fictions, then, is
not only not "debilitating" and "impossible," it is precisely
what gives them conceptual substance and heuristic power.
We found that Krieger's aesthetics begins much as Kant's
does, by defending poetry for its sacred, seductive, and self-
justifying beauty. But he betters Kant and his various formalist and contextualist descendants by refusing to concede
Plato's double attack: that poetry lacks such substance and
should lack such power. Replacing a representational with a
suppositional and pragmatic terminology enables him to de-

fine the poem's substance not as something it contains but as something it is. It also enables him to show how the self-consciousness of the illusion, its power to foreground its self-contradictory and opacifying dynamics, gives that illusion its substance.

Following Burckhardt, Krieger has taken the pun's self-substantiation as his paradigm, but he goes beyond not only Burckhardt but Derrida in showing that all self-conscious fictions or premises, whether used by the poet or the critic, are self-substantiating and suasively powerful in just this way. Just as Aristotle's elaborated definition of teleological plot, which announces his preference for the *propter hoc* over the *post hoc*, convinces us that tragedies so plotted surpass those that do not show their design, so do Krieger's own elaborate premises, which announce his preference for substantial, consistently reasoned, and immediately present explanations, convince us that such explanations surpass the "after the fact" mirrorings of traditional criticism.[20]

Krieger's defense of poetry, in sum, is as conceptual and ethical as it is aesthetic. By countering our tendency to literalize the fiction, either by losing "sight" of it in the "object" it "sees" or by hypostatizing it into myth, it concentrates our attention on the *process* of its operation rather than on its real-world or ideal-world ethical value, either of which is an always changing and frequently dubious guide. In other words, redefining the terms in which Plato's attack is mounted enables us to question a text's ethical value not statically but dramatically and pragmatically, in terms not of its content but of its power; can it enlarge and subtilize our capacity to live?

The answer to this question has, if only briefly, already been given: "The great instrument of moral good is the imagination; and poetry . . . strengthens the faculty which is the organ of the moral nature of man, in the same manner as exercise strengthens a limb."[21] The answer, which is Shelley's, is that poetry works its good by exercising our capacity to read. The contextualist rebuttal to Plato, then, rests finally—and fully—on a redefinition of the "good" text: it is one that challenges this capacity, one that is, as Stephen Booth has said of Shakespeare's *Sonnets*, "hard to think about."[22] Ethical and conceptual defenses here unite, as they must if either would succeed. And it is no accident that this union, in turn, brings us full circle to poetry's sacred and seductive delights: that is "*most* beautiful," announced Coleridge, "where the most obstacles to a full manifestation have been most perfectly overcome."[23]

5.

MURRAY KRIEGER
AND THE IMPASSE
IN CONTEXTUALIST POETICS

James Huffman

IN the early sixties René Wellek suggested that, in order to become a "coherent literary theory capable of further development and refinement," formalistic criticism "would need a closer collaboration with linguistics and stylistics," but it "would hardly need a radical revision."[1] In fact formalism has had to deal with several disciplines that Wellek did not anticipate, has had to be revised more than many New Critics are comfortable with, and still has not produced a fully coherent theory in the sense of a conceptual system free of contradictions which nullify it as a theoretical construct.

By the early seventies several French invasions had already hit the beaches or were on the way—existentialism with Jean-Paul Sartre, phenomenology with Georges Poulet, Structuralism via Ferdinand de Saussure and his students, Post-Structuralism through Jacques Derrida, and new insights in philosophy and anthropology by Maurice Merleau-Ponty and Claude Lévi-Strauss. Some of the formulations of Saussure and Derrida threatened the basic assumptions of formalism, that poetry creates its own unique contextual world un-like other forms of discourse, and that it thereby embodies a unique cognition. Instead of just suffering from a temporary theoretical impasse, or the constant "crisis" that Murray Krieger seems both to try to calm and to incite, formalism was being totally ignored or even pronounced dead by a number of commentators.

Krieger's constant paradoxes in his early career are signs of a logical impasse in contextualism, requiring one to examine Krieger's later formulations to see whether concep-tual progress has been made, or whether the basic impasse still stands—whether contextualism is dead, or whether reports of its death are exaggerated. The body of contextualism has had to survive strong attacks, and if Krieger has made some con-ceptual progress, much of the shaky theoretical ground on which formalism was originally founded still threatens to open up and swallow it whole. But I think the way out of the paradoxical impasse of contextualism is still open.*

Let me operate in reverse, trying first to refute those who assume formalism is dead, so I do not have to perform a sudden act of resurrection at the end of this essay. Grant Webster undertakes to bury formalism by claiming that it is an outmoded paradigm, and refuting his theory of paradigms, which he calls "charters," should at least establish the possi-bility that formalism still lives. Although Webster admits that Krieger is the most articulate formalist, achieving contextual-ism's most "systematic theoretical development" by creating its " 'normal theory,' the articulation of the theoretical impli-cations of a charter within its initial set of values," he also identifies Krieger as his generic "unrevolutionized critic," one who sticks to his guns long after the battle has gone somewhere else.[2]

To Webster, Krieger is a man whose "career time" be-gins unfortunately just when his chosen "charter time" is

---

*In the Richard Berg interview Krieger discusses the current status of contextualism in his work—Ed.

ending: "the charter he uses to form his opinion of the literary world becomes obsolete just as he finds his own voice; thus he becomes superannuated just as his career is beginning" in 1956 (*TRL*, 42). Most unkindly, Webster charges that in his "Republic of Letters critics also avoid or deny the problem of their aging by pretending that the old vision is still relevant (as have Krieger and Howe)," so that Krieger "remains unrevolutionized, our best example of the superannuated critic." The word "pretend" is particularly offensive here, since Krieger has worked hard at honesty and frankness in relating his ideas to new theories and revising his concepts as new insights appear. At any rate Webster is convinced that "the Gestalt has shifted, a critical revolution has occurred, and Formalism is finished as an active force among contemporary theorists" (*TRL*, 37, 201, 205).

By "contemporary," Webster means mainly young or in vogue. His theory of "charters" is very pragmatic, and all but overtly suggests outright opportunism to the young scholar. Since the critical theory a scholar follows is seen as totally the result of free-will choice, the "criticism of a literary work is essentially an act of morality"—but the smart critic amorally chooses the theory in fashion with the greatest apparent future.* Thus Webster is, paradoxically, an absolute relativist. He assumes that all current "fashions will become obsolete as have so many others in the history of criticism," and that any charter or "set of literary values" relies only on the intellectual authority of its main proponent and the document he produces, and "is limited in time and function." Fittingly enough Webster admits that "perseverence wins" at this game, so perhaps contextualism will survive, as Freud proclaimed about his psychoanalysis, just because its protagonist may outlive his enemies (*TRL*, 10, 13).

There is certainly justification for Webster's rather cynical and in some ways anti-intellectual view, since critical theories have indeed come and gone. But Webster does

* See Krieger's own comments on fashion and the critical stock exchange in the Richard Berg interview—Ed.

not see that critical movements leave important elements behind for others to build upon, or that new movements add
significantly to their insights. He refuses to admit any connections among the theories and schools, assuming that
movements are totally disjunctive:

Krieger's implicit view is that one movement derives logically and
historically from another, so that his Formalism can be related to
movements that come after it. The view of Kuhn and the view
maintained in this book, is that the change in movements involves
a "critical revolution," a shift in paradigms or charters, so that the
new movement is not, and *cannot* be, related to the old, since the
new movement asks different questions, expresses a different
charter, uses different critical procedures. (TRL, 201)

This central issue must be resolved if formalism—or any
other theory—is to have any lasting value even as a contribu-
tor to later developments. In the first place, Krieger's view (or
Frank Lentricchia's in *After the New Criticism*) is not so
simple as Webster's notion of critical paradigm shifts suggests; some movements are related both logically and historically, but even those which are historically disjunctive often
have logical connections because, despite Webster's claim,
movements do answer some of the same questions. One reason formalism still stands in a fruitful relationship with other
movements is that it deals with central questions, some of
which any theory must deal with: what is the nature of language? what kind of existence does language have? what kind
of knowledge, if any, may language involve? what is the relationship of poet to poem? poem to reader? poem to language?
poem to culture?
    Even if some of the questions of ontology, epistemol-
ogy, phenomenology, psychology, anthropology, linguistics,
or whatever are ignored or negated (as in Jacques Derrida),
Krieger is quite correct in seeing that all critical theories must
cluster around some of the same basic issues. As a result, he
says, there is still "a vital relationship between dominant
currents in present theory and my own work," and critics

should "see my work finding its shape at least partly as a result of that relationship" (PPI, 201).

Moreover, there is another reason Krieger's views are still current. Very simply, as he puts it, "If I do not continue to have a living relationship to the dominant movements in current theory, it is because I have worked at it, trying to keep my own position in motion, whatever the fidelities which I tried to retain" (PPI, 201).* His procedure is not the most empirical or objective, but it behooves any theorist to see whether his concepts stand up to new considerations and to revise them if they do not.

Webster oversimplifies the career of formalism to fit his own charter, which after all may not succeed even on his own terms if it does not become influential. His way to "evaluate charters, and distinguish the good from the bad" (terms with debatable utility here) is "on pragmatic grounds, by measuring the capacity of the charter to generate practical criticism that will reevaluate the literary tradition in terms of the Gestalt of the new charter; or, to put it another way, by measuring the capacity of the charter to become influential."

Thus Webster can only admire the pragmatic successes of early formalists, whose "easily teachable method of explication and their control of jobs and magazines combined to create a solid literary power structure which dominated the literary life of their time." But Webster sees only power and politics in his "republic," not representatives of different areas of thought and disciplines which may yet cooperate effectively in governing the world of letters. There is no productive heuristic cycle either in empirical or conceptual terms for Webster. According to his "principle of obsolescence: critical questions are never refuted but are changed when they are no longer of interest" (TRL, 85, 206, 203). No doubt the changes in critical theory are sometimes more temporal than logical, but whether this happens all the time, or should happen anytime, is at best debatable.

* Krieger's attempts to keep his position in motion and to appropriate new theories are discussed by Mark Rose and Vincent Leitch (essays 1 and 2)—Ed.

More serious are the deeper issues of meta-criticism that Webster raises. Since everything in any critical charter flows from "an extracritical standard of value or ideology" and the system covers only "the problems the theory is designed to solve, and the values it expresses," any critical theory "mediates between the observer and what he observes, or, more accurately, the informing conceptions of the observer that determine what he chooses to observe and the nature of what he observes." If this viewpoint is totally (and exclusively) accurate, it presents major problems for any theory making any claims of value. First, no incompatible data could get through to a follower of a charter to challenge his theory. Indeed perhaps no truly empirical data exist in the realms of criticism; or as Webster expresses it, "the point at issue is whether there is a reality, literary or physical, which exists apart from the critic or scientist and can be known directly by him." According to Webster, this point is problematic for Krieger because of his "assumption that one can experience literary works directly, without the intervention of categories." That is, "the difficulty—which Krieger admits as a possibility" is that "if one does not admit the existence of an unmediated aesthetic experience . . . , then Krieger's system must lose its preferred status and become another possible response among many" (*TRL*, 8–9, 196–97).

But Krieger has insisted repeatedly on the empirical fact of readers having aesthetic experiences, of being caught up in the context of a work to the point of experiencing in some way another world. (Dreams may be a useful parallel, or daydreams.) Krieger posits the totally intransitive experience only as a probably unreachable ideal, but comes back again and again to insist on the empirical repeatability of aesthetic experiences under the right conditions.

Lately he is more tentative on exactly what that aesthetic experience may be, but he still "must insist," even with all his "newly won self-consciousness and self-skepticism," on at least "the illusion of verbal and aesthetic presence in that beckoning structure that confronts the reader-critic" (*PPI*, 203). While he is aware that this experience could be the result mainly of training or brainwashing, the fact that anything approaching aesthetic experience can occur under any circumstances suggests that something else must be operating as well—that there must be something linguistic in order to make even a psychological illusion possible. At root, then, Krieger is trying to be empirical. He takes data from his own and others' experience, forms a postulate to explain the data, and derives a theoretical structure which would account for the phenomenon from beginning to ending, in poet-poem-reader.

For a time, then, Krieger takes leave of data in favor of deductive logic to create a theoretical system that would explain the phenomenon tentatively defined. At this stage the theory might be considered equal to other theories explaining the same phenomenon, as Webster claims, or in parallel but disjunctive competition with theories which define the phenomenon differently. Nevertheless, I claim that not all theories are equal at any stage. If a theory can be shown to be more logically consistent or complete or better able to explain all data available, then it deserves to be considered a better theory. If new data can be explained by the theory, the system has become more complete; if not, the contradictory data may suggest a revision in the original hypothesis, which in turn generates a better theory than the original. This theory, if heuristic, continues the cycle, presumably becoming more and more congruent with external reality by approximating and explaining its complexity.

Perhaps no single theory will ever correspond exactly to reality, since there may be too many factors for any one conceptual system to handle. Goedel's Proof, from metamathematics, suggests that the ultimate creation of a self-sufficient, coherent, comprehensive axiomatic system may be an impossible goal: if a system can be shown to be consistent, it cannot be shown to be complete; if a system is complete, it is not demonstrably consistent.[3] The impossible ultimate system need not concern us, however, just the possible ones, and their comparative heuristic and explanatory value. More than one equally consistent and explanatory system may be constructed, as in the discovery that Euclidean geometry, with its postulate that parallel lines never meet, was not the only possibility. Theories may compete on empirical grounds, or, if no data is available to help arbitrate, they can compete on grounds of conceptual sophistication and consistency. In other words, no matter how the basic issues are resolved, not all theories are necessarily equal. Not even Derrida's "decentering" necessarily disrupts this procedure, though it may lead us to greater conceptual sophistication (TWM, 1671).[4]

Since Krieger turns away at times from data of individual works and of readers reading to develop his theory only as conceptual system, I would like to examine its sophistication and consistency rather than its empirical accuracy, which is not possible to determine in a short space. In early work like The New Apologists for Poetry Krieger admits the value of both analytical and empirical methods, but has difficulty in coordinating them. Consequently in later work he sometimes denies even the possibility of empirical method in literary theory. It is appropriate, then, to judge his work mainly as analysis.[5]

From the very beginning, in The New Apologists, Krieger worried about New Criticism foundering upon the paradoxes that result from its eternal dichotomies. Then the paradox resulted from a "referential"/"contextual" dichotomy (NAP, 20, 168). In A Window to Criticism, a reformulation claimed that a "miracle" allows the totally contextual "mirror" of the work to become somehow a referential "window" on the world (WC, 17–18, 32–33, 67–70). This book marks the beginning of the claim that metaphor's capability of combining identity and difference at the same time, presence and absence, parallels what poetic use of language can do on the more cosmic scale of the complete work—the defining thread of Krieger's later essay collection, Poetic Presence and Illusion.

The Tragic Vision and its sister work pick up the dichotomy of chaos and order from existentialism, and rework the earlier paradoxes into the system. His late theoretical works, such as Theory of Criticism, are still full of dichotomy and paradox; in the third chapter, as Frank Lentricchia remarks, "his habit of pushing his thinking to unresolvable contradictions is brought to stark perfection" (ANC, 253).* In his later essays, where he has benefited from and appropriated the terminology and concepts of Structuralism and Post-Structuralism, Krieger finally seems more relaxed in what he sees as an essential yet non-logical formulation, though he still speaks of a crisis in formalism.

Nevertheless, the obsessive "both/and" structure of his formulation shows a part of his continuing struggle to move beyond traditional logic. He is trying to find a language and conceptual structure which can express how both a concept and its mutually exclusive opposite may be simultaneously operative. In his best late essay, he describes the problem as "justifying a theory which talks out of both sides of its mouth in order to encompass identity and difference" and his other polarities; "these paradoxical workings of poetic metaphor— so contrary to the permissible logic of discourse—can be accounted for only by a system of relations between opposites which defies our normal sense of contradiction." Always he assumes that the "paradoxical logic (or illogic) or metaphor" operates outside the permissible realms of logic: "In contrast to what discursive logic can recognize—the moment of opposition succeeded by the moment of compromise and reconciliation—in poetic metaphor the poles are to be seen as at once opposite, reversible, identical" (PPI, 152, 160, 157).

What Krieger does not yet know is that the resort to paradox and metaphor does not disqualify his theory as a logical system. As some recent philosophers recognize, in-

---

* Derrida is also in constant struggle to deconstruct and move beyond the oppositions of metaphysics, especially in "White Mythology," his own analysis of metaphor. See Adena Rosmarin throughout (essay 4) for further discussion of Krieger's dichotomies and paradoxes and of the problem of distortion in representational systems—Ed.

cluding Derrida in his treatment of Fontanier's catachresis, the resort to nonlogical statements to express insights may just suggest the need for more adequate terminology and logical systems:

There may very well be some things which in the terminology available at the time can only be said obscurely; either in a metaphor, or (still more disturbing) in an oxymoron or a paradox, that is, in a sentence which breaks the existing terminological rules and is in its literal meaning absurd. The man who says them may of course be just confused. But it is possible that he is saying something important. . . .[6]

Clarity is not always possible owing to the state of terminology in a discipline. More important, clarity and accuracy are hindered by the kind of conceptual distortion which causes antinomies in theoretical systems; inadequate terms and conceptual distortion are inseparable. Krieger needs conceptual terminology more adequate to his insights.

Perhaps the best way to proceed is to show how such concepts have already been used in other fields. Directly parallel theoretical developments in science and mathematics show how important and valuable more comprehensive concepts may be. Dualistic formulations like Krieger's have caused antinomies in physics and chemistry—antinomies which disappear when old dualistic concepts of matter and energy change. Einstein posited that matter can change into exactly equivalent amounts of energy and vice versa with his famous formula $E = mc^2$, but scientists still assumed that matter and energy have discrete characteristics. When observers examined light and other forms of radiation closely, however, these seemed to act at times like waves of energy (undulatory) and at times like particles of matter (corpuscular). Not until the formulation of the quantum concept, that energy is released in discrete units of bundles called quanta—a concept which unites characteristics of both matter and energy—could wave-particle behavior be explained as complementary rather than contradictory. Due to problems in conception, for a time early forms of quantum theory remained as "a contradictory addition to classical laws," like Krieger's antinomies, until the Heisenberg–Dirac forms of quantum mechanics altered "some definitions and the mathematical rules for manipulating physical symbols." By 1926 a "rational, self-consistent quantum mechanics" was developed, which "started afresh and evolved a mathematical framework and philosophy all its own."[7]

The new mechanics is not easy to comprehend, for like relativity theory, it disrupts the old dualistic concepts of space and time (examined also by Derrida), and suggests a possibly inseparable relationship not measurable by usual means. Among its many triumphs, quantum mechanics has explained what was a complete conundrum in the classic theory of photoelectricity. These major breakthroughs occurred primarily because scientists stopped conceiving of matter and energy as opposite and completely separable entities, and devised a concept combining the two, the quantum. Perhaps it is time that the concepts and terms in meta-criticism took a "quantum leap" as well.[8]

It may seem heretical to suggest a need for new mathematical and scientific logic for contextualism when the New Criticism so strongly denied the appropriateness of applying their concepts and methods to literary theory. But literary theory is not literary criticism; it is meta-criticism, and like meta-mathematics its basic foundations must be logical—despite Krieger's protests that a non-logical system is needed to apply to a nonlogical use of language. Krieger is correct in rejecting the old logic that governed mathematics and science, but these disciplines have now undergone precisely the kind of logical metamorphosis that contextualism needs and that Derrida seems to be proposing with concepts such as "differance" and "supplement."

Like Krieger, mathematicians discovered that "if one wishes to keep pace with the bold and restless mathematical spirit, one is faced with the comfortless alternatives of abandoning logic to preserve the classical concepts, or accepting the paradoxical results of the new analysis and casting horse sense to the winds." And like Derrida, "modern mathematics" is "faced with the alternatives of adopting annihilating skepticism in regard to all mathematical reasoning, or of reconsidering and reconstructing the foundations of mathematics as well as logic" (*TWM*, 1943, 1952). Post-Structuralism is dangerously close to adopting that annihilating skepticism for all critical theory, when the alternative of reconstructing (perhaps after deconstructing) the logical system is far more promising.

For this reason it will pay critical theorists to become aware of new systems. For example, Goedel's Proof, mentioned earlier in connection with Krieger's attempt to create a complete and coherent axiomatic system of aesthetics, has "provoked a critical reappraisal, not yet completed, of widely held philosophies of knowledge in general." If Krieger is going to use axiomatic methods of inquiry, then he should ponder the following discovery:

Goedel showed that the axiomatic method . . . possesses certain inherent limitations when it is applied to sufficiently complex systems—indeed, when it is applied even to relatively simple systems . . . He also proved, in effect, that it is impossible to demonstrate the internal consistency (non-contradictoriness) of such systems, except by employing principles of inference which are at least as powerful (and whose own internal consistency is therefore as much open to question) as are the logical principles employed in developing theorems within the systems themselves. (*TWM*, 1669)

No proof for the formal consistency of a system comprehensive enough to contain a whole aesthetic theory is possible without employing rules of inference and assumptions outside that system which are not self-evident. Such a system will be "*essentially incomplete*" because there is "an inherent limitation in the axiomatic method" as a way of systematizing wholes. The theorist cannot get a "formal system to speak about itself" without great antinomies (*TWM*, 1685–93).

The problem with a purely axiomatic method is that, like Krieger's "miracles," the meta-critical statements needed to complete and "prove" the system may be as presumptuous as the meta-mathematical statements needed to complete arithmetical systems, or the aprioristic "axiom of reducibility" invoked by Russell and Whitehead to try to prove mathematics equivalent to logic. As a result, "such proofs are in a sense pointless if, as can be demonstrated, they employ rules of inference whose *own* internal consistency is as much open to doubt" as the formal consistency of the system under consideration (*TWM*, 1694). This set of problems described by Goedel as inherent in axiomatic systems is a blueprint of one of the most persistent theoretical difficulties in contextualism.

Goedel's formulations suggest the need for a more comprehensive test of validity than mere consistency. Krieger's tendency to thrash about among inconsistencies like Emerson ("a foolish consistency is the hobgoblin of little minds"), while remaining content with his basic insights like Whitman ("I am large; I contain multitudes"), implies the inadequacy of consistency as the only ultimate test of theory.

To justify his supposedly neither synthetic nor eclectic approach, Krieger tries to create a system of organic theoretical constructs like the one outlined by philosopher Harold H. Joachim in his description of truth as "coherence." Joachim rejects the Cartesian idea that "truth is linked to truth until the arrangement constitutes that network of chains of truths which is the system of ideally complete knowledge"—a formula Krieger and Derrida struggle to escape also—and favors a more organic conception to aid formal systems in avoiding antinomies. Very like Krieger in rejecting the form-content antithesis inherent in the fundamental assumptions of formal logic, Joachim posits a theory of truth as "conceivability" rather than just consistency. As he explains the term, "to 'conceive' means for us to think out clearly and logically, to hold many elements together in a connexion necessitated by their several contents," a definition readily adaptable to Krieger's attempt to derive a consistent tripartite poetics. A properly conceived system results in a "significant whole" possessing "systematic coherence":

A "significant whole" is such that all its constituent elements reciprocally determine one another's being or contributory features in a single concrete meaning. The elements thus cohering constitute a whole which may be said to control the reciprocal adjustment of its elements, as an end controls its constituent means.[9]*

Struggling with traditional logic, Krieger has been continually frustrated with paradoxes which reveal the failure of his theory to attain full systematic coherence. One reason for his difficulty is that he has been unable to go beyond the concepts and methods of the older logic, and in attempting to do so has introduced some "inconceivable" elements into his theory. Philosopher P. F. Strawson describes Krieger's predicament, and solution, very well. Sometimes, he says, when thinking at an unusual level of generality, unacceptable but inescapable conclusions arise:

In this situation, some conceptual distortion has taken place; and, in general, the distortion is the consequence of an undue pressure exercised by some only of the features of the language in which we express the concept in question, to the temporary exclusion of others. To correct the distortion, we must clearly expose the full logical workings of the distorted concept, and perhaps of others too; and locate, if we can, the source of the distorting pressure.[10]

The main distortion in Krieger is his conception of all the dichotomies he describes as mutually exclusive opposites. As in the case of matter/energy in physics, or good/evil, beauty/ugliness, start/stop, and dozens of other pairs in Western languages, these words are not conceptually opposite but in fact part of a single more comprehensive conceptual unity. It is impossible to understand one part without the other, because the two are inseparable parts of the same unit. Intuitively Krieger understands this quality of language but states his understanding in an extreme fashion which distorts the

* See Krieger's own comments, in the Richard Berg interview, on the loss of logical ground in his theoretical development—Ed.

synthesis and becomes more than just a "friendly eclecticism which would embrace antagonistic positions," that he has so nearly achieved:

Indeed, the relations between the opposed claims which I develop, as I seek to affirm both of them, are not meant to be mutually supportive; they are rather meant to be polar, though in a duplicitous way that permits polarity to become transformed to identity, but without being any less polar. By polar I mean only the extreme form of difference, the logical consequences of the mutual exclusion between differential elements which turn them into binary oppositions. As mutually dependent as they are mutually exclusive, they undergo their will-o'-the-wisp transformations, leaving us unable to take our eyes off either of them without losing the other. (*PPI*, 156–57)

The elements he deals with are indeed "polar," but part of a single continuum rather than mutually exclusive as he conceives. Language itself is a continuum, whether we define its poles as poetry and prose or use newer terms such as *parole* and *langue*, or the more comprehensive *écriture*. It is not necessary for uses of language to be mutually exclusive in order for poetry to have a unique function or form of cognition; "degree" and "kind" are two more differences, like identity and difference (or "*differance*"), or even right and wrong, which are illegitimately conceived as exclusive opposites.

Krieger is constantly using the so-called "law of contradiction," the "law of identity," and the old "law of the excluded middle" in his formulations, but these are outmoded concepts from older logic. For example, he notes that "the fundamental law of logic is of course the law of identity, which is to keep us from confusing distinct entities, to keep them from overrunning the bounds of their distinctness." Consequently he finds that only "an utter miracle that violates the law of contradiction" and the law of identity can make an element of poetry "both itself and something else" (*WC*, 7, 23, 216). But the law of identity is not applicable to all supposed entities, and breaks down when applied to elements which are inseparable.

Similarly, by always defining his elements as mutually exclusive when they are not, he is misusing the outmoded law of the excluded middle, the idea that something cannot be both "p" and "not p" at the same time. Logic has learned that "p" can be "not p" and that there may be third possibilities even in binary systems. Interestingly enough, intuitionist mathematicians have created the only known mathematical systems which contain no antinomies precisely by rejecting such concepts as the law of the excluded middle and the idea (also a conceptual distortion) of completed infinities. And non-Euclidean geometries resulted from challenging the assumption that "logically incompatible statements cannot be simultaneously true," and that "if a set of statements is true . . . they are also mutually consistent."[11]

Misuse of infinity and other extreme concepts—such as Manichaean chaos, the instantaneous, and absolute uniqueness or "the utter autonomy of the particular"—is a major source of antinomies throughout Krieger's work, and even affects some of Derrida's formulations.[12] The Tragic Vision sees the protagonist's world in modern tragedy as a Manichaean chaos, a jumble of contradictory, discrete perceptions. The paired antitheses of dualistic Manichaean vision are presented as evidence of the chaotic nature of life at least on a phenomenological level. But the idea of Manichaean chaos is based on the concept of an infinite reality, which no finite observer can perceive. Krieger is misusing the notion of infinity.

The old point-line antinomy from geometry shows the problem. Since the mathematical point has no dimensions (like Krieger's "instant," which as no dimension in time just as the point has no dimension in space), it used to be said that any line "contains" an infinite number of points. Immediately Zeno's famous paradoxes proving the impossibility of motion between points arise, as does the antinomy on how any number of dimensionless points could ever add up to a one-dimensional line. Problems such as these arising from even the simplest uses of infinity have made the concept a very mixed blessing. Now mathematicians know that "special rules are required for operating with infinite series" and that "ignorance of these rules, or failure to observe them brings about inconsistencies" (*TWM*, 1956–76).

Perhaps, as in Derrida, we need to recognize that anything in metaphysics can only be a provisional abstraction, useful but not presumed to have theoretical validity. Nevertheless, I believe our understanding is increasing, contrary to Webster's implications. Krieger is always struggling valiantly to exceed himself, to go beyond his previous understanding, and in some ways each successive book achieves that goal. He and Lentricchia are both correct in seeing the long-term history of thought as developmental, not discontinuous. In his treatment of Krieger and many other theorists across several disciplines, Lentricchia sees a continuing attempt to struggle with dualism, and at least some hope, through Derrida and Michel Foucault, finally to break free. Even Derrida, who is a *bete noir* sometimes in his own eyes for presaging a birth now definable "only under the species of the non-species, in the formless, mute, infant, and terrifying form of monstrosity," has defined something that has constituted almost an historical universal in Western thought. And he is not truly turning his eyes away from "the face of the unnameable which is proclaiming itself," or trying to proclaim itself when we have the language/concepts to express it ("Structure, Sign, and Play," 265).

I do not have space to deal fully with Lentricchia and Derrida, or the representatives of so many disciplines which will benefit from this birth, including Lévi-Strauss, whose opposition between "nature" and "civilization" may disappear. We are ourselves nature, though in us nature may be civilized. We are part of the world, and part of the world is us, not just in us. That connection is what makes possible the relationship of human disciplines to each other and their relationship to the rest of reality, from which they are inextricable. Like Andrew Parker, I believe that there should be no "question of *taking sides* between these particular discourses," as New Criticism did against science, "but a question of indicating how such disciplines are (and are not) co-implicated in one another, 'historically.' "[13] And we may have to redefine our notion of history as Lentricchia and Derrida begin to, even though there seems now to be another "fundamental contradiction" between the idea of history and our "conceptual apparatus." Nevertheless, we will approach, we must approach, that contradiction; for as Fredric Jameson sees, that problem "contains within its structure the crux of a history beyond which we have not yet passed."[14] We may be moving toward systems of thought which are, finally, beyond contradiction.

PART II: EXISTENTIALISM AND HISTORY/ PHENOMENOLOGY AND DESIRE

6.

MURRAY KRIEGER: A DEPARTURE INTO DIACHRONY

Wesley Morris

The existential realm is, from the standpoint of propositional structure, a raging chaos.

The veil that the practical will must place between us and an infinitely varied mass of unique phenomena . . . turns out to be another veil as well: the veil of universal principles that our anti-existential need for moral order, for sanity, must place between our judgment or decision and the contradictory mass of raging and resistant particulars that make up the raw edges of our moral experience. . . . This is the veil . . . man in his social dimension . . . must hold before his vision if he is to permit himself to function, to believe in the legitimacy of his functioning. He must stalwartly stare at the veil and keep from looking beyond it—as if it constituted reality, all of reality.

Poetry breaks through because it alone dares construct itself in freedom from the equally false, equally comforting, veils of the stock forms of language.

The critic must follow in a similar spirit, disdaining
the ideological adaptation, the propositional use of
poems. . . . A not-quite-poet who also has been
given the charter for the freedom of his imagination
by the poem, the critic . . . is never again the
same. . . . (PPC, 247–51)

I BELIEVE we can find in these four passages the central concerns of Murray Krieger's remarkably productive career as a
theorist. They are relatively straightforward, although endlessly rewritten and readapted to meet new challenges. As a consequence, I find these basic concerns endlessly suggestive.

From these four quotes, and with some anticipation of
more recent versions, we can outline a fundamental schema.
1) The ground of poetic activity is the existential realm—a
reality of chaotic particularity similar to what Sartre termed
de trop. 2) The milieu of poetic expression or performance is
the realm of social activity with its veils of ethical and moral
ideology. The suggestion is that this is a world of bourgeois
values and reductive logic, a world of cultural bankruptcy.
Because poetry is a linguistic enterprise, this realm is what
we today call that of ordinary language, what the early
Krieger associated with prose or propositional expression
and which the more recent Krieger defines as a langue seen
as "generic expectations" or as a "system of minimal cues to
produce the stereotyped response in us" (TC, 187). Langue
thus becomes the structure of that coherent reality that bourgeois society takes as "given." 3) The poem is its own realm,
an inviolable, organic object in the early theory, a new Word
miraculously transubstantiated, incarnated from old words,
or more recently and less ontotheologically, a parole which
has violated its langue to the extent that it "appears to have
become its own langue" or "micro-langue" (TC, 188). 4)
Lastly, and "secondarily," the act of the critic, which must
keep its place without yielding the pleasure and freedom of
its near-poetic play, touches the realms of poem and existen-

tial reality but also has its own special and indispensable commerce with the prosaic realm of propositional and philosophical expression.

It is this last function that I wish to explore in this essay, for in it I find Krieger's most persistent struggle to break free from narrow formalism and articulate a powerful argument for the importance of poetry—or what we should call "the literary"—in contemporary society. Yet this is not to forget that these four realms are inextricably woven together, and that makes an approach to any one of them cumbersome and inevitably distorting.

And there are further complications to acknowledge before I begin. Krieger's strategy as a theorist has always been to confront and appropriate as many opposing theories as he could.* By this I do not wish to be understood as arguing that Krieger's work is fragmented or discontinuous; it is, in fact, remarkably consistent, insistent on its origins being included in the most recent adaptation. This process of appropriaton and rewriting seems to me to epitomize Krieger's idea of the critical function, and I wish to keep that focus before us even though we must begin far away from that issue, at the basic ground of his philosophy: existentialism.

I

Even at this familiar level the theory is problematical. In and of itself, Krieger's existentialism defines a vague anxiety focused on a terrifying reality characterized by contingency, by a chaos of particularity. It is not always clear whether this reality is merely the flow of raw sense data impinging on the brain or a metaphysical locus of evil, al-

*For further discussion of Krieger's appropriations, see Mark Rose and Vincent Leitch (essays 1 and 2) and Krieger's own comments on his theoretical development in the Richard Berg interview—Ed.

though there is a way to settle this confusion—somewhat. One of Krieger's representations of the existential realm is borrowed from Nietzsche. Here the chaotic reality is equivalent to Nietzsche's subversive nightmare of Dionysian revels. But Nietzsche insists, and Krieger agrees, that this Dionysian principle is irrevocably bonded to its opposite, the Apollonian dream of harmony.

Krieger adapts this paradoxical model of order-in-disorder to describe the function of the poem. This is not the same as the function of poetry, or of the poetic tradition; these latter are matters of the critical tradition, culture, and history. They are important concepts; nevertheless, Krieger here is bent on rewriting the old New Critical problematic of the form/content dichotomy. Every true poem is marked by the aesthetic harmony of Apollonian order, but not at the expense of failing to reflect the Dionysian chaos of existential reality. This paradox is necessary if the poem is to manifest itself in society's propositional, ideological realm of moral and ethical judgments, within the sane reality of society's repressive structure, in ordinary language, and yet touch the deeply schismatic existential realm of raging chaos.

The importance of this paradox is that it allows the poem to function "critically."[1] This is a term that Krieger would not likely use in this context, but the issue is an important one. The poem is critical in two ways. First, in its Heideggerian instability, its wavering between life and death, being and nonbeing. Second, in a Kierkegaardian sense, in its social functioning as skeptical of moral universals, covert metaphysical assertions, or easy propositional truths (TV, 11–12). In this way it destabilizes that reductive, static, bourgeois complacency that marks a culturally repressive social order. Although its medium is language, the poem is not, for Krieger, merely rhetorical. Its destabilizing function arises from its resistance to conceptualization. It offers itself as language, in language, masking as ordinary communication within the context of familiar meanings and values; but the harder we try to fix it according to one proposition or another, the more it slips away. Because it consists wholly of the language of the familiar, ethically stable world, this resistance is disturbingly subversive. The inevitable result is critical interpretation—after the fact—arising from our contemplation of the poem's paradoxical functioning and extending beyond the poem's immediate context into social meanings and values. The poem itself may make no statement, espouse no philosophy, yet it is the occasion for many philosophical statements.

The discussion has led us quickly toward the major issue of the critical tradition in Krieger; but what of the existential reality we began considering? It is still difficult to know what that is. One of Krieger's favorite expressions for it is the "Manichaean face" of reality. Thus what we perceive or experience is only a mask, and Manichaeanism is hardly a raging chaos. It is more nearly a psychical state of neutralization, the incessant counterpoise of antagonistic impulses. In this sense Krieger's poem is itself Manichaean, and the real reality behind the mask remains, in good Kantian fashion, unknowable. What is behind the Manichaean face, however, is important precisely because it is unknowable, meaningless, and I suspect that we should not even call it a raging chaos lest we step into the same trap that Robbe-Grillet snapped on Sartre for calling reality nauseatingly "absurd." "Chaos" and "absurd" are value-freighted, and in a bourgeois context function ideologically. "Chaos," for example, simply means the other, dark side of "proper" social order—the taboo, with all the suggestions of sin and punishment that accompany the thinking of the unthinkable.

Krieger's existentialism, a projection of a World War II *Weltanschauung*, argues that the poem in some sense imitates existential reality, but we must recognize that it is the poem's own Manichaean vision that establishes the mask that it is said to imitate. This circularity is not vicious; it merely argues that Krieger's existentialism is not a metaphysical assumption. The Manichaean face is always already within bourgeois society, and there is no simplistic nature/culture division proposed here. Beyond society with its veils and its subversive anti-veils is the world's body, implacably there.

I think the major objection to Krieger's theory today is that this existential vision is out of date.* This is a historical judgment which need not result in a rejection of Krieger's general theoretical position but rather would seek to rewrite it. And it does not mean that we are today without anxiety— just that the Manichaean vision of disorder strikes a contemporary reader as abstract and perhaps too deeply a private vision. Our anxiety is global: the threat of nuclear holocaust. It may be only an appropriate terror as we approach a millennial transition, but it has concrete referents and is prophetic of the extinction of humankind—ironically suicidal since the means of our disappearance from the universe is in the hands of our own ignorant armies.[2] It is a vision more terrifying and more incomprehensible than the remembered mad horrors of World War II. This fear is with us in our everyday lives, in the ever-present details of political gamesmanship contested on an international playing field.

What is most important here is that international politics, with its apocalyptic potential, is dispersed heterogeneously, situating diverse societies and special interest groups within any single social unit, whereas the existentialist vision is homologous, emphasizing an abstraction: the human condition. Existentialism, therefore, subsumes the pluralism, difference, heterogeneity of collective political interaction through a radical reduction of concerns to those of the individual (hence, representative) human in a struggle for personal authenticity.[3]

This is the struggle that Krieger's poem teaches us, and it can do so only by totally resisting commitment to political or collective action—sanctioning only a commitment to the abstract ideal of a recurrent assertion of individual freedom within an equally abstract vision of deadening, repressive bourgeois society.[4] But we have grown suspicious of this pri-

---

*In the Richard Berg interview, Krieger claims to have moved away from his early existentialism—Ed.

vate inner freedom, for it fails to address the concrete issues of outer, social life. Herbert Marcuse argued as far back as 1936 that when this ideal of inner freedom becomes the fixed center of an ideology "it is not difficult to accommodate the fact that the external sphere [is] primarily a realm of servitude and unfreedom, for this [does] not, after all, affect 'actual' [inner] freedom" (SCP, 128).

Clearly Krieger has no such consequence in mind, but these questions arise more insistently now than they did in the years immediately following World War II. So it is that Krieger's poem, subversive of those veils of cognitive distortion, contemptuous of the practical world of human functioning based on a too easy, familiar, propositional truth, "critical" as it is in its assertion of its own irreducible (almost unthinkable), impractical, non-propositional structure, can only help us understand ourselves in our world a little better; but its unrelenting Manichaean vision blocks all social/political action or commitment, for it equalizes, balances, flattens out ideological decision-making and judgment.

II

But should we ask the poem to function more immediately in the realm of political action? Is such functioning totally incompatible with Krieger's aims? Neither of these questions is easily answered, and I hope here merely to outline an approach to the basic issues involved. To do that I propose that we look at another phase of Krieger's theory, his appropriation of historicism. To this end let us again begin with quotations.

There can be . . . no question about history getting into literature; it is the very stuff of literature which, after all, cannot be created *ex nihilo.* But this history that enters literature as its raw material is the living, felt, pulsing history of breathing men and not the static formulae of ideology.

From the front end of history, our vantage point, the poet's activity may indeed look like the imitation of what has already been formulated elsewhere in culture; but to the extent that he has imitated truly existential and preconceptual forces, one cannot know what was being imitated until after the poet has made it perceptible—which is to say, after he has created it to show what it was he imitated. (WC, 59, 64–65)

The admission of history to the formula for the poem's functioning in society can be seen as perfectly consistent with the existential theory outlined in section I. Nevertheless, the use of the term "history" is problematical, for there are two histories here just as there are two "realities" to Krieger's existentialism. First, history is the "stuff" of the poem insofar as it is lived. Second, history is the "static formulae of ideology." The distinction is that of living beyond the veil in the Manichaean density of experience and living as functioning within the practical world of moral order and propositional truth. It is questionable whether or not "history" is the proper term for the former, but we can refer to it as existential history. Thus following the existentialist paradigm, existential history as imitated by the poem is a subversive anti-history within the realm of proper bourgeois social history.

What seems merely to be a principle of poetic anarchy here must be viewed in the larger context of Krieger's historicism—a "new historicism" as he designates it. This interlude in his theoretical career is rarely discussed by others, perhaps because the very idea of history has been so roundly attacked by the deconstructionists, but it is both interesting and important. It is, surprisingly, a step toward Krieger's later effort to appropriate Jacques Derrida, although in its earliest model, that taken from Eliseo Vivas, it represents, I think, a false step.

Krieger draws from the theories of Leo Spitzer, Eric Auerbach, and Sigurd Burckhardt to formulate his new historicism, yet it is Vivas' tripartite definition of the poem's "object" as "subsistent," "insistent," and "existent" that provides him with a foundation formula (*WC*, 59). Vivas claimed the poem could be said to have meanings and values which subsisted in society prior to the poem's composition. These meanings and values were only half-formed, waiting to be brought into poetic life by an act of visionary midwifery.[5] The poem expresses these meanings and values in completed form, and as such they are insistent, contextualized within the inviolable structure of that poem. Finally, through a process of reductive abstraction, these insistent meanings and values are conceptualized for society's use and are then said to be existent. It is clear, even though Krieger always avoids political terms, that these existent meanings and values function on the same level as the moral and ethical propositions of that bourgeois society that Krieger's existentialism seems ever to have in mind; and because of this, as we shall see, there are troublesome implications for the theory of historicist criticism.

That the poem builds on other meanings, even half-formed ones, is an important move away from the New Criticism through a radical historicizing of the formalist definition of creativity as a transformation of old words into a new Word (*TC*, 202). Vivas' subsistent realm, however, is metaphysical, and Krieger rewrites the model in order to embed the subsistent meanings and values in the realm of social functioning (*Creation and Discovery*, xv). Here they are not half-formed concepts nor the institutionalized ideas of a reductive abstraction but are "forces" for change that history recognizes after the fact as having been there. The poem, therefore, projects its own object of imitation, and seems also to reflect moments of social revolution—almost as if these forces were at work in the author's social and political unconscious. Yet as we look backward from history's vantage point, we recognize the "great" poems as those that contained and discovered the meanings and values that have since become functioning, reductive propositions.

For "subsistence" let us think of the indefinable subterranean forces at work in the Renaissance. Some of these find their way into every facet of the complex structure that is Marlowe's *Faust*. Here, and only here, this special grouping of them achieves absolute "insistence" . . . But the cultural interest in ideology can abstract from the complex of forces in the play and come up with the notion of "Faustian Man" which it can use anywhere, in an endless variety of contexts. The forces can thus achieve Vivas' "existence." (*WC*, 60)

This is indeed a radical departure from formalism if we see the critical historicist's interest focusing on the history of the social "uses" of *Faust*. For Vivas and Krieger, however, these uses are merely reductive appropriations by a pragmatic and culturally bankrupt society. Their interest is in the gap between these bourgeois appropriations and the subversive, resistant, authentic poem. Even this, of course, is a historical interest, a critical placing of the work (as prophetic of change) in its historical context (as evidence of the prophecy fulfilled). The work's greatness is measured, one might argue, by its appropriation, the fact of its having been made "proper" (reductive as this may be). The critical historicist tradition would, therefore, canonize only those works whose reflections of subterranean forces have successfully entered into the functioning of society, for only then would it "look like the imitation of what has already been formulated elsewhere." To this extent the canon established by historicist criticism "looks like" a mere confirmation of society's official history, and the historicist critic could do no more than assert the subservience (rather than the subversiveness) of the poem to propositional social order.

Vivas' tripartite theory plunges Krieger's historicism into a reactionary stance that the existentialist idea of the subversive poem contradicts. The poem, apparently a harbinger of change, is from history's perspective, that textualized and functional perspective that is all we have of history, little more than an affirmation of bourgeois society's enormously appropriative powers. We certainly can make distinctions between the uses of a work and the work itself, either with or without a formalist aesthetics; the problem arises when we define the work in terms of its imitation of meanings and values that can be known only after the fact of having been translated into propositions of use value.

We must measure the work's authenticity, consequently, according to the degree of its divergence from the inauthenticity of bourgeois appropriations of it. That is, we determine authenticity through an Idealist projection, what Krieger calls an "as if" assumption, by reading backward from society's misinterpretations and misreadings. Perfectly consistent with existentialist thinking, this yields a wholly negative poetics which fails to take full notice of the richly meaningful "misreadings" (uses) of the text that reflect the functioning of society's ideological machinery. Moreover, Vivas' model argues for no serious departure from society's institutionalized meanings and values; the function of all poems is to realize what is already on the way to realization, to better facilitate society's misappropriations. This is a circularity that is, at the least, politically vicious.

The borrowings from Vivas are significantly muted in Krieger's more recent work, and from the beginning Vivas' existent object gave Krieger some trouble—although it was hardly perceived to be as insidious as I have suggested. It is, I think, this aspect of the model that needs to be rewritten, and we can do so in terms of Krieger's earlier theory: specifically his conception of the "tragic visionary" (TV, throughout). Krieger's move into genre theory here defines an existential tragedy (parallel to the existential reality and history we have already discussed). In this genre there is a crucial division of functions assigned to the tragic visionary and the tragic existent—a twinning of the traditional figure of the tragic hero. Both of these characters are necessary to the presentation of a critical vision that subverts the complacency of bourgeois society with its static and repressive official history.

Krieger's "ideal archetype" of this tragic genre is Conrad's *Heart of Darkness*, and I believe that his discussion of this story says more to us today than it did at the time of its first appearance (TV, 155). It anticipates his new historicism and his more recent theory, which goes beyond the Vivas model. In Conrad's story Kurtz and Marlow, respectively the tragic existent and tragic visionary, depict also the man of action and the man of representation. The division between experience and language is sharply drawn; a skeptical nominalism questions the very act of writing about the world beyond the veil, the world that Krieger sees Kurtz daring to confront directly. Kurtz is Krieger's Manichaean, both the representative of static, bourgeois propriety and pagan violations of social taboos. Kurtz is the self-righteousness of moralistic imperialism taken to its own logical extreme in mad, amoral brutality. He is the civilized and the uncivilized, the cultured man and the natural man, joined so completely that we cannot sift out a propositional statement of his essential character.

Marlow, on the other hand, is wholly civilized, a man of the ethical sphere of social functioning, although as tragic visionary he wanders to the very edges of stable, sane bourgeois society. It is Marlow who must translate into words (through his "interminable" tales, as the unnamed companion among his listeners calls them—a crucial statement that Krieger does not discuss) the experience of Kurtz's plunge into extremity. Marlow is Krieger's poet, or perhaps it is better to say that Marlow is the tensional equivalent of the poem. He must function within the boundaries of ethical society yet undercut its bourgeois thinking with his critical tale of Manichaean experience. It is a formidable task, and not surprising that it is interminable—focused as it is on the voracious inclusiveness of Manichaean projections which defy closure.

However we interpret Kurtz's role in Conrad's story—as tragic existent to Marlow's tragic visionary or as a representation of the brutal immorality of late nineteenth-century bourgeois imperialism—narratively Kurtz functions as a name without a referent. Conrad withholds Kurtz from the plot as an act of mystification, allowing Marlow to patch together from scraps of secondhand conversation and fragments of Kurtz's writing a character that is completely enigmatic. Marlow's interminable story, therefore, is an elaborate interpretation of other texts, all of which are couched in the ideology of turn-of-the-century European imperialism and racism. As Edward Said remarks, "the heart of the matter—Kurtz's experience—is posited outside Marlow's discourse, which leaves us to investigate, if we can, the speaker's authority."[6] Kurtz is the dread chaos within the society of order and stability. He cannot be dismissed as merely mad (cast out of society to be ignored, forgotten, repressed) because he is so purely a representation of that society. Marlow (Conrad?) has built his poem solely out of the materials of ethical society itself, and thus we realize the Kurtz's existential reality is not only unknowable, as Krieger would argue, but ultimately inarticulate (as the existential inadequacy of Kurtz's famous speech, "the horror, the horror," demonstrates).

It is Marlow's monologue that adds profundity to Kurtz and to Kurtz's words, that establishes an alien mystery within the familiar. But his very mystification, the tragic visionary's "drawing back," as Krieger describes it, tells us more about Marlow's (and Conrad's) motives than any of the information we possess regarding Kurtz can tell us of his. Kurtz is Marlow's (and Conrad's) projection for the purpose of defining and closing the boundaries of bourgeois society. Kurtz, after all, dies as a kind of scapegoat to prove ethical order is what keeps the savage beast from our door. Even Marlow's disgust with the imperialism of his ethically pure society early in the tale seems to have been forgotten at the end.

But in projecting the mystifying Kurtz as Manichaean principle logically extended from society's highest goals, Marlow has indeed dared more than his companions (who charge him to keep a "civil" tongue). Conrad's poet/poem, Marlow, is critical even though the story's power lies not in the conflict between the extremes of the tragic existent and the complacency of bourgeois society, a conflict mediated by the Manichaean tragic vision of Marlow, but rather in the conflict between the awareness of society's repressive values accompanied by a desire to unmask them and a fear of doing so lest the foundations of civilization crumble, thereby casting all into unthinkable chaos—hence, the necessity of the mystified Kurtz, himself cast out only to be brought back to affirm society's transcendent stability with his dying breath.

For this conflict there is no mediation. What, then, of imperialist exploitation and racism? Clearly these issues must be raised, and Marlow's wavering critical position forces them on us. Marlow's interminable interpretation merely sets off a series of such interpretations, each encompassing and rejecting/rewriting/appropriating (as I have done here with Said and Krieger) those that went before. The poem's critical status, its power to embody contradictions that are unrealized, repressed, in society's institutional structure, frees critical interpretation for a truly historical analysis that not only considers the critical tradition of the work, the history of the uses of the text, but continues the interminable task of critically placing the text in its social context as it simultaneously establishes a social context to receive the text.

Have I departed too far from Krieger, employing much of his terminology to distort his theory? This will have to be answered by others. At this juncture I want to suggest that Krieger has always been concerned with the critical tradition and the function of criticism within society. If I have played down his concept of the poem as expressive of an existential reality and invaded his concept of the inviolable poem with the function of criticism, it is because criticism, with its complex ties to society, has become the central issue of our thinking about the idea of "the literary"—an occurrence in no small part due to Krieger's own efforts.

And this raises another point: why is the study of the critical tradition so important? Perhaps it is because the critic and poet (like the tragic visionary and tragic existent) combine their efforts to work within society against a tendency toward complacency and moral/ethical blindness. The critical poem and critical interpretation are in this way truly "de-constructive," an idea that Krieger comes to as a result of his reading of Derrida. Is there not, then, a range of actions combining poets and critics stretching between and within the extremes of anarchic rebellion and dogmatic affirmation? If so, this would provide Krieger with a break from Vivas' existent object, which could only function to serve the ends of bourgeois repression. The critical tradition (poem and interpretation) dwells within bourgeois society's own contradictions, is a product of society, but need not serve the same ends.

It is understandable, therefore, why Krieger's career has been so consistently devoted to the promotion of the history of critical theory, and his success here has been remarkable. It is a heavy burden he places on criticism, a sense of importance that can be traced directly to his interest in the literature of the eighteenth century. A significant portion of his published work is devoted to writers of that era, and Dr. Johnson emerges in Krieger's reading of the critical tradition as a heroic figure. A great critic caught in the transition between neo-classic and romantic philosophies, as Krieger interprets him, Johnson is a contradictory figure, a critic in crisis; so he too represents those subterranean forces struggling to emerge, and that makes him something of a poet-critic even when he was not writing verse (TC, 50–51).

It is Johnson's dictum that great poetry is measured by its continuance of esteem that initiates the very concept of a history of criticism which Krieger seeks to preserve and advance. Johnson's idea that the poem lasts because of its "general nature," of course, seems contrary to Krieger's faith in the poem's unique individuality; but from the perspective of the history of criticism it is the poem's individual, irreducible (to local meanings and values) character that is its general nature—that which measures the continuity of culture within and ever sensitive to the endless changes of society's history. The very tone of Krieger's concern for the critical tradition is more typical of the eighteenth century than of the

Romantic era which gave such support to his formalism. The aim of criticism is the improvement of taste through education. Every critic in Krieger's tradition is a scholar/teacher whose goals beyond mere *explication de texte* are to put us (critically) in touch with the history of our Western culture.

III

It is not a distortion to argue that Krieger is as interested in the critical tradition as he is in the poem itself. *Theory of Criticism* is an elaborate and self-conscious rewriting of the critical tradition since Aristotle in order to discover the poem as defined by the great critics, and from this tradition we establish the foundation of our literary canon. It is a tradition, as Krieger sees it, which describes the poem as an enduring, self-defining, articulate text, asserting its presence as a privileged moment of performance in the span of cultural history. Yet it suffers, necessarily, from Heideggerian fragility, for insofar as the poem endures so too does it risk fixity and transcendence with a resultant emptiness of meaning. It must, therefore, be self-critical of its privileged status, and as such it is a presence engaged in struggle for survival— a struggle with its historical moment that the poem will inevitably lose.

To this point I have avoided using the term "presence" in this essay because it is, I feel, less than useful in the climate of today's theoretical debates.* In its most radical, ontotheological implications it marks a dead end in poetics, and Krieger's efforts to avoid these implications are too often lost on inattentive readers anxious to espouse the American deconstructionist dogma. The least we can say of presence is that it is problematical; the most we can say is that it embodies a mythical projection. Krieger works out of the latter

*See the discussion of presence in Mark Rose and Vincent Leitch (essays 1 and 2)— Ed.

position. He employs the term in the context of a rather unexpected conjunction of the formalist doctrine of aesthetic distance with the Saussurean/deconstructionist obsession with the division between signifiers and signifieds. As a result he formalizes the deconstructionist hobby-horse of the freeplay of signifiers, rewriting it as his own concept of illusion of poetic fiction.

It is noteworthy that this conjunction accidentally calls attention to the similarities between deconstructionist theory and classical formalist theory; Krieger's appropriation of this American version of Post-Structuralism is easier than its advocates might wish. But for Krieger the primary aim is to argue that the poetic work represents the free play of humanistic fiction-making engaged in a struggle with the grander, inhuman free play of that differential structure of signifiers Saussure called *langue*. The freeplay of *langue* is appropriated by the poem's freeplay as *micro-langue*; freeplay is turned on itself to produce the poem.

Moreover, *langue* for Krieger (as the quote above on Augustan mock-heroic illustrates) is not the freeplay of empty signifiers. It is historical in the sense of defining what we used to call a period, a unified structure of meaningfulness defined by the history of ideas, and which we now have learned to designate under a more descriptive terminology as mythology, base structure, or *episteme*. Here the signified enters again, not as a "Real" which stabilizes language as referentiality but as a reality fully textualized. This signified is no more than a system of signifiers which produces a culture's knowledge, that which society takes as "given." As myth it is unconscious in Claude Lévi-Strauss' sense. As the discursive practices defined by Michel Foucault it eventuates in ideology. It is, of course, another version of that world of bourgeois abstractions, the "language of our evasions," that Krieger's early theory condemned, but here it is so much richer and more complex as the conscious and unconscious meaningfulness which anchors our social existence (*TC*, 195). *Langue* is historicized (in a more Derridean manner than the ahistorical deconstructionists are willing to recognize), and the struggle between *langue* and *micro-langue* becomes truly critical and deconstructive. Presence, consequently, is a name we give to the point of contact between critical poem and cultural myth; it is recognized only through the historical perspective of critical reading.

But what of the Johnsonian tradition, the work that endures and pleases many? Clearly such a poem must now be seen in its critical functioning, threatening a deconstructive practice that not only verges on its own self-destruction but which acts as an agent of deconstruction for the cultural mythology that is the *langue* of such a poem's *parole*. This is not simply a negative definition, for as an expression of cultural myth the poem also preserves as it criticizes.

We must wonder, then: is this too far from the New Critical concept of old words into a new word (now unfrocked of its ontotheological raiments)? And is not what lies within/ beyond bourgeois culture's mythology, its given reality, a raging chaos quite in the existentialist mode? Finally, is it not the case that works assert a critical difference with their cultural mythology to a greater or lesser degree? Presence, then, is rewritten as critical performance, and we understand such criticism as being capable of both affirmation (however uncomfortable) and revolution. The critical nature of poetry operates within the same spectrum which encompasses Krieger's classic and tragic visions, ranging from ethical retreat to radical (tragic) denial. This spectrum is the focus of our interest in the author's confrontation with his reality, and his fear of what Said poignantly terms "molestation . . . , a consciousness of one's duplicity, one's confinement to a fictive, scriptive realm, whether one is a character or a novelist. And molestation occurs when novelists and critics traditionally remind themselves of how the novel is always subject to a comparison with reality and thereby found to be illusion" (*Beginnings*, 84).

Said doubles the idea of misreading that we evolved in section II from Krieger's use of Vivas; here misreading describes both the author's critical appropriation of his culture's reality in his fiction and society's (the critical tradition's) misreading of that fiction in the name of its stable, sane reality. Said's terms, the "duplicity" of the "fiction," its "illusory" nature, are the same terms Krieger repeatedly uses throughout his theory with similar implications.

Krieger places duplicity in the structure of the work as its illusory presence which allows us (momentarily) to see the work free of the molesting threat of reality, *langue*, or cultural myth. Said is not so hopeful, feeling molestation as a strong presence in the author's consciousness that invests the structure of the work, a part of the undercurrent of undecidables that represents a political unconscious. Yet as both read Conrad's *Heart of Darkness* their theories converge on the character of Kurtz as the embodiment of contradictory cultural forces. Said's concerns approach that point from a perspective on Conrad and his culture, the author and reality behind Marlow's struggle for authority in his tale, and Krieger's interest in Kurtz, the bourgeois imperialist and savage, comes from his concern with the duplicitous structure of the work as it strives to express the contradictory extremes of the tragic vision. Unquestionably, both of these approaches are necessary and complementary.

Such complementary notions also help Krieger undo the confusions surrounding the idea of presence as he attempts to accommodate Derrida to his version of the critical tradition. He observes, "it is surely odd that the device of the pun, which for Burckhardt was the dominating, indeed enabling, act of presence, is for Derrida the instrument to undo any such notion as presence" (TC, 229). Krieger sees these two positions as negative and positive poles, but I would suggest that they are not opposed but merely different and complementary. Derrida's concerns are with the structure of discourse and the inevitable return of the duplicitous text to the anonymity of *langue*. Sigurd Burckhardt describes the focus of discursive practice, the speech act, or performance, that is historical.

Like a principle of indeterminacy, one cannot espouse both perspectives at the same time, but both are unconditionally subsumed within the differential structure of

language. The pun of deconstruction is rewritten as the poem
of critical practice, as the situating of the author as teller of
tales in culture and history. Perhaps this explains why
Krieger in *The Tragic Vision*, and its companion volume *The
Classic Vision*, was so often led to works which contained
tellers of tales, like Marlow, engaged in the struggle of authority and molestation. And perhaps we can speculate that
history for Krieger inevitably becomes an anthropology or
archaeology because the critic, still in Dr. Johnson's image, is
something of an archivist, a curator arranging and displaying
the monuments of man's literary performances that comprise
his cultural past—all the misreadings by an institutionalizing
society as well as the misreadings of that society through
fictional appropriations. It is the only means we have of
knowing our past as wholly textualized, intertextual.

We need not, therefore, see presence as miraculous,
although Krieger continues to use this terminology with full
awareness of its nostalgic implications.* Presence, however,
is recognition by the critical tradition, something more and
less than the Idealist "as if" commitment to the poem's objective status. Presence is the mark of discursive practice that
grounds our sense of history as well as issues in the formation of a literary canon, in the definition of "the literary."
Krieger's theory, now only faintly existential, nevertheless
locates that existentialist disorder-in-order within society
itself—so clearly manifest in a literary character like Kurtz,
who functions both as a Lévi-Straussian unmediated contradiction within late nineteenth-century bourgeois mythology
and as a Derridean undecidable in the texture of the work.
The battle between *langue* and *micro-langue* is a Hegelian/
Lacanian struggle to death. It is continuous, repetitious,
structurally consistent, psychologically enabling/disabling,
and endless. As such it is historical and social, a fiction that
must always admit that in the final analysis (critique) "the
diachronic never loses," (*TC*, 189).

---

* Mark Rose and Vincent Leitch discuss the quasi-theological nature of Krieger's
critical language (essays 1 and 2)—Ed.

7.

MURRAY KRIEGER AND THE QUESTION OF HISTORY

Bruce Henricksen

TWO concepts of history usually apply in discussions of the relationship between literature and history. The first names history as that vision, or those visions, of human life generated within literature itself, that particular knowledge of the human situation which, as Cassirer argued (following Kant), is constituted only within symbolic forms. Since no formalism can entirely avoid the "aboutness" of literature, asserting the constitutive power of literature is formalism's answer to mimesis—through the miracle of this constitutive power self-reference and mimesis are fused, and history becomes that which literature creates. This is the history that Murray Krieger had in mind in the introductory essay to *A Window to Criticism*, where he called for a "new historicism" as a corrective to the ahistorical tendencies of New Criticism. We must, he wrote, seek "to get through the poem's closed context back to history and existence" (WC, 3).

And yet this statement seems to point to an opposing concept of history as an extraliterary and extratextual given, which exerts its own shaping power on the literary text; history now exists outside of literature, and literature becomes that which is constituted within history. This is a properly Marxist concept which encourages the analysis of literature as ideology.[1] Is it possible to reconcile or sublate these two versions of the relation between literature and history? Krieger attempts such a reconciliation in his parable of the mirrors in *A Window to Criticism*. In this parable the reader, seeking refuge from a chaotic reality, finds sanctuary within the literary house of mirrors, its interior walls reflecting its own internal order. But then, miraculously, the mirrors turn to windows and, more miraculously yet, the windows project the interior order upon the outer world. Literature has ordered or in fact created our vision of history, but the order we see is now "really" out there, in history; that is, we are not free to see history independently of the forms literature has offered to us (WC, 67ff.). Literature has been the source of our categories of perception, and the phenomenological circle is airtight.

But it is precisely that airtightness which denies mediation with the Marxist view, a view which would ask, among other things, what conditions helped create the house of mirrors to begin with and therefore what interests are being served as the reader's perceptions are shaped by it—questions that require one to maintain an ontological distinction between the literary and the real.

This is not to deny the constitutive power of literary forms, but simply to argue for a give-and-take between the power of literature to constitute perceptions and the power of prior perceptions and social forces to constitute literature. Krieger has acknowledged the role played by prior, "subsistent" meanings and values that enter the poem, and he has therefore suggested a model of how literature can function as ideology.* But the poem, which to Krieger always maintains its innocence by acknowledging its own fictional status, is

---

*Wesley Morris discusses the "subsistent," "insistent," and "existent" aspects of the poetic object (essay 6).

always taken at its own evaluation, and the move is never made to unmask the poem's possible complicity with "subsistent" values which themselves require scrutiny. Thus criticism loses its potential for social action, for "criticism" in the full Arnoldian sense. Michael Clark, in essay 8, notices that when Krieger refers to the poem (in the words of Wyatt's sonnet) as "his mistress and a queen" he fails to refer also to the sonnet's warning that the queen belongs to the king. Krieger represses the political entanglements of the poem and, by extension, of the critic, although the repression seeks to acknowledge itself in Krieger's citation of such an obvious poem of intrigue.

At the outset of *Freud and Philosophy*, Paul Ricoeur posits two interpretations of interpretation: "interpretation as recollection of meaning" and "interpretation as exercise of suspicion."[2] The first is associated with the phenomenology of the sacred and corresponds to Krieger's notions of the miraculous powers of the poem to contain "presence."* The second is associated with such secular unmaskers as Nietzsche, Marx, and Freud, and it involves a recognition of the essential difference between a text and its object. Although the opposition between these two kinds of interpretation can be deconstructed—Ricoeur later alludes to the possibility of one inhabiting the other (pp. 60–61)—Vincent Leitch is correct in suggesting the greater power of a quasi-sacred hermeneutics of presence in Krieger's theory, as attested to by the insignificant place accorded to Nietzsche, Marx, and Freud in *Theory of Criticism*, Krieger's version of the critical tradition.[†] My contention is that a more thorough appropriation of a hermeneutics of suspicion is essential if one is to get beyond the closure of the poem and into the social and historical field.

In a recent essay Krieger discusses those theorists who, in a tradition fashioned by Marx, Freud, and Foucault, seek

---

*See the discussion of presence in Mark Rose and Vincent Leich (essays 1 and 2).

†And see Krieger's own statement, in the Konstanz Colloquy, of an "imbalance" in handling such oppositions.

to "expose allegiances not openly claimed" by the literary text. Their "darker suspicions," Krieger says, are "invidious." And since their own texts, which must also have undersides and repressions, are caught up in the very systems of power they would critique, the moral ground upon which they would stand "falls away." These critics emerge as the opposite of what they would be, not egalitarians but tyrants who "subjugate the text to themselves, the subliminal masters that make us distrust all that is said." Krieger concludes that we would do well to let the text "make its own claims and to examine them on their own, as if they were disinterested."[3]

But it is not clear that the necessary reflexivity of a theory of textual repression necessarily destroys the theory. Further, Krieger is being more combative than persuasive when he casts those theorists in the role of "masters" who "subjugate" texts. In his interview with Richard Berg, he has rightly critiqued the inappropriate use of political analogies by those who see the "privileging" of literature as undemocratic. But having here, in a dubious political analogy of his own, dispelled the suspicious reader as a tyrant, Krieger liberates the text, which now must be taken "as if"—a crucial phrase in view of Adena Rosmarin's exploration of the fictional nature of the "as if"—it were disinterested.

In another essay Krieger grants many of the assumptions of the suspicious reader, "that we are often self-deceived in our belief that we think and write as utterly free agents," that institutional pressures on thought and discourse are very real, and so forth. But nonetheless the reductionism of those who look for a "subtext"—the term Jameson uses in *The Political Unconscious*—is like that of "the gross Marxism" of the 1930s.[4] This charge rests on two assumptions: (a) that the suspicious reading involves "the easy dismissal of manifest content," and (b) that the latent content is more simplistic than the manifest. But the latent can only be discovered within the manifest, which is never therefore dis-

missed, and the discovery of the latent—like the interpretation of a dream—can only be enriching. When, for instance,
Jameson reads Conrad's subtext he works *with* Conrad's existentialism; he does not simply dismiss this prior reading.

Krieger's avoidance of a hermeneutics of suspicion and
his failure to reconcile the history constituted within literature with the history outside was, in his earlier work, a product of *his* existentialism. Although existentialism does not
necessitate the denial of political reality, as Sartre's career
demonstrated, Krieger's existentialism has served this denial.
It was a Barthesian "myth" in that it initiated a depoliticizing
transference of attention from the common to the particular; it
equated the history outside and prior to literature with a "raging" existential chaos from which "dazed" humanity flees to
the ordered house of literature.

This pre-literary "history" has no intentionality and no
structure and is unavailable to understanding or change—it is
that which produces nausea and the absurd. Literature imposes a vision of order upon it, creating "history" as something coherent and structured. The career of Krieger's persona, then, is like that of Sartre's Roquentin, who also flees
nausea by finding a way to create fictional history. Existentialism is the device that enacts the repression of the historical understood as that structure of interests which is itself
fiction's context. This is how Fredric Jameson analyzes the
ideological functioning of the existential in Conrad, a writer
who not coincidentally plays a major role in *The Tragic Vision*. Jameson argues that Conrad's foregrounding of Jim's
existential confrontation with destructive nature serves to
mask the true story of British imperialism—the true history—
implied in the plot.

We have indeed already discussed . . . the metaphysical, which
projects a proto-existential metaphysic by singling out Nature, and
in particular the sea—what crushes human life—as that ultimate
villain against whom Jim must do anthropomorphic battle to prove
himself. Nature in this personalized sense is fundamental if Jim's

quest is to remain a matter of courage and fear, rather than that quite different thing [an enactment of social contradiction] we have shown it to be.[5]

A similar functioning of existentialism can be seen when Krieger narrates the passage of chaotic, pre-literary "history" through literature, which transforms it into the ordered history of our post-literary perceptions.

Finally there is of course no denying some imitative role to literature: since history pre-exists literature, literature must in some sense imitate it. There can, then, be no question about history getting into literature: it is the very stuff of literature which, after all, cannot be created *ex nihilo*. But this history that enters literature as its raw material is the living, felt, pulsing history of breathing men and not the static formulae of ideology. So it is history as existential force that gets into literature by being there first; it is history as institutionalized in ideology that comes after, thanks in part to what literature shows us. (WC, 59)

If Jameson's analysis of existentialism as that which enables an ideological repression has validity, then this quotation is a strange moment in which Krieger's text reveals its own inner mechanism. On the one hand it makes the dubious claim that the history which exists prior to literature is "raw" and unencumbered by ideology. On the other hand it acknowledges that history as a structural model can only exist within ideology (no history is innocent) and that literature plays a role in or with ideology in producing such models. But Krieger's last sentence is unclear—the relationship between ideology and literature is imprecise, and the "in part" further suggests a need to escape implications.

Krieger comes close here to offering a definition of history that encompasses political and social processes as well as the non-literary discourses of people who call themselves historians, and he comes close to making literature available to political and social criticism.* But his own investments in

*See Krieger's remarks concerning history, in the Konstanz Colloquy, particularly his insistence on viewing it as an effect of discourse.

the ideology of formalism, with its assertion of the privileged status and constitutive powers of literary language, make it impossible for him to become appropriately suspicious of literature's ideological entanglements.

Perhaps the word "prison-house" in the glass house parable, anticipating the title of another of Jameson's books, further suggests what Krieger cannot acknowledge, that the way back to history demands a more thorough escape from his own poetics than he is able to attempt.

As we enter the work, before its system gradually closes upon us, like shades of the prison-house upon Wordsworth's growing boy, it appears—like other discourse—to be composed of elements that mean to relate obviously and immediately to the world outside the walls. (WC, 29)

The glass house is allegorical on a level Krieger does not fully intend, foreshadowing the growing exhaustion with history that has characterized much Structuralist and Post-Structuralist thought since the writing of A Window to Criticism. This is not to say that Krieger is unaware of his paradoxical position. Indeed, his very title poses the paradox in that a historian's window would normally be thought to open onto an external order (or disorder) of things, a window to history, rather than onto his own discourse, A Window to Criticism. The title therefore anticipates the image of the prison-house, and this image, coupled with Krieger's observation that literature functions to produce ideology, suggests a possible "other" Krieger who struggles against the limitations of his own critical language and who secretly alludes to Nietzsche, not Wordsworth, in mentioning the prison-house.[6]

This "other" Krieger, however, is held in check by the radical skepticism of the dominant critical persona, for whom the literary work is our only, last-ditch way of knowing in a world that is otherwise without rhyme or reason. In the following passage, the ability of the poem to reduce and then replace reality can be taken as a projection of the critic's need to dominate and annihilate existential facticity.

These illusionary worlds, as our imaged realities, may also appear to be satisfying simulacra of "the world" outside, though that world has now been reduced not only to the bounds of our intentional perception but also to the capacities of language to enclose within itself what would seem to open it outward (except for those moments when it is viewed from within what we intend as an aesthetic act). Nor is the world any longer cognizable except by way of such illusionary reductions, or what Gombrich terms "substitutes," even if the substitutes are our only free-standing prototypes. The illusion is all; it is the seer's imaged reality, since there is no independently available reality against which the image can be seen as distorted or false. . . .

Within our qualified sense of its presence, then, the poem remains as a reduction of the world to the dimensions of humanly imposed form, a human metaphor that is supposed to "stand for" extra-human reality except that, by way of the illusion which is as much reality as we intend, the metaphor is the formal expression of all that reality has become, has been compacted into. . . .

The poem, then, is a signifier which must carry its authenticity within itself since no external signified is accessible to us. (*PPI*, 142–43)[7]

These remarks reject a correspondence theory in favor of a coherence theory by which meaning is located solely within the internal structures of discourse. Moreover, they privilege literary discourse as the only lifeboat in the tempest, as though our colleagues in other departments already lie full fathom five without knowing it. The Konstanz discussion in this volume serves to modify or contextualize Krieger's earlier claims concerning poetry and the real, primarily by emphasizing the phenomenological and anthropological (as opposed to ontological) nature of his enterprise, which is to describe aesthetic perception as culturally conditioned. Krieger's phenomenology, however, can allow for the historical only as a repressed "presence" in the poem—or as something signified only by a "negative reference."[8]

"Contextualism" was the term used to label this argument concerning the absence of an external signified, referring instead to an all embracing "context" provided by the poem itself. But it was an odd name for a position that refused to contextualize the poem in a larger historical or intertexual world; it was a verbal appropriation of the move the position in practice refused. In "The Existential Basis of Contextualism" Krieger defines the poem as a unique engine against the "veils" of ordinary language which blind us to the truth beyond (PPC, 239–51). The poet is a knight of faith moving beyond these propositional veils. Thus Krieger sees his own existential poetics as linked to romanticism, with its thrust beyond the veils and propositions of neo-classicism, and specifically to the particularizing aspect of the Coleridgean I AM, which anticipates the existentialist's assault on essences.

This romantic notion of the radically free individual ignores the questions posed by such post-romantics as Marx, Freud, Lévi-Strauss, Lacan, Foucault, and Derrida concerning the shaping of the subject by structural and representational arrangements. The hermeneutics of suspicion associated with such names would view the poem not as an instrument against the veil but as part of the fabric. For Krieger the poem itself is radically suspicious of ordinary language, leaving no ground for the critic's suspicion of the poem. It is true that if the poem and the critical text are also seen as part of the fabric a certain Archimedean position has been lost, but it is a position that can only be maintained as a fiction. Seeking to maintain the poem's Archimedean position, Krieger isolates the poem from propositional discourse by offering the proposition that "experience . . . is never common," a belief that would render social life impossible (PPC, 249). Common experience—the political and the social—like neo-classical "general nature," is repressed in favor of a romantic privileging of the existential particular.

Krieger's criticism does of course focus on common experience—our common experience of the poem. But while apparently describing this common experience, the critic is in fact arguing for a particular mode of reading with its own particular blindnesses. In his recent formulations,

Krieger has claimed "anthropological" status for his descriptions. By this he means that his theory is descriptive of how the poem operates within culture as an intentional object, a projection of the desires of readers. While the poem may contain structural and linguistic features that push toward openness—just as the word "rape" in Pope's title opens the poem onto the reality of sexual violence which at the same time "The Rape of the Lock" represses—the reader's desire is always for closure.

Krieger has difficulty with the fact that a new generation of readers seems to have abandoned this desire, although an adequate anthropology would need to account for such changes in reception. As Gabriele Schwab argues (in the Konstanz Colloquy), Krieger's is only a "first step toward anthropology." One might probe the origins of the traditional desire for closure or seek to articulate it against the larger field of cultural and social behavior as, for instance, Claude Lévi-Strauss has analyzed the aesthetics of other cultures as projections of social life. One might ask, for instance, if New Critical closure is a projection onto aesthetics of the political conservatism and golden age nostalgia one finds in so many of its original theorists. If, as Krieger so often says, the poem is an object of desire, what desires, really, are being displaced upon it? Krieger's refusal to confront such questions shows that his historicism and his anthropology are indeed making only a first step. And if Krieger's statement that "the diachronic never loses" is an acknowledgement of the inevitable historical dimension in literary studies, the statement is more a lament than an affirmation, the diachronic being the province of Death (*TC*, 189). In the battle between Eros and Thanatos, history is the interim victim, whatever the ultimate fortunes of the diachronic might be.

The difficulty Krieger has in theorizing a historical dimension to formalist criticism finds an interesting metamorphosis in "The 'Frail China Jar' and the Rude Hand of Chaos" (*PPC*, 53–68). Here Krieger "historicizes" his own critical repressions, projecting them back onto "The Rape of the

Lock."* This poem and *The Dunciad*, Krieger argues, are companion representations of the conflict between art and existential reality. The reader of "The Rape of the Lock" is always aware of the destructive forces lurking on the edges or beneath the surfaces of Belinda's world of artifice, and this awareness engenders a certain sympathy and nostalgia for her world and what it represents. Like literature itself, her world relates to reality only metonymically or metaphorically, as the hair is a metonym for the body and the card game a metaphor for battle. The description of the coffee ceremony "opens" the poem by smuggling in references to the repressed realities of sex and of the swarming populations of a far off land, just as Krieger's language smuggles in representations of itself as a "prison-house" of "dilemmas." But the function of Belinda's world is to repress the real, or history, and that repression is justified by a theory that posits the real as an existential absurd. Thus the poem, to Krieger, self-referentially admits its own precarious status in a non-aesthetic world of conflict and chaos. When the poem refers briefly to real, unpoetic judges and hangmen, Krieger responds:

This brief, terrorizing glance at the alternative should send us clutching at the innocuous grace of the "toyshop" [Belinda's world], where we need fear neither hunger nor execution though we may have the make-believe equivalent of each. (*PPC*, 60)

Just as Krieger himself glimpsed the notion of literature's implication in ideology only to reject it, so the momentary return of the repressed reality principle in "The Rape of the Lock," which occurs through negative reference, forces the reader's dazed flight to the alternate, aesthetic realm that Krieger had allegorized in the glass house parable.[9] This, I think, is what Wesley Morris means by the "reactionary stance" of Krieger's historicism (see essay 6).

    The intrusion of reality could, of course, initiate other

*See also his discussion of this poem in *TC*, 165–67, 196–97, 201–2; and in the Konstanz Colloquy.

responses: a realization of the triviality of Belinda's world and of the need to pay attention to more serious matters, or perhaps a more suspicious interrogation of the ideological functioning of the mock-heroic in Pope's society. Although the plural pronoun in the above passage tries to hide the fact, a headlong flight from reality is not the only response to social injustice; it is a strange historian who presents himself as fleeing history, and "we" need not necessarily follow. Krieger is not innocently describing "the" inevitable, culturally conditioned response. While Pope's satire might warn many readers away from embracing the values of Belinda's world, Krieger's anxieties neutralize the satire and cause him to clutch at the innocuous grace of the "toyshop."

Thus, under the pressure of Krieger's reading Pope's poem begins to function ideologically as a justification of escapism. The subtlety of this justification is that the poem anticipates, and therefore defuses, all objections by acknowledging its own status as plaything, just as Krieger has acknowledged the fictional or "as if" elements in criticism itself.* The sophisticate need not appear deluded by the siren call of art, since the siren has confessed ahead of time. And since the poem has smuggled reality in, by the mechanism of negative reference, the critic is able to counter the charge of "empty" formalism, his escape from the real having occurred under erasure.

This should suffice to show that Krieger finds in the eighteenth century a staging of his own critical theories and their relation to his own existential anxieties.

I am here suggesting, of course, that "The Rape of the Lock" is Pope's testament of the aesthetic universe, one that reveals a nostalgic yearning for it along with a critical acknowledgement of its impracticability, and that The Dunciad is his bleak acceptance of the chaotic forces he most feared. (PPC, 68)

In The Dunciad, Krieger says, we move "away from art to the realities of history," which is to say that Pope, like Krieger,

---

*See Adena Rosmarin's discussion (essay 4) of Krieger's debt to Vaihinger in this regard.

had his classic and his tragic vision (*PPC*, 64). Thus Krieger historicizes his notion of "history" as the sum of those blind, inarticulate forces opposing art and order in the eighteenth century. If, on the other hand, one sees history as the sum of those discourses that have sought to conceptualize temporal change, then Krieger's "history" is that which is opposed to history understood as organized knowledge. Since Krieger's history is not something that has been thought in other, non-literary texts, it is not something with which literature can be articulated, as for instance one might wish to discuss *Absalom, Absalom!* in relation to a Marxist analysis of historical processes. This makes it impossible for Krieger to pursue the relation between literature and ideology, a relation the essay on Pope glances at but holds at a distance, or to examine the ideological implications of his own epistemologically skeptical definition of history.

To say that Krieger reads his own critical problematic back onto Pope and his work might sound like harsh criticism. Certainly an E. D. Hirsch would have to question the validity of such methods, but this essay is not written from the perspective of a Hirschean notion of historical meaning, nor does it assume that validity is a simple matter of establishing one-to-one relationships between a text and an outside reality. Krieger's readings are often instructive phenomenological moments in which the literary appears as a structure that mirrors the psychological structure of the critical persona Krieger has revealed with such candor. His procedure creates the fusion of present and past horizons that Hans-Georg Gadamer, in *Truth and Method*, has argued constitutes the only meaningful historicism. Thus Krieger tacitly accepts the insight that historical knowledge, to be knowledge, must have a firm grasp on the present, on that for which it is knowlege. Krieger allows the text to question him as a critic and a person, and few could argue with this procedure, since nothing can be said about literature that does not reflect local interests and values. What is at issue is not the projection of his own problematic upon literature, but the prior nature of that problematic and the kinds of exclusions it requires.

Because of the limitations of his entirely personal and "existential" problematic, it is inevitable that a book such as *A Window to Criticism*, which begins by announcing its historical intentions, should contain so little "history" as most people understand that concept. One wonders, for instance, if any historical critic today, responsive to the wider social concerns of our society, could offer a large scale discussion of Shakespeare's *Sonnets* that says nothing about their apparent anti-feminism or about the politics of the literary representation of women in the sixteenth century. While one can admire the subtlety with which Krieger's readings refashion the poems from the perspective of his own critical concerns and needs, one laments the constricted and private scope of those concerns.

I have tried to show a gap between theory and practice in Krieger's historicism: a theorizing that places strict limitations on the kind of historical discourse criticism can engage; and a practice that enacts a phenomenological encounter with the literary work which has historical implications but is never theorized on a historical level. In *Theory of Criticism* Krieger argues that major critics often inherit a critical discourse that does not allow them fully to articulate their new insights. Thus one can trace a kind of tension or fault line between the writer's language and his intention, an example being Aristotle's struggle to transcend the mimetic assumptions inherited from Plato (see *TC*, 85–97). Krieger's historicism is locked in a similar struggle to free itself, like a partially finished statue, from the formalist, neo-Kantian medium in which it is embedded. If this is so, Krieger's work represents the struggle within critical activity today to articulate the social and political nature of the literary work which the formalist tradition from New Criticism to Post-Structuralism has sought to repress.

The newer "new historicism" that is emerging from this struggle does not deny the power of the analytic tools provided by the other criticisms, but seeks to focus these tools upon the larger cultural text, creating (with or without apology) a *cultural* poetics rather than simply a literary poetics. For this historicism, literature is neither a toyshop one retreats to in dread of the real, nor an isolated and "privileged" island—-the only one worth inhabiting in a scattered archipelago of discourses. It is, rather, an organic part of culture, one region among many interrrelated and inseparable regions from which one can hope to aid the advancement of freedom. Krieger's criticism, his sacramental vision of the literary text, is a kind of Utopia, retaining its own validity as a Vaihingerian "as if" but never reaching a synthesis with alternate historical discourses.

And yet sophistication may be on Krieger's side. To speak with any confidence of extra-literary history as anything other than the raging chaos he makes it out to be is to court a "naive realism," although such naivete is not the necessary alternative. First of all, had Krieger spoken of extra-*textual* reality rather than extra-literary reality, many channels of communication would have become open. History then could be posited as constituted within textuality as broadly conceived. Literary textuality could profitably be placed in communication with the broader textual context, and without abandoning the cherished notion of the special nature of literary language. Nor would one need to argue that everything is a text.[10]

Fredric Jameson's appropriation of Jacques Lacan offers a solution to the problem of naive realism. It is essential, if we want to be able to do certain things as people involved in the world, to posit an extra-textual history that is social and political rather than existential. But like Lacan's Real, this history will remain an absent cause, and our dealing will always be with its shadowy emissaries within the Symbolic. Neither the Real nor the Symbolic (I ignore the Imaginary for these purposes) is experienced in isolation, although the Real is that which resists symbolization. Thus our entry into the symbolic carries with it an alienation, which Gilles Deleuze and Felix Guattari, in *Anti-Oedipus*, have sought to remedy by valorizing "schizophrenia" as liberation from the tyranny of the Symbolic. Theirs is a Utopian project quite the reverse of Krieger's, for whom salvation lies *within* the Symbolic. Of course Deleuze and Guattari's attempt to escape the Symbolic is precisely the move that is impossible to Lacan, and to a historian of Jameson's persuasion.

Jameson says that

it is not terribly difficult to say what is meant by the Real in Lacan. It is simply History itself: and if for psychoanalysis the history in question here is obviously enough the history of the subject, the resonance of the word suggests that a confrontation between this particular materialism and the historical materialism of Marx can no longer be postponed.[11]

The Political Unconscious is the result of calling off the postponement. But Krieger has anticipated Jameson in strange ways, as in those moments where his language reveals the "prison-house" aspect of his own formalism or where it acknowledges literature's involvement in ideology, the mistress's alliance with the king.[12] "The Rape of the Lock" *does* have a political unconscious as Krieger reads it, but while Jameson would summon that unconscious forward for examination, Krieger, once glimpsing it, labors to keep it out of sight. If Belinda's world is a mechanism of repression, it is with that mechanism itself that Krieger takes his stand.

8.

THE LURE OF THE TEXT, OR UNCLE TOBY'S REVENGE

Michael Clark

> The phallus is the privileged signifier of that mark
> in which the role of the logos is joined with the
> advent of desire.
>
> —Jacques Lacan

> My uncle Toby never understood what my father
> meant; nor will I presume to extract more from [his
> proverb] than a condemnation of an error which the
> bulk of the world lie under—but the French, *every
> one of em' to a man, who believe in it, almost as
> much as the REAL PRESENCE, "That talking of
> love, is making it."*
>
> —Tristram Shandy

AT the end of "Poetic Presence and Illusion II: Formalist
Theory and the Duplicity of Metaphor," Murray Krieger re-

To simplify references, I have used published translations of Lacan's work except
where noted. The epigraph is from *Ecrits*, Alan Sheridan, tr. (New York: Norton,
1977), p. 287. This text will be abbreviated as E in subsequent parenthetical page
references. I have used the Riverside Edition of *Tristram Shandy*, Ian Watt, ed.
(Boston: Houghton Mifflin, 1965), abbreviated as TS; the epigraph is from 486.

counts the episode near the end of *Tristram Shandy* in which Widow Wadman is desperately trying to find out if Uncle Toby has recovered from the wound he received at his celebrated battle of Flanders. Since her first husband suffered from sciatica, she is intent on discovering the exact extent of Toby's wound, "how far from the hip to the groin; and how far she was likely to suffer more or less in her feelings, in the one case than in the other." After a series of what she considers indirect questions—"Was it more tolerable in bed? Could he lie on both sides alike with it? Was he able to mount a horse? Was motion bad for it?"—she finally just comes out with it: "And whereabouts, dear Sir . . . did you receive this sad blow?" "In asking this question," Tristram continues, "Mrs. *Wadman* gave a slight glance towards the waistband of my uncle *Toby's* red plush breeches, expecting naturally, as the shortest reply to it, that my uncle *Toby* would lay his forefinger upon the place." He has, of course, promised to do just that, and he is as good as his word. Having been wounded in front of the gate of *St. Nicholas*, Uncle Toby pulls out his map of Namur, measures off thirty toises with the widow's scissors, "and with such a virgin modesty laid her finger upon the place, that the goddess of Decency, if then in being . . . shook her head, and with a finger wavering across her eyes—forbid her to explain the mistake. Unhappy Mrs. *Wadman*" (*TS*, 488–90).

Much of the controversy over Krieger's recent proclamations of poetic presence in the face of Derridean absence resembles this exchange. Sooner or later, the discussion inevitably returns to this topic, and Krieger promises to show us the very place where he has healed the wound left by the Derridean shot. After a quick account of the skirmish, he pulls out an exemplary verse, and with a triumphant flourish declares, "There!," directing our eyes to . . . the *illusion* of presence, "an illusory world which at once takes itself seriously *as if* it were reality, and yet shows us its awareness of its make-believe nature by being conscious of its artifice"; we must grasp "both the poem as object *and* the poem as *intentional* object," Krieger tells us, "mystification *and* demystification in the work's workings upon us . . . both fiction as reality *and* fiction as a delusive evasion of reality." With this, Krieger concludes—retaining all of Toby's confidence and none of his innocence—"I move . . . to my now-you-see-it-now-you-don't notion of 'the presence of the poem.' " (*PPI*, 193, 204, 208). Like Mrs. Wadman, many of Krieger's readers have been frustrated by such gestures. Unrestrained by any guardian goddess, Frank Lentricchia has attacked Krieger's latest work as "the criticism of the ever diminishing claim" that opens the door to "all-out relativism and all-out trivialization of literature and the critical effort." Despite Krieger's protestations that we must "try" to know the poem as object, Lentricchia argues, he "has, after all, come out epistemologically for a flat-out subjectivism" (*ANC*, 241, 253).

Lentricchia's argument is, in its general materialist sympathies, a familiar objection to the neo-Kantian epistemology that underlies so much modernist aesthetics as well as Krieger's poetics. In *Theory of Criticism* Krieger anticipated such objections to some extent by shifting his emphasis from the possibility of *knowing* reality through the figures of the poem to the phenomenological *experience* of reality as an "outside" beyond the limits of the poem's formal closure. So Krieger claims that Wallace Stevens, the "ultimate modernist," is able to avoid the "metaphysical gluttony of an all-inclusive monism" because "the presence of the world outside metaphor is suggested by the self-referential reminders of the poem's fiction built into the metaphor itself" (*TC*, 205). Drawing on Roman Jakobson's designation of the metaphoric and metonymic functions of language, Krieger describes those "self-referential reminders" as a combination of the metonymic reduction of the world to the word and the metaphoric celebration of that word as world. "Though locked inside those reduced, metonymic terms, those very terms," Krieger argues, "with their self-referential awareness of their own artifice—remind us of what is outside as well" (TC, 195–96).

If we are to measure metonymy as a reduction, however, we must have some sense of the world against which the reduction may be gauged; yet Krieger's increasingly careful epistemology led him in "Poetic Presence and Illusion II" to modify his earlier account of poetic language and do away with the apodictic sense of external reality that established the priority of metonymy two years earlier. In this later account metonymy is merely an effect of metaphor, and whereas before we allowed the poem to work its metonymic reduction of reality into the illusion of metaphor, we now must permit the metaphor to bring about the illusion of reality:

The illusion is all . . . there is no independently available reality against which the image can be seen as distorted or false, as a delusion . . . the poem remains as a reduction of the world . . . a human metaphor that is supposed to "stand for" extra-human reality except that, by way of the illusion which is as much of reality as we intend, the metaphor is the formal expresion of all that reality has become . . . Using the old-fashioned meaning of "metonym" considered as a figure of speech, we could say that it functions metonymically—except that, as in the case of metaphor itself, we cannot firmly say or point to the larger term (or entity) behind the miniature image to which it has supposedly been reduced. . . .

The poem, then, is a signifier which must carry its authenticity within itself, since no external signified is accessible to us. (PPI, 143)

This description of the self-sufficiency of metaphor would seem to leave no exit from the confinement of its illusory enclosure, and appears as gluttonous as the most supreme of Stevens' fictions. Nevertheless, like the traveler whose peaceful vision from the train window is suddenly clouded by the image of the passport that he left sitting on his dresser at home, our celebration in the discourse of metaphoric identity is plagued with that "lingering suspicion" that we left something behind when we entered the world of its word. Lacking a sure measure of metonymic reduction, Krieger accounts for the persistence of that feeling by transposing the metonymic effect of distance between the work and the world into a metaphoric effect of what might be called an "interior distance" between the two parts of a metaphor that suddenly splits in an apparently spontaneous mitosis:

close study of the signifier discloses its constantly enlarging capacity to be its own signfied and provide an ever-increasing sense of its semiological richness. . . . The poem's trick of being at once self-authenticating and self-abnegating enables it to proclaim an identity between itself as metaphor and its reality, a collapsing of the binary oppositions between signifier and signified, and yet enables it at the same time to undercut its pretensions by reasserting its distance from an excluded "real world." It is this acknowledged distance which seems to make the difference between signifier and signified impossible to bridge, since the signifier can find its formal nature only in the irreparable absence of the signified. (*PPI*, 144).

This "trick" that produces the signified as a mitotic offspring of the signifier certainly explains how the metaphor could collapse the binary opposition between the two. It also explains why we are able to view the poem "as a *micro-langue*, a *parole* that has developed its own language system by apparently setting up its own operational rules to govern how meanings are generated" (*PPI*, 149), since they are generated by an operational distinction between signifier and signified similar to that which occurs within the metaphor itself here. Even more importantly, as creator of both its word and its world, Krieger says that "the signifier, which is seen as struggling against its nature to create the signified it contains, seems to have forced its god into itself and thus to have become fully substantiated" (*PPI*, 151), a shimmering mirage of the Incarnate Word towards which our nostalgic longing for metaphysical presence gazes across the Derridean discourse of absence and disbelief. So, Krieger argues, "the worship of objects within the museum or within our poetic anthologies . . . has the characteristic of religious worship in that it satisfies those teleological demands of the mind that religion used to satisfy before disbelief intervened" (*AL*, 68).*

Krieger also attributes the "illusory doubleness" of the metaphoric fold that creates a signified within the signifier to the "primitive sense of metaphor" that we inherit from the "earlier ages of literal belief in the magical power of words," though of course he protects the poem from becoming a totemic fetish by insisting that our belief in the autosubstantiation of metaphor is possible only within the tradition of aesthetic fiction and so is "provisional and limited by the self-consciousness with which we address the nature of illusion" (PPI, 163–64). This qualification keeps his need to remain responsive to the word from lapsing into an indulgent mysticism, but its relation to the self-sufficiency of the poem's metaphor is puzzling. While we can easily understand why the signifier's division into its own signified would make the difference between them only "seem" impossible to bridge, it is not clear why the same stroke with which the signifier divides in two and marks its mitotic double with difference would necessarily reassert that difference as the poem's distance from an "excluded 'real world,' " regardless of whatever qualifications may be implied in Krieger's quotation marks.

Krieger addresses this problem obliquely by associating the phenomenological property of "self-consciousness" with the formalist property of the poem's self-reference. "Thanks to self-reference," Krieger says, "that self-consciousness which illusion reveals about what it is and is not—the totality of self-assertion for the sake of illusion is to be matched by the totality of self-immolation before an unyielding if unenclosable reality" (PPI, 195–96). Whereas the New Critics were committed to "an aesthetic closure that substitutes the work for the existential world," Krieger claims "that the apparently self-conscious character of this closure . . . leads it also and at the same time to deny itself, thus opening

---

*For discussion of the religious overtones of Krieger's theoretical language, in which poetics seems to replace theology in a secular age, see Mark Rose and Vincent Leitch (essays 1 and 2)—Ed.

itself outward to the existential world which it would exclude but now, by negation, must include" (*PPI*, 206).

Through his association of self-reference with the work's "self-consciousness," Krieger establishes the poem's relation to the world as a phenomenological sense of the "otherness" of a reality that resists the forms in which the poem would constrain it. This is also the way that the critic comes to a sense of something other than the solipsistic subjectivity of his or her own consciousness:

Though the work seems to exist for us only as our categories permit it to be defined . . . still there must be something in the work as it must exist . . . on its own, outside our categorical structures and symbols. This something can force our structures and symbols to work radical transformations upon themselves, in response to their own commands, as it were, though prompted from beyond their autonomous realm. What more persuasive indication can we have that there is something out there . . . ? (*PPI*, 321–22).

So just as the world is perceived by the poem as that which resists and undercuts the autonomy of the word, the poem undercuts the autonomy of the critic's categories of perception, and the "thematic double relation between the words-as-aesthetic-work and their object" becomes an exact "existential reflection" of the phenomenological character of "the aesthetic double relation between us as reader-interpreters and the words as our object" (*TC*, 242). The captured deity that we perceived in the poem as the juncture between the word and the world of metaphor thus comes to resemble nothing so much as our own sense of ourselves as readers reading language in the world, and our self-consciousness of that language as illusion appears before us as the poem's consciousness of itself as fiction: "The work functions for us as a myth that—if we watch it closely enough—knows itself to be one. This characteristic is an inevitable accompaniment to our sense of it as a fiction, emanating from the work as an inner skepticism about itself and its peculiar status in being" (*PPI*, 191–92).

The attribution of consciousness to the work thus serves

a crucial double function in Krieger's aesthetics: it establishes
the distance between the work and the world and so limits the
power of the work to illusion; and it establishes the work as
"other" to the critic's own consciousness, thereby rescuing
criticism from a relativistic subjectivism. Further, as Krieger
shows in a remarkable recapitulation of his argument in *Theory of Criticism*, it is only *as* consciousness that the work takes
on the force that constitutes it both as the illusion of the presence of a world in its word and as the presence of that illusion as a word in the world beyond the epistemological limits
of our perception:

This poem before me—as an alien "other," outside me and my
consciousness—imposes upon me to make it no longer "other."
My habitual willingness to indulge the myth of total interpretability
makes me a willing subject for an experience that, restricted to
appearance only, is properly termed "aesthetic." This experience
would convert the object from "other" to part of myself. ... I
willingly reject my prior norms and follow the deviations to the
new center, the new fiction, the new master metaphor of vision to
which these point. Then the poem as "other" has become a form of
consciousness that can alter my own. (*TC*, 203–4)

And, Krieger says, "if, in this outside reality which persists,
there is an objective embodiment of human consciousness
within a humanly created form, then it will be humanity
itself that persists" (*TC*, 64).[1]

The embodiment of consciousness in the poetic object
is the principal component in what Krieger calls "aesthetic
intentionality," and it serves as the hinge with which he
joins formalism and phenomenology. "Poetry is the only object, fixed in a final form, that does not objectify and de-
stroy—that embodies to preserve—the object as universal
subject." How does this embodiment of consciousness in the
object—indeed, the object as subject—come about? Through
a very special relationship between the poem and its reader
that turns the poem from an object into the object of desire.
Just as the poet "explores his freedom in his affectionate
toying, his love-play with the world's body," Krieger argues,

"the critic must follow in a similar spirit." He must play with poems "as converted objects of his love that deserve no less than his unwillful, sportive resting among them. ... After all, as the poet, confronting the world, must transform it into an object that has become his subject, so that critic, confronting the poem, must create it as an object that has become his subject" (PPC, 251).

Desire is thus the means with which the critic experiences the poem as consciousness, attributing subjectivity to the object and thereby establishing the object as other to himself and the world. Desire appears frequently in Krieger's descriptions of the poem as a "beckoning structure" (PPI, 203) that can "seduce us toward the willfulness of an indulged illusion" (TC, 161), and an "enrapturing aesthetic object" (TC, 17) that draws the critic to it in an idolatrous worship that grants the poem its capacity to "entrance us" into complicity with its illusory vision (PPI, 149).[2] And in Theory of Criticism the very formal closure that we perceive as the "aesthetic intentionality" in the work is attributed to an attitude that recalls the melancholy realization of all long-suffering lovers that the perfection of the loved one is more the product of their desire than its source:

All any of us has, then, is our subjective experience of the object, an experience that is never as good as we would like it and would want to demand it to be, so that we atone for our lapses by acknowledging the object to be potentially better than we find it to be. ... But it is not only the imperfections of our experience in time that we seek to overcome; it is also the imperfections of the poem itself. As we try to compensate for the inadequacies in our actual response by an act of "objective" criticism, we may tend also to make the object better than it is as we seek to put it in control of the experience we wish we had. (TC, 40–41)

Yet despite the importance of desire to Krieger's account of the experience of aesthetic intentionality in the poem, it nevertheless functions in his work more as a metaphorical motif than as a theoretical concept, and he usually mentions it as part of an impressionistic description of the poem's effect rather than as a property of the poem's linguistic form. So the aesthetic experience fragments into a self-contradictory state in which "we remain conscious of the common-sense view of language . . . and yet we permit the poem to seduce us into a magical view of language as creator and container, creator of what it contains, collapsing all . . . into an identity within itself" (*PPI*, 157–58). Krieger's aesthetics thus splits between the aesthetic permission of illusion and the self-conscious proscription of its limit; and his efforts to insist on their connection through the "systematic duplicity" of his both-and paradoxes suggest not so much an explanation of that connection as Krieger's stubborn fidelity to the experience of the poem at the expense of theoretical consistency.*

The connection between desire and language that Jacques Lacan describes makes an interesting gloss on this point in Krieger's account of the aesthetic experience. Like Krieger, Lacan associates the poetic effect of language with metaphor, which he also claims stems from the apparent collapse of signifier and signified in a creative spark. Lacan also argues that the metaphoric effect produces the impression of "Other" that we perceive across the Symbolic order of language as one who dominates not only the words we read but our entire being as well—what Krieger calls a "universal subject" in the poem. The convergence of these two accounts of our experience of metaphor is striking, coming to that experience as they do from the very different perspectives of neo-Freudian psychoanalysis and humanist aesthetics. But they differ significantly in their explanations of the cause of that effect.

Krieger suggests that our ability to indulge the illusionary sense of presence in the poem despite the Platonic proscription of belief in that presence may simply be a habitual indulgence made possible by our acculturation to the tradition of *aisthēsis*, which grants to the world of appearance an

---

*See James Huffman's discussion (essay 5) of the issue of theoretical consistency in contemporary thought—Ed.

affective power that does not need the prop of metaphysics.[3] He also speculates that the persistence of that tradition "probably derives from human need as well as habit" and attributes that need to "our cultural nostalgia over the myths of presence which earlier ages could uncritically maintain but which growing skepticism has been draining away" (*PPI*, 153). Lacan, however, ascribes our awareness of an Other across the domain of language directly to the semiotic properties of metaphor and metonymy as they mimic an originary juncture of proscription and permission that constitutes us as subjects in culture through the path of our desire.

Echoing Krieger's description of the self-sufficient metaphor in "Poetic Presence and Illusion II," Lacan attributes the formal properties of the signifier to an "irreparable" exclusion of the signified from the signifier, which then establishes our relation to the excluded world of signifieds as it "conditions them by its presence as a signifier" (*E*, 285).[4] He credits our awareness of this separation to Saussure, who he says inaugurated modern linguistics in his "primordial placement of the signifier and the signified as being distinct orders separated initially by a barrier resisting signification."[5] Drawing on Roman Jakobson as Krieger does, Lacan goes on to characterize the semiotic properties of language as an interaction of metaphor and metonymy. The isolation of the signifier from the signified, Lacan says, generates a combinative sequence of signifiers which pursues the missing signified in a metonymic series that "always anticipates on meaning by unfolding its dimension before it" (*IL*, 110). But since the exclusion of the signified was the origin of the signifier, this pursuit can only result in a constant "sliding" of the signified under the order of signifiers, which suggests that all the "enigmas which desire seems to pose . . . its frenzy mocking the abyss of the infinite . . . amount to nothing more than that derangement of the instincts that comes from being caught on the rails—eternally stretching forth toward the desire for something else—of metonymy" (*IL*, 127).

In addition to the serial order of this chain, Lacan

adds, there is a paradigmatic "articulation of relevant context suspended 'vertically' " from each point (*IL,* 112). This context is established by the metaphoric substitution of one signifier for another, which is then suppressed from the chain of signifiers but remains latent in the operation of suppression.[6] Lacan expresses this metaphoric operation as an algebraic function, $f(\frac{S'}{S})S \cong S(+)s$, which means that the metaphoric suppression of one signifier S by another S within the signifying chain is "congruent" to the crossing of the bar between S and s in Saussure's formula $\frac{S}{s}$; this "crossing" is represented by the vertical stroke in the $+$.

The parallel between Saussure's formula for signification—$\frac{S}{s}$—and Lacan's formula for metaphorical suppression of one signifier by another—$\frac{S'}{S}$—expresses what Lacan calls "an effect of signification . . . which is creative or poetic in the metaphoric function and that results from the illusion of a "leap over the line" separating signifier from signified (see *IL,* 124). It is only an effect, of course, because it takes place between two signifiers or, in other words, only within the domain of language, and this point helps explain why Krieger's metaphor seemed to provide its own signified: rather than truly creating a signified, the metaphoric signifier functions through its relation to another signifier. There is indeed a binary opposition between them, but it is not an ontological opposition, and since the second signifier can function in the chain only through its position above the bar over the first, its very existence presupposes the latent presence of that first signifier as that-which-is-suppressed or, in Krieger's terms, "its" signified.

Lacan therefore describes metaphor as an "expression of the condition of passage of the signifier into the signified" and claims that this passage is "provisionally confused with the place of the subject as the link between world and word (*IL,* 124). Lacan then asks the same question that was raised— but not asked—by Krieger: what is our relation to that illusion of subjectivity in the work? Or, in Lacan's terms, "the place that I occupy as the subject of a signifier: is it, in relation to the place I occupy as subject of the signified, concentric or ex-centric?—that is the question" (*IL*, 125). Lacan's answer integrates the semiotic properties of language with his psychoanalytic understanding of the nature of the subject. Metaphor raises the question of subjectivity, Lacan says, because it "reproduces the mythic event in terms of which Freud reconstructed the progress, in the individual unconscious, of the mystery of the father" (*IL*, 116). That is, the formal structure of metaphor repeats, in language, the moment at which the child escapes the Oedipal trap of wanting to be the object of the mother's desire (i.e., the father or, in Lacan's lexicon, the phallus) through the "*nom du père*," which is Lacan's term for the totemic ruler of Freud's *Totem and Taboo*, an absent but omniscient locus of proscription that is also the source of discourse, cultural forms, symbolic order, and social power.

This "paternal metaphor" effects a symbolic castration of the child by introjecting a lack into the illusory harmony of the Imaginary couple of mother and child, but it is only through this experience of castration that the child can redirect that desire through the system of cultural values that Lacan calls the Symbolic or, more generally, language.[7] Lacan's "return to Freud" thus consists in his recasting Freud's sexual etiology of cultural forms into a semiotics. The phallus, Lacan argues, "is not a phantasy . . . nor is it as such an object . . . in the sense that this term tends to accentuate the reality pertaining in a relation. It is even less the organ, penis, or clitoris, that it symbolizes" (*E*, 285). In fact, Lacan says, the phallus is a signifier, the "signifier of signifiers," the "ultimate significative object": "the phallus represents . . . what cannot enter the domain of the signifier without being barred from it, that is to say, covered over by castration" (*LS*, 187).

What is "covered" by castration here is the signified, the Real. And because the phallus is always the property of an Other, i.e., the Symbolic Father, the place of the subject marked by the phallus is always constituted in language as radically "excentric" to itself: it is split into two places—that of the Other, recognized in and through the Symbolic, and that of what Lacan calls the "barred subject" that exists only as a "fading" before the Imaginary object as that object is replaced by the phallus. So, by reenacting Freud's drama of castration in terms of language, metaphor simulates the effect of subjectivity in language as the desire of the Other—Krieger's "beckoning structure," soliciting our indulgence—named and renounced as our own through the primal repression that distinguished the Real from the Symbolic. The perception of a "subject" in language is therefore intimately related to the separation of the signifier and the signified as that separation maps our desire in the discourse of the Other. For this reason Lacan calls the phallus the "signifier of desire" (LS, 187), the "privileged signifier of that mark in which the role of the logos is joined with the advent of desire" (E, 287).

Which brings us back to . . . widow Wadman.

It takes little insight to imagine the relevance of Lacan's emphasis on the symbolic role of castration to a story told by a man whose own amours were cut short early in life by a loose window and a careless maid who, as Tristram tells us, "did not consider that nothing was well-hung in our family" (TS, 284). Indeed, the "Amours" of Uncle Toby that take up so much of the narrative literally proceed through the widow's desire for exactly that "place" that stands out so prominently in Lacan's account of metaphor. And since Krieger returns to the exchange between Widow Wadman and Uncle Toby as an allegory of the metaphorical process he describes in "Poetic Presence and Illusion II," the function of her character in Tristram Shandy makes an interesting point of comparison between Krieger's aesthetic theory of metaphor and the psychoanalytic properties of the trope as described by Lacan.

The widow, whose title inscribes her lack within her name, first enters the novel as the very embodiment of desire, its perfect signifier. The story of Uncle Toby has been pro-

ceeding as smoothly as anything does in Tristram's narrative
when it hits a snag on its crucial term: "All I contend for is,
that I am not *obliged* to set out with a definition of what love
is; and so long as I can go on with my story intelligibly, with
the help of the word itself, without any other idea to it, than
what I have in common with the rest of the world, why
should I differ from it a moment before the time? . . . At present, I hope I shall be sufficiently understood, in telling the
reader, my uncle *Toby fell in love*" (TS, 356). But Tristram
immediately finds himself lost in what he calls "this mystick
labyrinth" of the word: "To say a man is *fallen* in love—or
that he is *deeply* in love,—or up to the ears in love,—and
sometimes even *over head and ears in it*,—carries an idio-
matical kind of implication, that love is a thing *below* a
man:—this is recurring again to *Plato's* opinion, which with
all his divinityship,—I hold to be damnable and heretical;—
and so much for that. Let love therefore be what it will,—my
uncle *Toby* fell into it." The gap in the signifying chain
through which Toby has fallen is widow Wadman, "and possibly, gentle reader, with such a temptation—so wouldst
thou: For never did thy eyes behold, or they concupiscence
covet any thing in this world, more concupiscible than
widow *Wadman*."

Clearly, the signifier "love" is not up to this most concupiscible of signifieds. Tristram must differ from it absolutely in order to present the full meaning of the word to the
reader. So, just as he brought the endless slide through the
field of the signifier to a stop on the snag of heresy with the
anchor of his faith, he sets out to anchor his narrative on the
reader's desire by providing the very image of desire itself:

To conceive this right,—call for pen and ink—here's paper ready to
your hand [i.e., a blank page].—Sit down, Sir, paint her to your
own mind—as like your mistress as you can—as unlike your wife
as your conscience will let you—'tis all one to me—please but your
own fancy in it.

—Was ever any thing in Nature so sweet!—so exquisite!—Then,
dear Sir, how could my uncle *Toby* resist it? (TS, 356–58).

Of course, we have already seen how Toby resists it: he draws a map of Namur in the space provided by the ambiguity of the widow's words, and then lovingly directs her finger to the very mark he has created as their signified. By leaving the blank, however, Tristram claims he has protected himself against any such misreading at this most delicate point: "Thrice happy book! thou wilt have one page, at least, within thy covers, which MALICE will not blacken, and which IGNORANCE cannot misrepresent" (TS, 358). Secure in the significance of this gesture, Tristram proceeds with Uncle Toby's story "in a tolerable straight line" (TS, 359).

That security appears paradoxical, since it is founded on the absence of any signifiers. But Lacan says that this is exactly the mode in which the signifier of signifiers appears. Operating under the cover of castration, the phallus "can only play its role when veiled, which is to say as itself a sign of the latency with which any signifiable is struck, when it is raised (aufgehoben) . . . to the function of the signifier." In fact, Lacan says, "the phallus is the signifier of this Aufghebung itself, which it inaugurates (initiates) by its disappearance" (E, 288).

So the widow—who here achieves the Oedipal dream of really being the object of her desire—is able to suspend Tristram's wandering in the etymological maze of the word "love" because her presence as the signifier of desire recapitulates that "mythic moment" in which the Symbolic and the Real were distinguished as desire passed into the metonymic chain of discourse or, in this case, narrative. Tristram's strategy of pinning down the slippery signifier of love with the reader's desire corresponds to Lacan's own designation of desire as the means by which the "signifier stops the otherwise endless movement (glissement) of signification" (E, 303). Because desire marks the birth of language in an originary separation of the signified from the signifier, Lacan claims that its persistence in language forms a "point de capiton" or "anchoring point" that orients the metonymic flow of language toward the real without making the impossible jump over the barrier behind which the real ultimately resists signification.

Krieger's interest in the relationship between the widow and Uncle Toby stems from his broader interest in *Tristram Shandy* as one of the works in the literary canon "which recapitulate these teasing powers of metaphor and thereby become allegories of the metaphorical process itself" (PPI, 164). Earlier, in *The Classic Vision*, Krieger proposed the novel as an allegory for his general poetics because like the self-conscious poem, Tristram is able to combine within himself "a transcendent awareness that can indulge the hobby-horse [of illusion] without losing sight of the deadly actual" (CV, 285, 283). Despite his fascination with the linguistic miracles of his narrative, Tristram proceeds with what Krieger has called the poem's "grudging acknowledgement of its limitations, of that world beyond in which the non-linguistic fact of death withstands all metaphorical reductions and transformations" (PPI, 208). The illusion of Tristram's narrative is all-consuming, Krieger says, but in the end death "unmasks the miracle for what it is" (TC, 244): "All of Tristram's metaphors are undone—Tristram the supreme hobby-horse rider—as he is pursued on horseback by Death, in a metaphor that signals the end of metaphor, that threatens to empty all metaphor into the common refuse heap of factual, time-ridden history" (TC, 61). Like Lacan's concept of the phallus, here death is the "signifier of signifiers," whose eruption into the work demetaphorizes its world and anchors it in the real to that non-linguistic fact that the miracle would bar forever but inevitably raises to our vision.[8]

It is all the more surprising, then, when in "Poetic Presence and Illusion II" Krieger relinquishes this negative connection between the word and the world and concludes: "we watch all the hobby horses . . . while we are probably mounted up on our own. Tristram acknowledges as much when he shows himself mounted up on his and riding, that is, writing this book. Or is he, as he suggests in volume 7, *literally* riding as he flees through the continent, trying to escape that 'arch-jockey of jockeys' who he feels is mounted up behind him and is in pursuit? But of course in this form death itself becomes just another metaphor, another hobby horse and hobby-horse rider. There are, then, no horses but hobby horses, though man is never anything but a jockey" (*PPI*, 167–68). Here Krieger seems to have been caught up in the same "mystick labyrinth" that confounded Tristram earlier: "Where is the metaphor and where is reality in this discourse?" Krieger asks. "Looking for reality, where can we find its 'place' in this novel in which . . . nothing holds its 'place'?" (*PPI*, 166).

The novel constantly turns away from such substantial signifieds as presumably real towns and real genitalia (only "presumably real" since the novel does no more than note their absence) to let us dwell among those newly substantiated signifiers—the maps and make-believe replicas which turn into linguistic realities . . . it is the language which is the reality, creating instantaneities of metaphor which collapse all the varied versions of reality into its own single identity of the word. (*PPI*, 167)

Krieger acknowledges this confusion, of course, as merely the "fallacy of verbal reification," and claims that "our sympathy for the seriousness of the illusions of the characters is cut short . . . Sterne encourages our hold-out, antiverbal skepticism by stimulating our sense of absurdity" (*PPI*, 167). But as we saw above, the explanation of metaphor that Krieger offers earlier in this essay cannot really account for the "lingering skepticism" that would cut short our absorption in these illusions, so Krieger's predicament comes to resemble that of Uncle Toby who, as Krieger says, "lives, on hobby-horseback, in mimesis of the one act in his life which has meaning, confounding ambiguous signifiers and signifieds in all-out sacrifice to the symbolic reality of his wound, the sole isolated fact" (*PPI*, 167).

Sterne's many-leveled language, which would appear to be our only reality, is the one sure presence in a world where everything resists our touch and points us to a verbal map. Where signifieds and signifiers reverse and re-reverse their roles, what, besides the poet's language, is "here"? Where is the body of this reality before us and how does it relate to the body of words, if Sterne has persuaded us to grant his words body? . . . What, then, is the book *about*? Where is its object of imitation? How can we touch the wound with which it has left us? We discover how difficult it is to answer precisely when, like Uncle Toby and the widow Wadman, we try to put our finger on the very place. (*PPI,* 168)

Like Uncle Toby, here Krieger seems to have lost his bearings because he has no means of distinguishing in the text between the "sole isolated fact" of the *symbolic* reality of Toby's wound—its role in the story of Namur—and the "non-linguistic fact of death" whose mark Toby carries beneath the waistband of his red plush breeches. The widow, of course, has no such problem, guided as she is by her desire. Yet it is just that desire that Krieger's theory renders invisible to him: "Clearly," he says, "the issue between the not-quite-lovers is semiological and hermeneutic, revolving about words like 'whereabouts' and 'place'. . . . There are four 'wheres' and 'places' to which Uncle Toby may have been referring" (*PPI,* 165). True, but only one that the widow is interested in; and from her perspective, the issue is hardly semiotic. But ignoring the fact as completely as Krieger, Toby is able to seize the widow's words and map her desire onto the symbolic site of his wound to tell the tale of Namur one more time, just as Tristram's own story of Uncle Toby's amours proceeds before the veil of the perfect signifier of desire.

But just as Tristram knew that only desire could protect that one signifier in his narrative from the endless drift of the signifying chain, so do we find at the end of his narrative that the absurdity of Uncle Toby's obsession with his maps and models can be measured securely only against the anchor of the widow's desire. When that desire finally erupts in a virtual orgy of revelation in volume 9—we are told that Toby finally finds out what the widow really wants from Corporal Trim, who got it from Susannah who heard it from Mrs. Bridget who learned it from Tristram's mother, to whom the widow had confided her plight, and that Susannah had "instantly imparted it by signs" to Jonathan, who told the cook who told the postillion, who told the dairy maid . . . (TS, 494)—Uncle Toby's illusions, the story of Toby's amours, and the novel quickly come to an end.

The difficulty Krieger experiences in trying to put his finger on the place where the word confronts the world in *Tristram Shandy* recalls the dilemma he described in *Theory of Criticism*, where the critic "vainly seeks to capture in his language the object whose language has captured him" (TC, 39). Although it is the critic who constitutes the poem as an object of desire by "putting the soliciting power out there" in it as an "idol that serves his needs," the position of the master in this relation is never secure. Confronting us as Other, the poem "resists being reduced to the determinances of the perceiving self" and "would seem to define [the critic] rather than he it"; the enrapturing beauty of the poem turns it into a lure, a "bait" or "entrapping structure" that appears before us "formally sovereign," seeking "to enclose the reader within its symbolic world" (TC, 63, 43, 40, n.2, 44; PPI, 121; TC, 39, 18).

The experience traced through Krieger's texts in these metaphorical terms closely resembles Lacan's account of the specular capture that threatens to trap the subject in the Imaginary. Should the individual's passage to and through the Oedipal stage be interrupted by a rejection or "foreclosure" of castration, Lacan says that the seductive trap of the Imaginary snaps shut. The operations of consciousness by which the other comes into being are obscured, and the subject becomes "riveted to the Imaginary, which is taken for real, to non-distinction between signifier and signified."[9]

This is, of course, exactly how Krieger describes the state of aesthetic intentionality, which "would see the poem as a mode of discourse in which the signifier has swallowed its signified" (PPI, 153). Yet Krieger's poetic illusion is not a neurotic regression to Imaginary delusion, for it functions only within the boundaries of the tradition of aesthesis that constitutes the illusion as illusion under the succinct rule of the Platonic "No": "One cannot appreciate the verisimilar without being aware that it is not the thing itself," Krieger says (*PPI*, 147).[10] "If we choose the illusion, we must play in full knowledge of what it is: that is, in effect, knowledge of the reality that resists being embraced by our play with an ultimate language. The language of the poem, in providing its own limits, provides this knowledge as well" (*TC*, 173).

But as Lacan shows, the knowledge by which the poem would disclose the illusion of its mirage comes to us only through the language of desire. If we cannot name that desire, we cannot situate the imaginary object of our love-play within the law of the Symbolic, and our account of the luxuriant fold of those two orders within the poem's illusion cuts that fold in the very gesture with which we would open it to inspection. Suspended between our Imaginary appreciation of the poem as what it is and our Symbolic knowledge of what it is not, the knot of desire that joins pleasure and knowledge in illusion has therefore remained resistant to Krieger's aesthetics, an object "we must try to know but theoretically, of course, we cannot," its presence marked only by the theoretical paradoxes with which he has recorded the strands of logic that twist in its coils.

In one of the many moments of exquisite sensitivity and hard-nosed honesty that pervade his work, Krieger noted the inevitability of that resistance several years ago at the end of an essay introduced by these lines from Sir Thomas Wyatt's "Whoso List to Hunt"?:

> Yet may I by no means my wearied mind
> Draw from the deer, but as she fleeth afore
> Fainting I follow. I leave off therefore,
> Since in a net I seek to hold the wind.

Comparing his plight as a critic to that of the weary hunter/lover in Wyatt's poem, Krieger claims that the "apparently self-contradictory" propositions of his paradoxical argument deny themselves, and

in denying themselves, deny their appropriateness as defining tools for this object of definition. I have tried to speak firmly, definitively, about the will-o'-the-wisp literature, whose very being undoes this mode of dealing with it. . . . I feel like the lover in my epigraph from Wyatt, who cannot find the equipment appropriate to his beloved quarry, and finally retires, exhausted. . . . But as I do, I remind myself that the elusive deer in Wyatt's sonnet was very likely—as poetry is for me—his mistress and a queen. (*PPI*, 196)

In such passages, desire does emerge in Krieger's work, but only as the residue of the critical act, a testament to its failure and a witness to his defiant will to remain responsive to a promise he cannot name. Yet Lacan teaches us that desire joins us to discourse through the same gesture in which the Imaginary object falls before the law of the Symbolic, so it can serve as the bond that ties the lover's illusion to the proscription of its limit. If Krieger had examined the quarry in Wyatt's poem a little more closely, he would have discovered that lesson. For there, immediately after the lines Krieger quotes in his epigraph, the poet tells us that the elusive object of his pursuit bears the interdictory mark of the Other that submits it to Law even while putting it out of reach as the perfect object of eternal desire:

> Who list her hunt, I put him out of doubt,
> As well as I, may spend his time in vain.
> And graven with diamonds in letters plain
> There is written, her fair neck round about,
> "*Noli me tangere*, For Caesar's I am,
> And wild for to hold, though I seem tame."[11]

9.
THE PHENOMENOLOGY OF SPENSERIAN EKPHRASIS

Herman Rapaport

AT a certain point in "The Ekphrastic Principle and the Still Movement of Poetry," an essay written in 1965 and collected in *The Play and Place of Criticism*, Murray Krieger writes that,

Poetry must be at once immediate *and* objective: neither the mediated objectivity of the normal discourse that through freezing kills, nor the unmediated subjectivity that our idolators of time philosophy would want to keep as the unstoppable, unrepeatable, un-entitled all; neither life only frozen as archetypal nor life only flowing as endlessly empirical, but at once frozen and flowing (like the urn), at once objective and immediate, archetypal and empirical. I would share the interests of the Georges Poulets and the Maurice Blanchots; but I would give the special liberating license to our best poetry, insisting on its ekphrastic completeness that allows us to

Editor's note: Krieger discusses ekphrasis in this volume in "Both Sides Now" as "the intrusion of the spatial imagination on the radical temporality of pure sequence." In the dialectical relation between the spatial and the temporal, the "spatial vision . . . sustains itself only through acknowledgement that all may finally be nothing but time."

transfer the human conquest of time *from the murky subjective caverns of phenomenology to the well-wrought, well lighted place of aesthetics.* (PPC, 127; my concluding italics)

In large part, my reading of Krieger's interpretation of ekphrasis in literature is a critique which takes issue with the italicized portion of the quotation above. Indeed, I will shortly begin with remarks on Maurice Merleau-Ponty's discussion of perception in his *Primacy of Perception* with regard to Edmund Spenser's *Faerie Queene,* book 3, in order to show how what Krieger would have to acknowledge as ekphrastic moments in a literary text can best be understood phenomenologically. Especially Krieger's early and New-Critically inspired account of ekphrasis as the textual oscillation between two modes of perception—stasis versus movement— seems, from my point of view, quite inadequate for the instances I have selected, even when one generalizes the poles of ekphrasis to include, as Krieger would like in the quotation above, the vacillations between objectivity and subjectivity (i.e., form/process). Without doubt, Krieger modifies various aspects of his position with regard to ekphrasis in his more recent work, assimilating various critical approaches introduced by the new wave of European influence in the seventies. However, even in as recent an essay as " 'A Waking Dream': The Symbolic Alternative to Allegory," we can read that,

The poem unifies itself aesthetically around its metaphoric and its counter-metaphoric tendencies, even as its oppositions remain thematically unresolved. It is, then, self-demystifying, but as such it does not fall outside the symbolist aesthetics so much as it fulfills what the aesthetic, at its most critically aware, its most self-conscious, is able to demand: nothing less than a waking dream.[1]

Indeed, my paper is also about a waking dream, one in which a girl sees something in a crystal glass, and to this extent I wish to take my departure from a Kriegeresque ekphrasis, which, for me at least, does not suffice in the particular instance I have in mind, for it is by developing a phenomenological reading in terms of some Lacanian clues, themselves indebted to Maurice Merleau-Ponty, that I will make the suggestion that in Spenser's representation of an hysterical feminine consciousness in whose gaze one is situated we find that it is precisely Krieger's more formalistically inclined ekphrasis as literary freeze, monument, or (and this is the term I would stress) erection which is refused by a feminine stare. Whereas Krieger sees the poem unifying itself aesthetically, I see a certain disturbing disarticulation, that deconstructive horizon from which Krieger's symbolist aesthetic retreats for the sake of a much more detached and perhaps rational glance. In part, my point in developing such a line of thought is to show, simply, that in the "murky subjective caverns of phenomenology"—and, I should add, phenomenologically oriented theories of psychoanalysis—the well wrought arguments of formalist aesthetics find themselves challenged.

In *The Primacy of Perception*, Maurice Merleau-Ponty speaks of perception as a grasping or captivation and notices that no perception can be decomposed or made into a mere collection of sensations. The gazer has vision, in other words, by which is meant a "field" of perception, though one that is not merely intellectual or conceptual. The "field" makes up an infinite sum of "an indefinite series of perspectival views in each of which the object is given but in none of which it is given exhaustively."[2]* Merleau-Ponty's analysis of perception is by no means gestaltist, for in his opinion the field is not to be taken as a form but as the space or locus in which the possibility of form intuits itself ahead of the perceptual concretizations. This space is the possibility of continuity and synthesis, an arché—structure, as it were, by means of which perception can be thought. "Let us say with Husserl that it is a 'synthesis of transition' [*synthèse de transition*]—I anticipate the unseen side of the lamp because I can touch it—or a 'horizonal synthesis' [*synthèse d'horizon*]—the un-

*For Krieger's own comments on his perceptual and phenomenological claims, see the Konstanz Colloquy—Ed.

seen side is given to me as 'visible from another standpoint,' at once given but only immanently" (*Primacy*, 15). The structure of the object is always posed in terms of an anticipation or premonition concerning the unseen, the not-yet-given, and it is by means of this anticipation or expectation that the object is grasped.

Yet, perception itself is not reducible to the overall unity of any arché-structure; rather, perception is discontinuous, fragmentary, fleeting, intermittent, and only partially conscious. "We experience a perception and its horizon 'in action' [pratiquement] rather than by 'posing' them or explicitly 'knowing' them" (*Primacy*, 12). That is, our experience of perception is built up as a layering of discontinuous perceptions which transpire in action rather than in a *mise en scène* which we can safely watch from a distance. About perception, then, there cannot be an adequate meta-language; there cannot be an adequate model or representation which will speak in place of it, but only a continuation of the perceptual process itself.

The unprejudiced study of perception by psychologists has finally revealed that the perceived world is not a system of objects (in the sense in which the sciences use this word), that our relation to the world is not that of a thinker to an object of thought, and finally that the unity of the perceived thing, as perceived by several consciousnesses, is not comparable to the unity of a proposition [théorème], as understood by several thinkers, any more than perceived existence is comparable to ideal existence. (*Primacy*, 12)

Merleau-Ponty adds elsewhere that the "world" (the totality of perceptible things) cannot be understood as a mathematical object but as a "universal style" of all possible perceptions (*Primacy*, 16). By "universal style" Merleau-Ponty does not mean a single, logocentric and uniplanar mode of expression, but rather a plurality of styles, what in Mikhail Bakhtin is termed "heteroglossia." Such a "universal style" is possible from Merleau-Ponty's view, because he argues that the objects of perception do not impose themselves as true for every intellect. Yet they do impose themselves as "real for every subject who is standing where I [the subject] am" (*Primacy*, 17). By means of such experiencing of the "real," the "universal style" is, if not understood, at least accepted by everyone on a provisional and potential basis.

Given these leads from Merleau-Ponty, I wish to consider an example chosen from Edmund Spenser's *Faerie Queene*, book 3, canto 2. We recall that in this canto the chaste Britomart asks the Redcrosse Knight to describe her beloved, Arthegall, a man whom she has only seen in a "mirrhour plaine" that she had once found in her father's "closet." The mirror is convex and very much reminds one of a crystal ball. It was given by Merlin to Britomart's father in order that he should know all that would happen for the better protection of his empire. That Britomart asks Redcrosse to explain something she already knows may be no accident, because this request itself mirrors the condition of those who possess magical mirrors: they know the reflections before having seen the substance. They perceive even though they do not have the experience of the real. Yet, it would be fair to say that if Britomart does not encounter Arthegall as substance in book 3, she uses Redcrosse's position with regard to having really encountered Arthegall as ground for perception, even though it is a ground achieved by listening to Redcrosse's flattering style and observing his courtly gestures. We notice, then, how in Spenser what Merleau-Ponty would call the "real" is disclosed in terms of perceptual modes.

Indeed, while Redcrosse is extolling the virtues of Arthegall to Britomart, we experience a shift in perceptual mode by means of a digression.

> Yet him in every part before she knew,
> How ever list her now her knowledge faine,
> Sith him whilome in *Britaine* she did vew,
> To her revealed in a mirrhour plaine,
> Whereof did grow her first engraffed paine;

Whose root and stalke so bitter yet did tast,
That but the fruit more sweetness did containe,
Her wretched dayes in dolour she mote wast,
And yield the pray of love to lothsome death at last.[3]

Apparently one mode of perception is substituted for another, because while Redcrosse is speaking of Arthegall, Britomart daydreams about what she has seen in the spherical glass, thus using her perceptions to accompany the ground or certainty which Redcrosse's praise establishes. At the same time, Spenser provides essential narration through which the reader can grasp the romance. Such modes or styles of perception are all rather fragmentary: Redcrosse's perceptions are cut off and superceded by Britomart's intermittent thoughts while third-person narration is providing a stream of discontinuous perceptions for the benefit of the reader.

Within the point of view of Britomart's revery (as told through third-person narration to the reader), other fragmentary perceptions become noticeable. For example, there is a very odd shift from the perception of the beloved in the mirror to "engraffed paine" and the ensuing talk about trees and fruit. What is particularly odd about this shift is that it is "condensed" in the Freudian sense of the word in the phrase "Mirrhour plaine," a condensation which occurs because "mirrhour" rimes with the name of a fleeing maiden in mythology, Myrrha.

James Nohrnberg, in The Analogy of the Faerie Queene, calls our attention to the importance of this mythological figure with regard to Florimell, who, like Myrrha, is a fleeing maiden and whose name recalls metamorphosis into a tree.[4] Myrrha was chased by her father, with whom she was innocently seduced through Aphrodite's wiles to make love. Just as the father, who has been similarly deceived, expresses his outrage by approaching his fleeing daughter with a sword, she turns into a Myrrha tree, is cut by the father, and gives birth to Adonis, whom Venus spirits away to the underworld. Florimell's beloved, Marinell, is also a kind of Adonis figure, not unlike Belphoebe's beloved, Timias.

This aspect of the Myrrha allusion is prominent elsewhere in book 3 of *The Faerie Queene*, where the Venus and Adonis myth is set forth in the tapestry scenes of canto 1 and the Garden of Adonis in canto 6. A psychoanalytically inclined reader might say that the Venus and Adonis myth functions as a deep structure or unconscious content which receives numerous conscious or surface articulations. Not only that, but the myth is an expression of female desire, the sexual mastery of woman over man. It is in this sense that the myth re-emerges in so many forms as a figure of captivation, for what a French psychoanalyst might term *l'emprise* as *l'empire*, captivation as empire.[5] That Britomart, the source of a peculiarly British empire, should be captivated before a convex mirror which gives her mastery over men and yet enthralls her to the one man whom she sees as her double, Arthegall, can come as little surprise.

Nor can we be shocked to find the syllepsis Mirrhour/ Myrrha. The mirror is the tree, the family line which will give birth to royal Britons. But the tree is also the mirror of woman's desire, the place where Britomart will find her Adonis. The syllepsis also suggests incest, since Myrrha slept with her father. Britomart's finding the magic glass in her father's closet suggests that the image she sees is paternal or at least connected with the paternal. This hint is reinforced by the usual association of the Myrrha plant with aphrodisiacs and by the suggestion that Britomart's wound received by looking into the glass is not just that of a lover but of a father, for Mirrhour = Myrrha. Lastly, the relationship of the Adonis figures in Spenser's poem to the females, Belphoebe, Amoret, Florimell, and Venus suggests that the male is placed in the role of a child as sexual object for a mother. Perhaps Britomart's looking into the Mirrhour/Myrrha is to be associated with this series of relations. If so, incest is mirrored in a bifocal manner in which woman commits incest with father and child. Spenser, of course, does not seem to be reducing the "meaning" of the perceptions to incest, but merely allows the resonances of such associations to be associated with female desire.

It would be incorrect to say that any of the strands of allusions I have mentioned can be limited to a mise en scène, for Spenser has produced a series of intertwining perceptions which are constituents of a universal style that is not reducible to a uniplanar or logocentric vision. Still, this universal style has distinct modalities or orientations. Psychoanalysis is helpful in identifying one of these orientations in the stanza above, for it is clear from a psychoanalytic view that Spenser's narrative is about woman's fear of the sexual: hence the allusions to incest in the mirror. Incest is both desired and forbidden, just as the desire for Arthegall is wished for and denied by his inaccessibility. The allusion to Myrrha suggests a woman in flight, and Britomart throughout the third book of Spenser's *Faerie Queene* is also very much in flight, though it looks very much like pursuit. The mirror, of course, allows us to perceive these traces of female desire, and in that way the mirror is a structuring agency, that which gives a forum through which we can see. But the mirror is also more than that, for it is like a *stade du miroir* or mirror stage in the Lacanian sense. Here an imaginary or narcissistic relation is articulated by way of Britomart's seeing in the mirror an ego ideal (Arthegall) who is to be realized for the time being in Britomart as female warrior.[6]

The function of the mirror as a stage for narcissism works also as a defense mechanism, promoting an illusion of sexual union while preserving Britomart's chastity and solitariness. The mirror stage, which accompanies Britomart as an imaginary construction, becomes that mechanism taking the place of desire, becoming the thing which woman takes in place of the traumatic object of sexual wishing. Within the Mirrhour/Myrrha we notice Father, Arthegall, and Adonis (Father, Lover, Child), yet these images only consolidate Britomart's inviolability, her code of chastity. This is the code of the mirror or defense against what has been seen, a defense which curiously will investigate what is behind the mirror in Faerie land.

Penetration and investigation turn out to be a mode of flight or defensiveness, something which psychoanalysts notice is characteristic of hysterical behavior. This hysterical code of chastity, if I may call it that, is not, properly speaking, woman's, but that of Spenser's phallocentric society, and it is through this perceptual intersubjectivity that the fantasy structure of woman's desire can be reflected, but only as a modality of male consciousness. Thus, where we see woman gazing at man through the mirrhour, we must recognize how men are gazing at women through their social glass. A Lacanian would point out, then, to what degree hysteria is encoded in a mirror-möbius strip, one upon which recto/verso are twisted so that two modalities of desire, that of male and female, are bound within and without one another: invaginated.

The mirror not only points to hysterical bindings, but also refers us to family lineage. In this sense, the mirror yields its priority as a major focal plane for our reading as it is quickly transformed into the image of trees and their grafting. This slip reminds us of the perverse crossings alluded to by incest (Myrrha as tree), since trees are grafted to mix species against nature's law. In the trees, strangely enough, the mirrhour is mirrored. Thus the syllepsis, Mirrhour/Myrrha, is not so much an object as a forum or structure through which we can perceive errant semantic slippages and the surfacing of hidden allusions and resonances. The reference to the convexity of the mirror into which Britomart looks is but one clue that in any given stanza there may be many distortions or anamorphic deformations.

Indeed ,what we have is a world view made up of what Merleau-Ponty calls "an indefinite series of perspectival views in each of which the object is given but in none of which it is given exhaustively" (Primacy, 15). The mirrhour is not so much a centerpiece of the stanza above as it is a component of a complex of relations which invites the eye to gaze. Through the aperture of the mirror or glass we are asked to pay attention to many details which surface and recede, yet it is not through the glass itself that all is seen, for the glass itself is reflected in other images, such as the trees. What is posed, therefore, as an ekphrastic image in which Faerie land itself is represented as a whole, with Arthegall in only one of its zones, is, in fact, deconstituted the more we gaze at the stanza above and those which elsewhere address this moment of Britomart's wounded sight.

If the styles or modes of perception emerge and decompose, or even align themselves in a series or what could be called a palimpsest, these modes or styles do not solidify into an ekphrasis. Spenser's poem allows us, at certain points, to rest our readerly gaze upon certain figures or suggestions which render the possibility of perceptual continuity and synthesis, perhaps even what Merleau-Ponty calls a synthesis of transition by means of which we anticipate the unseen aspects of Spenser's Faerie land. Yet these unseen aspects are suggested in the crossing or engrafting of different styles— even literary styles like Arthurian romance, Greek mythology, Petrarchan convention, etc.—the articulation of disparate and fragmented perceptual resonances which through careful reflection or even random thought can be intuited as part of an overall texture. In Spenser, the series of perspectives elicits what Merleau-Ponty specifies as "visibility from an other standpoint," or what Roman Ingarden calls "schematized aspects." Ingarden develops Husserl's notion of the "horizon" to argue that a property of literature is the schematized aspect or intentional perception which apprehends meaning in terms of both determinate and indeterminate concretizations, thus subjecting interpretation to a manifold of perceptual shifts or realignments which, as Merleau-Ponty suggests, are intermittent, though available to temporary unifications and stabilizations.[7]

In the *Journals*, André Gide constructs a literary mechanism which gives rise to what phenomenologists call horizonality. This is the *mise en abyme*, the narrative space which never yields itself up to analysis, but offers itself by way of energizing infinite perceptual constructions. Already in the late 1800s, Gide noted that if one wants to write a psychological narrative, one must always structure an *abyme*—that is, a mirror or chiasmus—into the text.[8] This could be done by doubling or overlapping structural relationships, thus repeating perceptions in displaced form. The mirror in Gide's fiction is precisely that of an *overlapping structure* rather than that of a specific image. When we read a novel like *The Immoralist*, for example, we find a text folded over on itself at almost every point and in so doing establishing and eroding our certainty in the oppositions which at first seem so clear: sadism/masochism, good/evil, proper/improper, Michel/Marceline, etc. We are asked to perceive through an abysm of reflections which cannot be saturated by textual content, cannot be grounded or filled up by significance generated from the code of oppositions, what Roland Barthes in *S/Z* calls the "symbolic code."[9] The abyss is the invisible, the chiasm, as Merleau-Ponty might say, which elicits cognitive evaluations even as it forecloses these very cognitive acts from usurping the abysm's place. The abysm or mirror is not something we look at, an object in the text's semantic weave, but a structural aperture through which the reader constructs the text's various codes or systems of relations.

Merleau-Ponty addresses the notion of chiasm as reflection and mirroring, in *The Visible and the Invisible*, when he writes:

As there is a reversibility of the seeing and the visible, and as at the point where two metamorphoses cross what we call perception is born, so also there is a reversibility of the speech and what it signifies; the signification is what comes to seal, to close, to gather up the multiplicity of the physical, physiological, linguistic means of elocution, to contract them into one sole act, as the vision comes to complete the aesthesio-logical body.[10]

If the mirror that Britomart finds in her father's closet is less of an ekphrastic object than an aperture which constitutes and de-constitutes relations, it is also the signification that seals and gathers up the multiplicity of elocutions, that contracts them in one act or completed vision. Yet it must be kept in mind that such a seal is but a temporary concretization, but a momentary perception of the mirror. The mirror is not a fixed formal representation with a static signified, but is a broaching or spacing whose horizonality cannot be eradicated by an interpretation. If the mirror seals and allows vision to complete the multiplicity of elocutions, it is because this is but a specific modality of perception, one that, in fact, is capsized in plurisignation. The mirror binds the images momentarily into a world or Faerie land, a space of desire, a field of history, a representation of a man, the reflection of a woman (Britomart), etc.

In this world all fantasies and doubled relations can be articulated as a tissue of universal style. Without this locus we cannot place ourselves before anything, cannot intuit the other *Schauplatz*, as Freud might say. Without the forum or arché-structure of the mirror, Britomart's desiring relations would never be perceivable. More importantly, perhaps, for the reader, without that glass, one would not be able to locate the invisible within the visible, would not see Myrrhas in Mirrhours. The glass establishes the gaze upon the land of Faerie in which the reversibility Merleau-Ponty addresses is possible. The mirror is the abyme, the rupture of which enables the seal of signification to be established in what is its temporary ascendancy.

Without doubt, the mirrhour plaine is what some critics would isolate as an ekphrastic image, one that would conform to Murray Krieger's notion of ekphrasis in *The Play and Place of Criticism*. That is, the mirror appears self-sufficient and transcendental with respect to the temporality of the protean poetic flux. The ekphrasitic image, Krieger believes, calls attention to an authorial recognition that art raises itself above mere life. Moreover, the ekphrastic image, such as the famous urn in Keats' ode, functions as a meta-poetic figure pointing to the unreducibility of poetry to mundane, linear time, to its dependency upon things of the real world. The urn is a figure for the autotelic, self-sufficient, and hermetic or miraculous nature of the poem. And yet, Krieger argues, this spatial figure will be subject to questions of a temporalizing order which deprives the poem of its self-sufficient illusion. Ekphrasis, then, is a dialectical shifting between art and life, space and time, objecthood and process, reading and textuality, the moment and eternity. And perception is the subject's recognition of this intellectual play and place of the poem, this temporalizing and objectivizing interrelation. Indeed, it is this dialectical play which saves poetry from the "murky subjective caverns of phenomenology" and carries it "to the well-wrought, well lighted place of aesthetics."

Such ekphrasis is extremely classical in the sense that it presupposes any frozen moment to belong to a narrative temporalization from which it has been momentarily isolated. Hence the ekphrastic moment is like a position or step of a ballet dancer when arrested and isolated from the whole of the dance. Indeed, in ballet, it is not unusual to see such positioned freezes, whose tension is controlled with respect to the movement of the steps and positions within a sequence. Gilles Deleuze speaks of this in *L'Image-Mouvement* when he discusses classical movement as an order of poses or privileged instants as in a dance.[11] This order is nothing less than a series of ekphrastic moments and as such cannot organize perception as intermittent or tentative, only as a homogeneous field or ordering in which a particular position may become a synecdoche taking center stage as a coherent illusion or figure whose presencing captivates the audience's attention, even as the audience recognizes in this freeze a failure to arrest completely movement or temporality. In literature, the poem may be represented as an ekphrastic figure whose contradiction is dialectically reconciled, though in Krieger's more recent writings, this dialectics has been subjected to a greater emphasis on the free play or openness of the signifier and to a concomitant softening of the notion of form such that it takes on a less reified aspect.

In " 'A Waking Dream,' " for example, Krieger revises
his earlier reading of the Grecian urn in Keats with a brief
and subtle reading of Keats' bird in "Ode to a Nightingale."

As the bird's song leaves the speaker's consciousness, it
'fades' away, a very different fading—apparently—from what occurred early in the poem when the speaker sought to fade away
into the world of the nightingale's song. As before, seeking an act
of self-dissolution, he tried to fade out of the world of human
time, collapsing the distance between himself and the bird, so at
the end the bird's song fades away from the speaker back into the
differentiated world of time and distance. Now 'buried deep' in
the next valley, it is—separated by time and distance—an absent
part of the speaker's dead past. Yet repeating the word *fade* suggests a similar activity in fading out of or fading back into the
realm of worldly experience. The repetition functions at once to
move us toward the identity of opposites (as in the symbolic aesthetic of spatial form) and to remind us of the unbridgeable differences between apparently repeated elements (as in de Man's definition of "repetition").[12]

Krieger's focus upon the bird's song is hardly ekphrastic in the sense of the Grecian urn in the essay written some
fifteen years earlier. Indeed, his later account of ekphrasis
stresses the fading of the bird and its song. And quoting
Keats, Krieger asks, "Was it a vision, or a waking dream?"
But notice how quickly Krieger turns this into a dialectical
opposition.

I have borrowed the phrase 'a waking dream' for my title because I
find in the oxymoron the two sides of the dialectic I have been
tracing. As in dream, the symbol creates for us a surrogate reality,
claiming the completeness of an irreducible domain within its ec-
centric terms . . .

And,

Whatever the incompleteness of the vision, later seen as such even
by the speaker, the poem that contains it contains also the vision of
that incompleteness. The poem unifies itself aesthetically around

its metaphoric and its counter-metaphoric tendencies, even as its oppositions remain thematically unresolved.[13]

In other words, however incomplete the materials of the dream, the vision as poem unifies and re-presents through the presentation of *mise en scène* or space the temporal slippages or fadings of the nightingale's song, recovering it as aesthetic vision and, too, aesthetic form.

That " 'A Waking Dream' " ends with an objectification, especially in terms of the subject's waking, by means of which the dreamy elements of the vision are distanced as well as recollected as poetic artifact, signifies, perhaps, that Krieger wants to re-establish a gaze in which the critic surveys and maybe even masters the whole. The critic, then, is given the opportunity to turn a logocentric eye/I upon the work. Subjectivity (sleeping or dreaming) and objectivity (vision or poem) stabilize from this distanced perspective on well balanced dialectical and aestheticized figural ground. This would be congruent with the aesthetic assumption that theory can discuss art as a logically coherent form which, however complicated by disruptive elements, can be at some point recovered as an artistic or visionary presencing.

Of course, in " 'A Waking Dream,' " Krieger has taken his distance from presencing in the naive metaphysical sense—hence the discussion of Paul de Man in that essay—and has moved closer to a phenomenological attitude in that it is clear his analysis is not quick to prestructure vision as crude *Gestalt*. He entertains the destabilizations inherent in the interplay of the objective and the subjective, vision and dream. Still, the return to an objectification and the stress on aesthetic vision or form suggests closure and even a certain reification or ekphrasis of vision.

My brief discussion of the Mirrhour/Myrrha in Spenser's *Faerie Queene* demonstrates how ekphrasis in Renaissance literature strongly resists even Krieger's later and more sophisticated formulation of the ekphrastic principle, for in Spenser the historical gaze is not unifiable from a formalistic

point of view which rests, ultimately, outside of the poem
and, therefore, can project closure. To that degree a phenomenological reading is not a dialectics of subject and object
but an intersubjective process which frustrates the more formalistically inclined assumptions.

Indeed, if the mirror in Spenser resists closure (and I
think it would be hard to argue otherwise), it also resists acces-
sibility to the kind of critical gaze Krieger sets up. An interesting detail which is "invisible" in Spenser's mirror is the fact
that written on Arthegall's coat of arms is an inscription
telling us that Arthegall has Achilles' armor, which can only
mean that he must also have Achilles' shield, itself an ekphrastic image in which the whole of Homer's Greek world is
reflected. One mirror is captured, or "emprized," within
another. Yet it is not just two worlds or mirrors which scintil-
late within one another. There is also Faerie Land, the realm of
Britomart's father, and the history of Britain as disclosed in
canto 3. If so much is compressed, so many worlds folded over
on one another, it would be difficult to say a gaze can be easily
established in all these reflections. The more we look into
such a mirror, and from the wrong side, since we are always
already in Faerie Land, the more we recognize that perception
is broken into many perceptual fragments haunted by invisible allusions.

This occurs not only with the mirror but with the tapestries in Castle Joyous and the House of Busyrane, where
so many scenes show and hide themselves from our gaze.
Spenser himself comments on this showing and veiling when
he writes,

> For round about, the wals yclothed were
> With goodly arras of great majesty,
> Woven with gold and silke so close and nere,
> That the rich metall lurked privily,
> As faining to be hid from envious eye;
> Yet here, and there, and every where unawares
> It shewd it selfe, and shone unwillingly;

> Like a discolourd Snake, whose hidden snares
> Through the greene gras his long bright burnisht
> backe declares.
>
> And in those Tapets weren fashioned
> Many faire pourtraicts, and many a faire feate,
> And all of love, and all of lusty-hed
> As seemed by their semblaunt did entreat.
> (FQ, 498; book 3, canto 11, stanzas 18–19)

However much we are invited to see tapestries, portraits, processions, mirrors, and inner rooms in which we discover enigmatic Amorets chained to pillars, our gaze is trapped in the "hidden snares" where closure is refused by disclosure, where the gaze cannot so easily congeal even upon the metaphor of a snake whose "long bright burnisht backe declares."

My suspicion is that Spenser's *Fairie Queene* refuses closure because it is an hysterical mode of textual production, and not in a pejorative sense. It is a point that could be demonstrated from a Lacanian point of view compatible with what has already been said regarding Merleau-Ponty and the primacy of perception. This can be substantiated at length. But let me just say here that we see it constructed in a feminine gaze which results in various somatic effects. Britomart, upon seeing Arthegall in the mirrhour, is forced to acknowledge "loves cruell law" which occupies the paternal site upon which Britomart looks "under erasure."

> Nor man it is, nor other living wight;
> For then some hope I might unto me draw,
> But th'only shade and semblant of a knight,
> Whose shape or person yet I never saw,
> Hath me subjected to loves cruell law:
> The same one day, as me misfortune led,
> I in my father's wondrous mirrhour saw . . .
> (FQ, 370; book 3, canto 2, stanza 18)

The cruelty of the law is not just a reference to a cliché from the rhetoric of a lover's discourse, but is in terms of Spenser's context rather more problematic in terms of the doubling of

Arthegall with the Father. We recall that Britomart will experience side effects from her gaze: ulcers, perceptions of poison-
ous substances in her bowels, bleeding sores, and so on.
These give way to reflections of the self as analogous to hor-
rid females: the Arabian Myrrhe, Biblis, Pasiphae, etc. Here
the law of love is constituted as the formation of a gaze in
terms of a deterioration and destabilization of a frame of reference, one connected not only to the gaze but to that of the
body as well.

This is precisely analogous to the kind of deconstruction which Dora performs in analysis with Freud even as she
places him in the role of knight in shining armor.[14] As Freud
observes in the "Postscript" to the analysis, "At the beginning it was clear that I was replacing her father in her imagination, which was not unlikely, in view of the difference
between our ages."[15] By means of such transference the
analysis was manipulated by the relays of Dora's fantasies,
which were based on the mischievous premise of seducing a
father whose sexuality was, strictly speaking, used up. Freud
noticed that the hysteric masters an arena in which the phallus cannot intrude, thereby upholding the law while sexually
profaning against it by means of defying the father with what
will turn out to be auto-erotic and homosexual attachments.

In *The Faerie Queene* this is developed in terms of
both the mirror in canto 2 and in the doubling of Britomart
and Malecasta in Castle Joyous (*jouissance?*). We notice
something similar in canto 12 with respect to Britomart and
Amoret where the phallus appears extremely traumatic in the
construction of a feminine gaze, what Luce Irigaray calls the
speculum de l'autre femme.[16] It is here that the representation of woman is mediated by a masculine law which is at
once constituted and deconstituted by the phenomenology
and psychology of a feminine desire, one which passes
through the place of the Father, though not without resis-
tances, not without hesitations which reflect as well upon a
certain masculine order of things which Spenser is, quite
obviously, re-presenting in *his* text. If the Law appears in the

mirror, it is not so much foreclosed as it is sublimated into an auto-erotic and ekphrastic moment in which the Law is superseded by phantasmic constructions.

Given these hints, I will say that it seems to me a great liability for any critical theory to ignore two important aspects of literature, particularly with respect to ekphrasis: (a) the phenomenology of perception and the articulations and disarticulations of gazes as intuited through a network of signs; and (b) the psychoanalytical formations of perceptual styles, what in my previous work on Lewis Carroll I consider in terms of a "pathology of seeing."[17] Anyone who carefully reads *The Faerie Queene*, and especially books 3 and 4, will recognize that a specific modality of female desire plays a crucial role in constituting perception as well as the ekphrastic constructions, those textual phalluses which predictably fail to establish themselves under the limpidity of a feminine gaze, ever vigilant and watchful, lest Adonis rise and seize his prey.

PART III: CRITICS AND COLLEAGUES/ FATHERS AND SONS

10.

AFTER THE TRAGIC VISION: KRIEGER AND LENTRICCHIA, CRITICISM AND CRISIS

Sandor Goodhart

> Hostile reviewers may blame their father
> for all failures.
>
> Frank Lentricchia,
> *After the New Criticism*

IT is not surprising that Murray Krieger turns out in a recent book by Frank Lentricchia to be the primary object of attack. In *After the New Criticism*, Lentricchia undertakes to write a history of criticism in America since the New Critics. The task, he concedes at the outset, is beset with difficulties. In the first place, because "New Criticism was in fact no monolith but an inconsistent and sometimes confused movement, the differences among variously identified New Critics and their progenitors . . . are real" (*ANC*, xii–xiii). And, in the second place, because the attempt to get beyond New Criticism as reflected in the burgeoning Structuralism and Post-Structuralism succeeds, ironically in Lentricchia's view, only in extending it. "If my title suggests . . . that the New Criti-

cism is dead I must stipulate that in my view it is dead in the
way that an imposing and repressive father-figure is dead. I
find many traces (perhaps 'scars' is the word) of the New
Criticism in contemporary theory." Such "traces" or "scars"
are particularly troublesome for Lentricchia, for whom a
"fundamental concern" is to develop an historical methodology that gets beyond the "evasive anti-historical maneuver"
of contemporary theory. Such New Critical remains "produce, in turn, another effect, not easy to discern: an intertextual mingling among contemporary theorists," a phenomenon
which, Lentricchia feels, endangers his very project.

I am arguing not only that the ruptures separating nineteenth-century aesthetic traditions, the New Criticism, and contemporary theory are not absolute but also that the differences among contemporary theories are not clean discontinuities. In my opinion it is the
very condition of contemporary critical historicity that there is no
"after" or "before" the New Criticism. (ANC, xiii)

In the middle of all this stands Murray Krieger. Krieger
is one of four critics whom Lentricchia identifies as the "major theorists in America since about 1957" (the others are
Harold Bloom, E. D. Hirsch, and Paul de Man.) But even
within this grouping, Krieger is given special status. Soon
after the publication in 1956 of The New Apologists for Poetry (a book that Lentricchia ranks, with another by Gerald
Graff, as "the most important scholarship done on the New
Critics"), Krieger was "recognized as a pioneering figure in
the United States for the discipline called literary criticism."
Three professional honors punctuate at once Krieger's achieve-
ments and the "burgeoning prestige of theoretical study in
this country." "Krieger's career," Lentricchia notes, "becomes in a number of important ways a miniature history of
what has happened theoretically in the contemporary scene"
(ANC, xiii, 213–14).

It is not surprising, then, that when Lentricchia comes
to summarize Krieger's achievement he does so in terms that

reflect his assessment of New Criticism at large. In a chapter entitled "Murray Krieger's Last Romanticism," and with a nod to T. E. Hulme whom Krieger admires, Lentricchia writes:

Krieger will not be surprised by the title of this overview of his work. He might, however, be dismayed at the attribution of a romanticism that is not only unambiguous but also the desperate finish of a theoretical tradition opened by Kant, Coleridge, and company. . . . From the very beginning of his career . . . to the present, Krieger has been a self-conscious, agonized, and, in part, an unwilling connoisseur of postsymbolist aesthetic isolationism. . . . (*ANC*, 214–15)

Apart from the strangely forceful tone of Lentricchia's remarks, the substantive claims that he makes—that Krieger carries forward a tradition of formalist aesthetics that has its roots in Coleridgean organicism and Kantian metaphysics—are not unfamiliar. Krieger himself has alerted us in "An Apology for Poetics" to the formalist origins of his current position and to the idea that formalism, if conceived broadly enough, could encompass all that we have identified as Structuralist and Post-Structuralist invention. And if we continue today to take sides for or against Krieger's work, do we not do so precisely on this same basis, embracing it to the extent that we value new critical aesthetics, shunning it to the extent that, like Lentricchia, we feel the need to move beyond its borders? In short, of everyone on the contemporary scene, is not Murray Krieger the representative par excellence of New Criticism in America?

But there is another level on which Lentricchia's attacks against Krieger make sense and on which such "intertextual mingling" may begin to become evident, one which may have at least as much to do with his professional or institutional affiliations as with his subject matter, and one, moreover, which may help to explain his fascination with the possibility (or impossibility) of succeeding the New Criticism (and thus of writing his book). Krieger and Lentricchia are not unfamiliar with each other's work. Krieger was for a number of years Lentricchia's senior colleague in critical theory at the University of California at Irvine, and the influence of the elder critic upon the younger, particularly in the present book, seems marked.[1]

We have already noted that Lentricchia defers to Krieger's work for his primary scholarship, an odd phenomenon since Krieger is the object of critical scrutiny. But Krieger's influence is also marked in a number of smaller ways. Titling a particular section of his book, for example, "A Critical Thematics" Lentricchia borrows an idiosyncratic use of the word "thematics," which Krieger has himself developed in The Tragic Vision. Or, again using the word "place" to help describe the work of Northrop Frye in the way that he does, Lentricchia employs a peculiar usage that Krieger seems to have originated in The Play and Place of Criticism. The "intertextual mingling" of which Lentricchia spoke seems borne out bountifully in these and other ways in the book, as Lentricchia, no doubt, would be the first to acknowledge.

But sometimes these traces of the elder critic crop up in Lentricchia's work in ways that are less manageable, as true "scars." An example is the title of his book. In an essay entitled "After the New Criticism," published in 1962 in The Massachusetts Review, and subsequently as the first chapter of A Window to Criticism, Krieger attempted to sketch a move beyond formalist organicist aesthetics. It is less important that Lentricchia has borrowed Krieger's title without referring to it (although he does, in fact, play with the title in the preface) than that he seems to have borrowed without reference Krieger's project, a borrowing, moreover, that takes Krieger as its primary object of attack. Lentricchia's note, in his chapter on Krieger, that "Krieger will not be surprised by the title of this overview" acquires in this light an unexpected power.*

And perhaps in this same way we can begin to under-

*See Krieger's remarks on Lentricchia's title and reading of him in the Richard Berg interview—Ed.

stand a certain excessiveness in Lentricchia's tone when he writes about Krieger, a certain aggressive—even pugnacious—quality that surpasses the requirements of "historical" description. Referring, for example, to what he calls Krieger's "romanticism," as "not only unambiguous" (a problematic claim a priori), "but as well the desperate finish of a theoretical tradition opened by Kant," Lentricchia seems as much "out to get" (another meaning of "after) Krieger as to describe the difficulties of succeeding him.

Fredric Jameson, whom Lentricchia cites in the preface as one of his "mentors" in the historical methodology he envisions, draws our attention to this aspect of Lentricchia's style in remarks on the jacket of the paperback edition of the book. Lentricchia's analyses, Jameson writes, "draw blood, cause pain, spare no one." For Jameson these qualities are admirable, and he calls Lentricchia's book "brilliant" and "courageous," adding, with something of the assurance with which older critics used to justify parody, that Lentricchia's analyses are "always informed by a secret sympathy for the work and achievement of the master thinkers he here challenges."

Both Lentricchia's "sympathy" and the necessity of its "secrecy" may be more complicated than Jameson has indicated. Krieger himself, of course, has been very much concerned with relations to literary and literary critical ancestors, both as a professional critic—as in his relations to Eliseo Vivas—and within the subject matter of his criticism—as in The Theory of Criticism. And so it is hardly surprising that the kinds of struggles that would be familiar to readers of Freud should surface here. Lentricchia himself has described his attempt to get beyond New Criticism (a movement which he identifies preeminently with Krieger) as like trying to shake off an "imposing and repressive father-figure," an attempt, that is, that always leaves "traces," or "scars," and an "intertexual mingling," with the result that the "differences among contemporary theories are not clean discontinuities." To suggest, however, that there are age-old parameters to Lentricchia's position or that in trying to get beyond Krieger he appropriates him and extends him is not to devalue Lentricchia's achievement as much as it is to place it, especially since it is such ironic extension that Lentricchia finds at the root of the contemporary scene.

What may also help us to locate Lentricchia's work and what may, indeed, take us by surprise, is that the very same dynamics of displacement and repetition internally organize Krieger's own work. Although it is true that Krieger often embraces with certain qualifications Coleridgean organicism, at other times he takes a position fundamentally at odds with what he then identifies as New Critical or formalist aesthetics, a position which stages the limits, the origins, and the dangers of the romantic implications of the organicist or pure contextual position.

The Tragic Vision is a case in point. In chapter 1 Krieger defines tragedy as a rendering asunder of the literary form we have come to recognize through Aristotle as tragedy before a demonic vision at its center, a vision that begins as the hero's vision of the world—his "view and version of reality"—but ends as an all encompassing moral and ethical absolutism that swallows up all it meets. In the face of this absolutism, the framing impulse of forms, the soothing aestheticizing, totalizing, and objectifying impulse of the ending, can only engage itself by lying about the vision at its center. Backing off from its extremity, betraying it for the more illusory perspective of the everyday world, the ending of these works creates a difference between tragic form and tragic vision which it was the experience of that vision to have rendered impossible, the tragic vision itself being nothing other than such a distinction between form and content made monstrous and violent (TV, 1–21).

And in the final chapter, Krieger relates this view to formalist aesthetics itself. Borrowing the notion of "Manichaeism" with which Wimsatt, in the conclusion to his famous history of criticism, dismisses both organicism and Platonism before a perspective which, in his view, is more encompassing (that of the Christian Passion), Krieger at once poses the limitations of organicism and specifies what would be necessary to supersede it (*TV*, 240). Making a breakthrough with the notion of contextualism, organicism finally stumbles, in Krieger's view, before its romantic liability—aesthetic isolationism. Organicism can succeed only if it finds a way of linking art to the world, if it finds an umbilical cord which Krieger spots in the notions of self-reflexivity, the Manichaean "strife of principles," and a certain logic of extremity which he will then develop (See *TV*, 1–21, 246, 256, 266).

That Lentricchia seems less concerned with *The Tragic Vision* than he ought to be (if he is really on the track of New Criticism and out to challenge what he identifies as Krieger's formalism) is less curious than the fact that Krieger himself at other points seems to back away from that book. In the preface to *The Classic Vision*, for example, written ten years after the earlier book, Krieger writes: "I recall quite clearly my awareness, even before I had finished with *The Tragic Vision*, that *The Classic Vision* would have to follow it in order to right the balance" (*CV*, ix). And then later in the first chapter he writes:

When I opened *The Tragic Vision* with the assertion that "the tragic is not the only vision projected by our serious literature and philosophy, nor is it necessarily the profoundest vision," I was trying even then to leave room for the alternative of the classic. If much of the earlier volume concerned itself with distinguishing the tragic as an authentic vision from what I saw as aesthetically (and existentially) deceptive or self-deceptive pseudo visions, I must open this volume by preparing for a distinction between what I see as two authentic (if mutually exclusive) visions. (*CV*, 3)

But this later view is itself already an altered retrospective position. For in the earlier book there was no felt need to "right the balance," the very idea of "balance" being already an aesthetic idea, issuing from the ending of tragedy. Krieger indeed spoke about "two authentic visions," but the other vision was the religious in the earlier book, a vision he developed around the work of Kierkegaard. "In the Kierkegaardian universe," Krieger wrote, "there are two authentic visions— those I have termed the tragic and the religious—that can be earned through crisis" (*TV*, 15). The Kierkegaardian universe being the modern universe, in Krieger's view ("Kierkegaard," Krieger writes, is "its spokesman"), it is clear that the other vision, the more profound vision for the "crisis-mentality of our time," is the religious (*TV*, 17,1). To say as much is not to suggest that the classic vision is already present in *The Tragic Vision*, but it is introduced in quotation marks, as it were, as "authentic" only from within the self-assuring (and self-deluding) perspective of the ending of tragedy which expels "the errant tragic vision it contained within it." In the first chapter of *The Tragic Vision*, Krieger writes:

From a less severely Protestant point of view, other "authentic" visions would be sanctioned. One that concerned me earlier is what I called the classic vision. . . . It is what I have tried to talk about in discussing the formal and thematic triumph of tragedy over the errant tragic vision it contained within it. (*TV*, 17)

From the point of view of the earlier book, that is, the classic vision could be read as something of an illusion, a hangover from an older world-view that, in giving birth to the tragic vision, gave birth to something of a monster, an "*agent provocateur*," as Krieger calls it, "rebellion incarnate" (*TV*, 17). It is as if, having written *The Tragic Vision* and having distinguished between the demonic center of *The Tragic Vision* and the illusory aestheticizing of its form, Krieger, in the later work, jumps into that aesthetic form and from that perspective rewrites his own earlier critical production. The re-issuing of both *The Tragic Vision* and *The Classic Vision* from a different publisher in a new "balanced" and complementary format (the two books now form a "set") is not at odds with the very tension Krieger describes in the earlier book as constituting tragedy.

In retrospect, the dynamics complicating Krieger's work lend to Lentricchia's a new dimension. Turning against

Krieger, he has only appropriated him all the more profoundly. Lentricchia's rebellion against the father is neither
the forging of a genuinely independent path (the marks of
Krieger's influence are everywhere), nor even simply a negative imitation of the father (which reproduces Krieger's work,
if not directly, then in opposing him systematically), but an
unwitting and undesired positive imitation as well. For
Krieger himself has already turned against his own earlier
work. The central tension of Krieger's own work is already
the battle between a violent and monstrous *agent provocateur* ("rebellion incarnate") born in his midst (his conception
of the tragic vision and of the Manichaean) and a humanistic
classical conceptualizing that is constantly trying to encompass it only to give birth to it once again. Lentricchia's attempt to repudiate Krieger turns out to be a proper extension
or extreme of the very drama in which Krieger's whole corpus is critically engaged. Lentricchia's negative imitation is a
positive duplication of Krieger's own negative imitation of
the tragic vision. Even there Krieger has anticipated him.

To assert as much is not, of course, to claim that
Krieger and Lentricchia are doubles. The absence in Lentricchia's work of any significant account of *The Tragic Vision*,
the unwitting quality to Lentricchia's duplication, is a particular blind spot that is itself absent from Krieger's work.
What is more, Krieger has already erected within his work
the perspective by which the whole of his corpus may be
read. There is a "Lentricchia" in Krieger in a way that there
is no "Krieger" in Lentricchia, no "tragic vision," but only a
"classic vision" (to borrow Krieger's terms again) trying with
increasing difficulty to encompass the "intertextual mingling" and "traces" from a source beyond itself.

Krieger's work, in short, is able to make a reading of
Lentricchia's in ways that Lentricchia's is unable to make a
reading of Krieger's. If, to borrow the brilliant characterization by de Man of the relations between criticism and crisis,
there are only two interpretations—those that are blind and
those that are (more or less) aware of their blindness—then

Krieger's text is unquestionably the richer, more sensitive to the stumbling blocks which Lentricchia persistently reflects.[2]

We should be careful, however, not to carry these distinctions between Krieger and Lentricchia to an extreme, for Lentricchia may not be completely oblivious to these limitations. There may be traces of his awareness of them, for example, in the concluding paragraphs of his essay on Krieger, where he draws attention to a remark Krieger makes in an essay entitled "Theories About Theories" (ANC, 254).[3] "Somewhere in my argument," Krieger writes, within Lentricchia's quotation of him, "I have anticipated most objections by trying to include them too within my paradoxical contours in advance—if one can accept my tactic just at the outer edge of what may be permitted to argument." For Lentricchia that inclusiveness is already going too far, and he notes: "To accept the tactic is to grant Krieger's later works the status of nondiscursive symbolist poem. . . . It is to grant, as I have not, that, in more than one sense, he is beyond criticism" (ANC, 254).

Apart from the playfulness with father-son relations in the final sentence (a kind of trace in itself), the appeal of Lentricchia's rejection is to the old Platonic distinction between criticism and literature in which literature is considered inspired but mute and criticism parasitic but alone able to speak (an idea that Northrop Frye takes up in the opening polemical chapter of his Anatomy of Criticism). To grant Krieger the paradoxical inclusiveness he asks for would be to grant his work the status of literature (a "nondiscursive symbolist poem"), which is to say that he is "beyond criticism," not responsible for what he says and therefore not able to be challenged. Lentricchia is too close to Krieger for that. He can see the oppositions, the contradictions, the monstrosity too clearly. There is nothing magical or mystical about it by which he could externalize it from himself or from Krieger's background, by which he could "sacralize" or transcendentalize it.

And yet Krieger's argument has been—in The Tragic Vision, for example—that our greatest literature is made up precisely of such demonic opposition, such Manichaean and monstrous duality, and that such opposition is none other than a form of criticism itself, the most profound criticism we have, a criticism of the very formal oppositions by which it is contained. In the face of Krieger's demystification of literature, of his revelation of the Manichaean criticism that is its center, Lentricchia undertakes the oldest move in the book: he remystifies it. He divides it. He invokes a distinction between literature and criticism which would reestablish "clean discontinuities," barring criticism from literature and vice versa.

On the other hand, it is Lentricchia who has chosen to include this paradoxical literature from the Krieger canon, who has perceived these contradictions as "summarizing with sterling candor" Krieger's position, who has perceived an identity between literature (a "nondiscursive symbolist poem") and a certain exceeding of limits. Moreover, it is Lentricchia who, in introducing the notion of "criticism" in a familial context, would seem to call attention to the proximity of Krieger to himself. At one point in this final moment he even calls Krieger's ethical position "courageous," and although he backs off from the compliment ("he cannot earn his ethical spurs," he immediately adds) he does so in terms that could be taken as sympathy: "too much in his work gives aid and comfort to his enemies," Lentricchia writes, as if he is on Krieger's side (*ANC*, 254). It is as if his hostility toward Krieger's work originated less in a rejection of it than in a more profound admiration of it, an admiration that has not yet been acknowledged and that he feels Krieger has blocked.

The implications of these critical dynamics for the study of Lentricchia's work may be far-reaching. Suddenly they enable us to understand how Lentricchia's entire project, his critical history or "thematics," echoes Krieger not only when he is concerned with Krieger's work specifically, but also when he becomes unaccountably vehement about matters that seemingly have nothing to do with Krieger: for example, his treatment of Paul de Man.

Lentricchia incessantly condemns in de Man what he

identifies as a "rhetoric of authority," an "impression" that
he feels de Man has "always given" of "having a grip on
truth" (an attack he wages with the constancy he condemns
in the supporters of de Man—among whom he counts Harold
Bloom, Geoffrey Hartman, and J. Hillis Miller). De Man addresses us, Lentricchia asserts, from within a form of transcendental rhetoric that can be identified as essentialism
(*ANC*, 282–317). In speaking in the preface of the difficulties
of superseding the New Criticism, Lentricchia noted the existence of a "crisis" in its midst which contemporary theory
"has not resolved but deepened and extended." "The crisis is
generated," he remarked,

> by, on the one hand, a continuing urge to essentialize literary dis-
> course by making it a unique kind of language—a vast, enclosed
> textual and semantic preserve—and, on the other hand, by an urge
> to make literary language "relevant" by locating it in larger contexts
> of disclosure and history. (*ANC*, xiii)

Lentricchia's appeal is to the traditional division of
critical response into formal or generic approaches and historical approaches which are often identified with Aristotle
and Plato. Between these two alternatives, in Lentricchia's
view, de Man chooses to enclose literature within a privileged space, a choice which makes him a formalist and a
literary apologist, which are, of course, the charges he also
levels upon Krieger. Presumably, Lentricchia would identify
support for his position in a critic like Stanley Fish, who, in
his recent essays on language, would seem to wage the same
anti-essentialist battle against literary apologists.[4]

Now we may feel that Lentricchia is not wrong in identifying a certain apologism in the work of de Man, or for that
matter of Krieger. In fact, this aspect of de Man's criticism
has been unduly underplayed in favor of his more ironic
positions.[5] In the case of Krieger, if there is any thread that
spans the entirety of his career—from *The New Apologists for
Poetry* to the recent "An Apology for Poetics"—it is such a
notion. Moreover, there may be important ways in which an

anti-essentialist position is more comprehensive and explains more than essentialist views. But it may turn out—and
here is the point that Lentricchia misses—that it is de Man
and Krieger who in their very apologism are the real anti-
essentialists. For if they would confer upon literature a special status it is not from within a Platonic-Aristotelian philosophic fortress (theirs is no apologetics of the kind M. H.
Abrams described in his introduction to *Literature and Belief*) but against that fortress, in an effort to turn the tables on
a critical tradition that has always expelled literature for its
dangerous mimetic properties and rewritten it according to
idealist specifications that would deprive it of its Manichaean and violent truths.[6]

Indeed, it may turn out (ironically enough) that it is
Lentricchia and his allies who are the real essentialists. For if
they oppose the essentialists for what they perceive as the
assignment of arbitrary privilege to literary discourse, it is
not with the aim of reintroducing literature (the tragic literature that the Platonic-Aristotelian idealist tradition has implicitly or explicitly expelled) but with the aim of further
developing the resources of that expulsion, of reducing the
discourse of literature to just another form of institutional
practice. Far from undoing the distinction between literature
and philosophy, from recognizing that literature is already
philosophy, their aim is to bar forever from the philosophic
fortress the kind of monstrous writing that within the framework of the old system became "literaturized." If de Man and
Krieger argue for literature it is not on behalf of this "literaturization" (which is, in effect, only a transcendentalizing of
its monstrous qualities of violence) but on behalf of exposing
both the monstrosity (that gets aestheticized in this process)
and the mystification or domestication of aestheticization itself. It is the avowed anti-essentialists who would, in the face
of the inefficacious domestication of violent writing, carry
the sacrificial process to its logical extreme and complete it
by expelling the whole muddled corpus.

But, and here is perhaps the most striking point, Lentricchia could have found precisely this argument in Krieger's own work. For in the last chapter of *The Tragic Vision* this is the very argument Krieger uses to disarm the detractors of contextualism—those who would claim that the New Critics have enclosed literature within an autotelic formalism and isolationism. Such detractors, Krieger argues, depend upon the very form-content dichotomy that they would attack the New Critics for abandoning. They themselves are "trapped," Krieger writes, within the very formalism (or essentialism) with which they would confront a criticism that—through the notion of self-reflexivity—would uniquely relate literature to the existentialist complexities from which it has arisen (*TV*, 229–32).

To suggest that Krieger is more aware of the limitations of his own work than some of his critics is not to claim that Krieger is immune from falling at times into the same trap himself, particularly when he encounters a critic of comparable insight. In a series of essays on deconstruction, and with particular reference to the work of Paul de Man, Krieger misses, it seems, the same point as Lentricchia.[7] He fails to see the way in which he and de Man place the same demystifying value in literature. Allying himself in one essay with Derrida (Derrida is doing in philosophy, Krieger feels, what he is doing in literary discourse), Krieger would charge de Man with the same misunderstandings that Lentricchia, in a much less sensitive way, would level upon Krieger (*TC*, 224–33). The richness of Krieger's text does not hinder it from being blind to the same point in others. What is important is not whether or not a text is blind—there are no non-blind texts—but whether or not (and to what degree) it offers us a perspective from which that blindness can be read.

But the implications of these "Kriegerian" dynamics ("Krieger" in German means warrior) may be even more far-reaching for the study of Krieger's own work. Future theorists of Krieger's work will no doubt want to pay closer attention to *The Tragic Vision* and to the particular ways in which, already within its boundaries, Krieger engages in the kinds of self-distancing strategies that will characterize some of the tensions between that book and later theories. They will want to understand, to take just one example, how Krieger's theory of the miracle of metaphor and duplicit illusion both completes and displaces an organicist project begun in *The Tragic Vision* around the notion of self-reflexivity. This notion is initially attributed to the New Critics (it is, in fact, in Krieger's view, the way the New Critics escape the charge of a "barren formalism" or aestheticism, and make art responsive to the "phenomenological data of moral experience") and subsequently reintroduced by Krieger in the face of a pure contextualism or organicism that has been abandoned by its practitioners for the "real dilemmas" (the isolationist tendencies) it promoted.[8]

But they should be most concerned with the central tension in Krieger's work, a tension between a tragic vision conceived as a critique of formalist aesthetics and the re-presentation of that vision from the less extreme position of an aesthetic closure, a duplication which both maintains the traces of that former vision and thoroughly represses it, which produces, to borrow Lentricchia's phrase, an "intertextual mingling." In the paragraph in which Lentricchia feels Krieger "summarizes with sterling candor" his position, something of this "mingling" may be seen.

I have tried to hold fully and press simultaneously both halves of the following oppositions: both the poem as object *and* the poem as *intentional* object; both the concept of a discrete aesthetic experience *and* a notion of *all* experience as indivisible and unbroken; both the discontinuity of the poem's language system *and* the continuity of all discourse as a system; both spatiality *and* temporality, mystification *and* demystification in the work's workings upon us; both the poem as self-willed monster *and* the poet as a present agent subduing a compliant poem to his will. . . . Finally, then, both the verbal miracle of metaphorical identity *and* the awareness that the miracle depends on our sense of its impossibility, leading to our knowledge that it's only our *illusion* of identity held within an awareness that language cannot reach beyond the Structuralist principle of difference. (Quoted in *ANC*, 254)

From the perspective of *The Tragic Vision* these "oppositions" are not oppositions at all but the two "extremes" of one and the same conceptualization. They are not unlike the two apparent "sides" of a Möbius strip in which there is really only one continuous side, the other being always a future or a past of the same side, and the illusion that there are two sides being fostered by our obviating of the twisting path between them. From the point of view of *The Classic Vision*, however, Krieger is here attempting, from within a propositional Platonic matrix, to articulate a certain Manichaeanism or strife of principles within his critical practice, which is not unlike the demonic Manichaean dualism he has identified at the heart of the tragic, an articulation which can only present this "opposition" as a form of contradiction and monstrosity.

Which is the more accurate account of what Krieger is up to in this passage? For Lentricchia there is no choice (although the inclusion of this passage may bespeak a fascination on his part for its confusions). He will reject the passage itself from within the confines of a traditional rigid Platonic distinction between literature and criticism. Krieger's work is either literature or criticism but not both. And since Lentricchia will not allow him the status of literature, it must be criticism that does not succeed at what it attempts. For Krieger, on the other hand, at one moment in his career the first perspective dominates and at a later moment the second takes over and rereads the first.

It may be however that in formulating the opposition between the two in this way we can recognize the continuities between Krieger's and Lentricchia's texts, whether within Krieger's text or without. For it may turn out that all of Krieger's work is engaged in a sliding from one option to the other, from an intertextual mingling to a differential expulsion—two options that may turn out, like the tragic vision and tragic form itself, to be two extremes of the same option. And it may be that between these two choices—between "Krieger" and "Lentricchia," between the new apologism and the new essentialism—all of contemporary theory in America writes itself.

To see all contemporary theory as inscribed between these poles would only be to say, in a way that Lentricchia may not have anticipated and for which Krieger may not wish to take credit, that Lentricchia is right. To the extent that it is between the extremes of Krieger and Lentricchia that we find ourselves, and that Krieger already contains within his work the extremity of Lentricchia, it is within Krieger's text that we continue to theorize. Murray Krieger would be, then, something like the "father" (to borrow Lentricchia's word) of contemporary theory in America, a father who is certainly not "beyond criticism," since it is he who would teach us, above all, that literature is already criticism, that our "greatest" literature is none other than our most profound staging of the limits of our perspective (although this criticism can only appear—from within our Platonistic distinctions—as a "self-willed monster"), but who, in his very expansiveness, already includes in one form or another the debates in which we would now engage.

Lentricchia himself may have said it best. In an unusually protracted note at the beginning of his "acknowledgement" section, and offered as "fresh evidence for Harold Bloom's anxiety of influence," Lentricchia relates the fantasy of his children that they wrote his book. They would like me "to credit them with writing it" he tells us. Where did they get such an idea, we may wonder. "I can't put their names on the title page," Lentricchia writes. "But I can say it here: Amy and Rachel wrote this book. Hostile reviewers may blame their father for all failures" (*ANC*, ix).

Where is "here"? Where is the space that allows children to be credited with writing their father's book, a fantasy that deconstructs the book Lentricchia has just written and yet within which it is contained? Where else but in the margins, in the "acknowledgement" section, in an anecdote about a fantasy of appropriation—in short, within literature.

And in Lentricchia's decision to relate it to us, the comparison we have been developing is brought to completion. They are his "Lentricchias" before his momentary and fleeting "Krieger." And all the themes we have noted suddenly reappear: imitative appropriation and rivalry with the father, self-creditation, hostility, misplaced blame, criticism, failure, and so forth. And between the two interpretative extremes to which the final sentence in his anecdote is subject—on the one hand, that the children did not do it, that their father is responsible (and hostile critics, who would project upon others their own bad faith and therefore need a scapegoat, may blame him) and on the other hand, that hostile and critical children are entitled and justified in blaming fathers for the failures they themselves exhibit (extremes which contrast generous protective fathers with hostile angry children)—Lentricchia traces out, as he has in the book at large, his relationship to Krieger.

No wonder, then, that Lentricchia chooses the title that he does. "After" can mean "what follows," "on the track of," or "out to get."[9] And if we take the "New Criticism" in the familiar sense, then we can render the title to mean: (a) the criticism which historically succeeds the New Criticism—i.e., Structuralism and Post-Structuralism; (b) the intertextual mingling between the New Criticism and its would-be successors—so that there is no "before" and "after" the New Criticism; or (c) the frustration that such a dilemma engenders.

But by dint of the first rendering and the sense that contemporary theory has become the "new" New Criticism, the title comes in retrospect to assume a number of other possibilities which compound the difficulties for reading it: (a) the kind of criticism that can be written in the wake of contemporary theorizing—for example, Lentricchia's own envisioned historical methodology; (b) the lack of clean discontinuities between contemporary theorists and the difficulty of tracing distinctly the current debates; (c) the frustration that this new dilemma poses.

And, of course, if we add Krieger's essay "After the New Criticism" or the name of Murray Krieger itself to this collection of referential matrices, then the difficulty of rendering the title has increased exponentially. What began as the designation of a piece of criticism has become the designation of a crisis. In displaying meanings and attitudes

which vary from historical, objectifying, informative accounts to angry, subjugative invectives, the title of Lentricchia's book, like the anecdote that straightaway follows it,
traces out Lentricchia's relation to Krieger. By the end of the
book, "After the New Criticism," whether understood now
to issue from the pen of Krieger or Lentricchia, has become
an impossible title—monstrous, out of control, in short, a
piece of literature.

And we are suddenly back where we started.
"Krieger's career becomes," Lentricchia writes, "in a number
of important ways a miniature history of what has happened
theoretically in the contemporary scene." Krieger's criticism
is a kind of tragic vision which Lentricchia's would struggle
to contain. But Lentricchia's criticism is also an extreme of
the same criticism, a monstrous *agent provocateur* born
within its midst which would supplant its critical progenitor.
And between these extremes, which pose for us at one moment the truth of monstrous writing (and "literaturization")
and at another moment dissolve "literature" before the analysis of institutional practices, within language and within history, we continue to find our own. In the curious mixture of
gangsterish street talk and psychosexual metaphors by which
a critic like Lentricchia can speak of being "forced to finger
Paul de Man," one may detect the traces of a "sympathy"
with a growing anti-intellectualism in this country (all the
more punchy for having to be kept secret), a new turn of the
Platonic essentialist screw, which, in the face of a progressive
manifestation of violence and monstrosity from behind the
mask of a domesticated "literature," would rid us of the literary subject entirely (*ANC*, 283). Romanticism, the denial of
the blindness which is the condition of our possibility, the
blindness to our blindness, continues to flourish in this
country and to define the parameters of all our theoretical
discussion. As Lentrichhia put it so well, in a phrase that can
serve as a motto for the whole endeavor, "hostile reviewers
may blame their father for all failures."

11.

A MATTER OF DISTINCTION:
AN INTERVIEW
WITH MURRAY KRIEGER

Conducted by Richard Berg

I'd like to begin with two monumental questions: first, how did American literary theory get where it is today from where it was twenty-five years ago; secondly, where is it?

WHEN you say twenty-five years ago, I asssume you are speaking of the heyday of the New Criticism, just about the time from which we begin to trace the decline of its dominance. 1957 was the year of the publication of Northrop Frye's *Anatomy of Criticism*, which was, I suppose, the first major post-New-Critical, which is to say anti-New-Critical, statement. It was also just one year after the publication of my book, *The New Apologists for Poetry*, which sought to sum up the theoretical consequences—as well as the deficiencies—of the New Criticism.

As I look back to the several candidates since Frye to succeed the New Criticism, I am struck by the extent to which they seem to function as corrective reactions to the various excesses of New-Critical orthodoxy. In reaction against the over-ardent suppression of biography and authorial intention, there sprung up a new interest in consciousness criticism on the one hand or visionary criticism on the other. We associate the first with the Geneva School and Georges Poulet and the second with the followers of Northrop Frye, perhaps most impressively in the early work of Harold Bloom (that is, the pre-anxiety Bloom of *The Visionary Company*). This emphasis was accompanied by the urgent rediscovery of Romanticism—that period much maligned by the New Criticism—which, as yet, has not again been removed from the center of critical interest and authority. I suspect it was the revival of interest in authorial consciousness, intentionality, or vision that largely accounts for the (then) new centrality of the one literary period—the Romantic period—in which authors are most explicitly invested in their works. On the other side, the excessive neglect by the New Criticism (through its concentration on a normative, unyielding object) of the role of the audience and of social forces has in part sponsored a number of antagonistic responses, whether arising out of speech-act theory, information theory, German reception aesthetic, or neo-Marxism. Finally, the New Criticism's excessive concentration on a discrete poetic object, seen as a unique discursive entity cut off from the generic language system, has helped justify the antithetical response of Structuralism and Post-Structuralism: the deconstruction of the isolated work is accompanied by the deconstruction of the very notion of literature itself into an indivisible realm of *écriture*, of undifferentiated textuality, in which—however paradoxically—the principle of difference reigns monolithically supreme.

It is rather unjust to the facts, as well as self-serving, to suggest—as I have—that all movements in the last twenty-five years receive their impetus from a desire to reverse some of the tendencies of the New Criticism. Clearly, many of them—especially those from abroad—have purposes and functions historically unrelated to the New Criticism; indeed, a good number seem hardly to be aware of the New Criticism. Yet I believe that, within the context of American academic criticism, we find an antithetical relationship between the New Criticism and subsequent movements, perhaps growing out of the need to overthrow the austerity of parental dogma and to restore to critical interest the place of works and of kinds of works long neglected.

The several criticisms I have named seem to me, then, to represent the variety of theoretical movements which have sought to hold sway these last two decades: criticism after Frye or Poulet, criticism responding to various theories of audience or society, and the several kinds of criticism thought of as Structuralist and Post-Structuralist. Criticism and critical theory have doubtless always been products of current fashion, but it is certainly the case that, in recent years, the pursuit of what is fashionable—together with the attempt to discover at each moment what is fashionable—has dominated the realm of criticism far more completely than we were used to expect. Indeed, of the movements I have named, surely the first group—those critics concerned primarily with authorial consciousness, intentionality, or vision—is pretty well out of it now, being about as much out of fashion as the New Criticism itself. These approaches were doomed to be set aside as part of the general rejection of anything that could be related to the "myth of origins." What origin could be more obviously vulnerable to textualist attack than the quaint notion of the author himself, the speaking presence which such critics confidently found reflected in the words spoken or written? Of the others mentioned, Structuralism itself has been superseded by any of several Post-Structuralisms, with the "post" itself guaranteeing obsolescence.

I would say that the main contest at this moment is between Post-Structuralist proponents of an infinite textuality (or rather we should say intertextuality) and those who would move beyond the world of texts to search out the extra-linguistic role of naked power which those texts reflect or disguise. The interpretation of the world *as* text is thus confronted by the interpretation of a world hidden or suppressed *in* texts and thereby revealed *through* texts. In one the text is the world, while in the other the text is the verbal manipulation *by* the world, through which the world-as-power (whether Marx's, Nietzsche's, or Freud's) creates its authority and control.

There are, of course, several camps within each of these two sides, both of them in their varieties seeking to dominate the world of critical fashion and to demonstrate that domination by forcing upon it a hegemony of special language. As a result of my experience for five years as director of The School of Criticism and Theory, during which time I examined many hundreds of applications from our brightest younger theorists, I have some sense about the sway of fashion and indeed even thought of having some sort of stock market index recording the relative popularity of our several competing schools. I would guess that, just about now, Derridean deconstruction, still very widely followed, may be losing just a bit, with Marxism-cum-Foucault moving up. But that was as of about a year ago. Perhaps we should check with Geoffrey Hartman, who read the applications for the School this year. Sometimes a year can make a big difference in such matters, if—as too many do—one tailors his theoretical allegiance to keep it fashionable.

Do you see this movement in theory as a continuum or as some radical break with the past?

Of course, as with most such questions, you probably expect my answer to insist that in some ways it is both. And I won't disappoint you. First, as my earlier answer indicates, I would insist on saying "movements" rather than "movement." But even if, collapsing all the recent movements, we were to speak of a common tendency, then I would find myself beginning by describing it as a radical break which, upon closer observation, betrays many elements of continuity. The revolutionary tendencies of deconstruction, as it has become domesticated by the American academic tradition, seem to have been tamed by the critical habits common to it and to its antithetical precursor. It has certainly become common, in recent days, for socially oriented critics to complain that the deconstructionist movement is vitiated by the varied formalistic objectives of the early formalisms which it would deconstruct.

Is "deconstruction" then the "telos" of certain tendencies in earlier Anglo-American theory?

I look at your last question as followed by this one, and I can easily deduce that it is your own conviction that deconstruction is *the* movement to which the recent history of theory has arrived. As you know, I am less sure about this monolithic claim. Similarly I would hesitate to privilege its historical role by projecting anything like a "telos" upon it. If you are asking whether in any sense some deconstructionist notions are implicit—if hardly ever realized or understood as such—within certain New Critical practices, then I suppose I feel that they are. But of course the two movements for the most part shout their differences to one another. Still the problem of telos bothers me more in your historical model. Since I feel that in some ways American criticism is already showing signs of moving beyond deconstruction, the application of anything like teleology (that is, of an Aristotelian final cause) to it is hardly appropriate.

How does your earlier work relate to this unfolding movement, and particularly deconstruction? Would you say that it

*acted as a vanguard for these present developments; didn't
you help open the door for these once new French fashions?*

Let me proceed with this answer, using deconstruction as the
movement which interests you. It is, as a matter of fact, the
movement among current ones of which my own earlier work
contains a number of curious foreshadowings. These go as far
back as the passage, in *The New Apologists for Poetry* (1956),
which deals with Donne's undoing of his own metaphorical
construct in "The Canonization." My notion of the metaphor
that at once encloses the work and, by denying itself, opens it
up—this notion persists, from my earliest work right through
to my claim in *The Classic Vision* (1971) that "all poems
must covertly contain their anti-poems." Indeed in that book
I argue in several places for the need for "systematic duplicity." My dear colleague and theoretical cohort at Iowa, the
late Rosalie Colie—though well outside the French theoretical tradition—provided brilliantly for what becomes in Paul
de Man the poem's self-deconstructive tendencies, when she
traces the moves by which the metaphor "unmetaphors" itself. Her essay on Marvell's "The Garden," perhaps the best
chapter in her splendid book on Marvell, is developed by
means of the device of "unmetaphoring" within the assumed
totality of metaphorical composition. This is another version
of my own claim, which is as old as my book on Shakespeare's Sonnets (*A Window to Criticism*, 1964), that the metaphor functions as a miracle, though it is most like a miracle
in its counter-movement, which negates itself: for a miracle
can function only in conjunction with our rational fore-
knowledge that it cannot exist at all.

    The issue here ought not to be reduced to a fight for
priority, to a claim for my earlier-ness. But you have framed
your questions in so historical a way that I could not
resist—especially when the relationship between an Anglo-
American theorist like me and the new (but not so new)
deconstructionist tradition in our academy (though mainly

borrowed from France) is at issue in your questioning. I know that Gerald Graff has charged me with being in part responsible for the deconstructionist mode.* He sees me as helping to open the way for its rejection of the simple referential function of words, for its concentration upon the internal entanglements of the text which allows for a play of signifiers, thereby depriving us of the sure stay of signifieds which should pre-exist them and control them. But recent movements have gone well beyond any precedents which one might find in my work when, making no distinction between fiction or poetry and other writing, they appear to resort to a monolithic method of analyzing the textual (and intertextual) play of signifiers. Nor, I might add, is their notion of the free play of "undecidables" to be confused with my own notion of a controlled doubleness. I seem to hold out much more hope (perhaps an old-fashioned hope) for the possibility—and the desirability—of consensus among readers confronted by the same text, however qualified or downright skeptical my epistemological concessions.

It could be argued, I think, that your earlier work, prior to The Play and Place of Criticism, *not only helped establish criticism as an academic discipline, but also set the style and mode of the argument within the critical debate. After all, you laid the New Critics to rest in* The New Apologists for Poetry *because of their lack of philosophical rigor. Now that you have somewhat changed your style, has this earlier mode come home to haunt you? Would it be off the mark to say that even though your style has changed, your work still shows a continued commitment to this project, that literary theory and criticism should be firmly grounded in philosophical rigor even if that means abandoning the sureness of that ground?*

*See Graff's "Tongue-in-Cheek Humanism: A Response to Murray Krieger," ADE Bulletin (Fall 1981), no. 69, pp. 18–21—Ed.

No, I don't think it is off the mark. I think that I have always searched out the systematic assumptions beneath the critical statements of others and have tried to worry about my own. Nor do I believe that my more recent work marks a significant break with that project. What *has* happened, though, as you suggest, is that the ground—and my style with it—has lost its sureness, if it hasn't slipped away altogether. I now find myself more sensitive to the need—and the need to yield to the need—for counter-logical moves that force me to acknowledge the paradoxical; even, I suppose, to welcome paradox into the would-be logical precincts of theory.

Nevertheless, this change should not be seen as a resignation from system-hunting, nor should I be seen as substituting for system-hunting a search for the aberrant, the stray moment of discourse, which has its own decentered authority apart from any systematic context. I recognize, in other words, that my continuing project of theoretical analysis presupposes now, as it has all along, an argumentative discourse which seeks to center itself about a principled closure. In other words, I hang onto a notion of argument that is clearly pre-deconstructionist. At the same time, I see the logic of system subverting itself, working to undo the very assumptions which allow it to function. But the discursive habit of submitting terms and propositions to a logical closure still, for me, creates the assumptions behind my reading of other critics and of myself, even where such assumptions are undercut in the very act of seeming to be assumed. So you can see how some of what I say may appear similar in feel and temper to the work of Post-Structuralists, even while it undoubtedly springs from a more old-fashioned devotion to the notion of theoretical system than they could allow. I just do not believe that the theorist has to give up the notion of discursive system in order to account for the anti-systematic in discourse.

This welcoming of paradox would then also account for what Frank Lentricchia in After the New Criticism *sees as the retreat of your later work.*

You are probably right: I suppose Lentricchia does find himself disturbed by my resorting to the "both/and" and the "even-as," thereby retreating (in his eyes) from straight assertion to self-denying assertion. With his interest in the historical and socially "real," he finds this practice a retreat to the equivocal and hence the politically paralytic, a retreat whose only possible justification, he claims, is hedonistic. So he would find in my more recent work an aesthetic resignation that has given up its commitment to the existentially real (as seen in The Tragic Vision) for the fictional being pursued for its own sake. I think he gives less attention than he should both to the equivocal character of the existential as it appears in my earlier work and to the cultural impact of the fictional in my later work. The difference is less severe than your question—and perhaps Lentricchia's chapter—suggest.

Lentricchia's attack on what he calls my hedonism is central to his chapter on my work. The enemy for him is what he thinks of as the hedonistic fictionalism of Wallace Stevens, who, curiously, was one of the heroes of Lentricchia's first book, The Gaiety of Language (1968), the title itself a quotation from Stevens. It is, I think, this insistence on reducing me to Stevens that leads him to ignore my interest in the cultural function of literature. Thus in the book of mine which he treats in great and knowing detail, Theory of Criticism, he overlooks what was for me its most important chapter, Chapter 7: "The Aesthetic as the Anthropological: The Breath of the Word and the Weight of the World." In it I make my fullest argument yet for the process by which the double movement in the literary work's master metaphor unlocks for us not only a culture's momentary grasp of its visioned reality, but also what it represses in the excluded realm that the metaphor evades.

I find in Lentricchia's antagonism toward what he claims to be my hedonism a strange echo of Yvor Winters' violent attack on what he claimed to be John Crowe Ransom's hedonism. And that in turn suggests a relationship I don't enjoy contemplating between Lentricchia and Gerald Graff, who has never fully recovered (who does?) from his apprenticeship to Winters' dedication to the real. Both are disturbed, as Winters was, by those critics who would trap us inside texts, within a world as fiction, thus putting in question the very existence of a world beyond fiction, beyond its involute language. I don't mean to suggest any literal indebtedness to Winters by Lentricchia, or any real kinship to Graff, but there *are* similarities in this protection of the extra-linguistically real and, consequently, the antagonistic obsession with the hedonistic, a label that is being too freely passed around.

As, according to him, I have retreated from logic in my own theory and from a vision of the existential in poetry to a paradoxical play of criticism that seeks to focus upon an internal fictional play in poetry, I have—as Stevens did before me—joined the ranks of the "theoreticians of deliberate triviality." And we know which theoreticians he means by these. He sees me swallowed up by that deconstructionist gang, as my tactic of seeking to swallow them up has been turned inside out. And he sees my cultivation of the paradoxical in theory as leading to a self-destructive system that is no more useful to expose reality and its social determinants than is the "nondiscursive symbolist poem" which I apparently mean my theoretical work to resemble. So much, then, for my anthropological quest and for the distinctions I would place between myself and the deconstructionists. Needless to say, what Lentricchia sees as a retreat I would claim to be an advance in my self-awareness. And I worry whether it is not his movement, back to Winters or—moving from right to left—back to social reality, that is the retreat from what these past decades have taught us.

Wasn't "After the New Criticism" a title you once gave to an article? Isn't Lentricchia's use of it a surprising comment on his own work?

Yes, I published an essay with that title in the *Massachusetts Review* in 1962. It was, as a matter of fact, an ambitious essay, and I think it was pretty widely known—even was translated. I know Lentricchia knew of it and has acknowledged it, and I find the suggestion of his acknowledgement of it at one point in his preface. Of course, my own essay, now twenty years old, had a quite different set of after-New Critics in mind, although chief among them was Northrop Frye, who is also the first post-New Critic considered by Lentricchia's book. Hence Lentricchia's *After the New Criticism* begins, as he tells us in the preface, in 1957 (presumably with Frye's book), in effect, after *The New Apologists for Poetry*.

If I work at it, I can come up with a number of curious speculations about the significance of Lentricchia's title, especially the extent to which there is a ghostly trace of my own earlier essay's title in it. Lentricchia is seeking to create a new—his own—*After the New Criticism*, turning upon mine and taking it back—also, to a great extent, taking back his own earlier self which was to some extent tied up with that earlier "After the New Criticism." Lentricchia's early work found its source in the kind of post-New Critical suggestions I was making in the late fifties and early sixties. So my earlier post-New Criticism (After the New Criticism) then was to a great extent his. Seen this way, his recent *After the New Criticism* indeed does come *after*, after his own, now rejected, version of New Criticism. In this sense, Lentricchia's title—and the *after* in it—is autobiographical in relation to his own project and his own development, although the *after* here again means not only coming later but also coming in response to, in reaction against. This double sense of "after" is familiar to us, thanks to the work of Harold Bloom. Something of this sort of historical succession I think moves Lentricchia to his own new *after* in its relation to his own earlier work and mine. In turning against his earlier self, he must make his former ally the now rejected hedonist that he sees himself as having been. For he is also coming after his own earlier version of Stevens' romanticism.

So perhaps, finally, we see yet another sense of "after." We have had not only "after" as coming later, and "after" as the reaction against, which turns out to be the obligation of those who come later; but, despite that rejection, we also have not merely *après* but *d'après* in the French manner of citing the adaptation of an earlier by a later version, the sense in English of "after" as "according to" or "in the manner of." In his desire to fulfill a function for this historical moment in a manner that echoes the way that function was fulfilled for another earlier moment, Lentricchia may be seen—in his repetition of my exact title—as writing his *After the New Criticism après* and *d'après* mine. But all this is extravagant speculation on my part. I have so used his title as to turn it (and his work) into an allusive, intertextual, and antithetical criticism all at once. As I relate his title to mine, I have found his work to be in the genre of *after*, that is, to be an after after, a *d'après après*, *d'après* "After the New Criticism." No wonder his chapter on me must take on so antithetical a character, since it is my "after" that he comes after, my "after" that must be wiped out by his—which perhaps is why there is no explicit reference to it. But for me the twenty years between the two "afters" call for no such negation as his, but permit a greater sense of theoretical continuity. Perhaps because it was I who wrote the earlier "After the New Criticism."

Probably all this .is not only an extravagent speculation, but an immodest, even an egocentric one as well. That is the danger of interviews, I fear, in the free range they give to the responding self.*

Let's turn to Lentricchia's critique of your work. He is trying you for the anti-logical tendency of your recent work, the advance of self-awareness, and not the argument itself. He finds that it has become a theory of contradictions; then he

*For an extended discussion of the Krieger-Lentricchia relationship see Sandor Goodhart's essay throughout—Ed.

goes on to discover more contradictions. Yet doesn't each discovery give your argument more density, complexity, and substance?

I would of course enjoy agreeing with you. I think it is true that Lentricchia tries to have it both ways: he says that I seek a theory that self-consciously nurtures contradictions (in effect, "Both Sides Now") *and* that I can be found out as contradicting myself in spite of my most proper theoretical intentions. He is unhappy about the first of these because he fears it makes me consciously forgo proper theory-writing to indulge a false poetry, and then he finds me veiling my theory and muddying its system by stumbling into contradiction, apparently against my will. Yet even in the latter case he usually concedes that I am aware of, and acknowledge, the particular contradiction without struggling against it. As you suggest, then, he seems uncertain about the status of statement, of logical discourse, in my theorizing, so that he does not seem to me to strike home either when he claims to prefer another sort of discourse than mine or when, claiming a foul, he finds my discourse erring by doing what it confesses it has to do.

Lentricchia seems, then, to be showing a decided nostalgia for an earlier Krieger, one less poetic and more logical.

I am pretty much in agreement with what you are suggesting. I would like to remind you that, while I do not completely deny that there are significant changes between those of my writings influenced by existentialism and the later ones which are consciously addressing the Post-Structuralist challenge, I would prefer to stress the extent to which, in my earlier work, the equivocal was already undermining any momentary attraction which the "real," as an ontological element, held for me. In that earlier work I suspect that I was not always as constant as my later theoretical context reminded me I would have to be, and that my wording sometimes slipped; but the evasiveness which annoys Lentricchia was there, I fear, much earlier than he seems to allow.

My first theoretically self-conscious projection of it appears as early as *The Classic Vision* in 1971, in the anti-Hegelian diagram which I originally invented in order to explain certain thematic duplicities that characterize what I was calling the tragic and the classic visions. I resurrected that diagram more recently, in my second "Poetic Presence and Illusion" essay in the book of that title, when I discovered how effectively its terms and relations characterized what I wanted to say about the operation of literary metaphor generally. The diagram is intended to indicate a pattern in accordance with which apparent polarities, for all the exclusiveness of their opposition to each other, criss-cross, even turn into one another, so that difference is at once sustained and converted to identity. This double relation between convertible poles, in which their distinctness ends by being confounded, I have more recently expressed in the model of the prisoner's dilemma game, which frames my notion of *Poetic Presence and Illusion*. My MLA rejoinder, "Both Sides Now," pursues this extension into the prisoner's dilemma. All this is indeed the paradoxical play upon logic that I find at the heart of poetic metaphor and that any theory seeking to account for literary discourse must confront with its own subversive self-consciousness. I suspect that, whatever slips one may find in the language of my early work, the counterlogical subversion—with its threat to the logic of a self-consistent theory—is a consistent tendency (perhaps the only consistency) within all my work.

Yet, for me, this intratextual play, which seems to cut the work off from an extratextual reality, has strong cultural implications, and hence references to historical realities, after all—so much so that I wonder whether, if he was aware of them, Lentricchia could still make the charges of mandarin-ism and isolationism which he does. I find that the enclosing, totalizing pretension of the poem as metaphor seeks to impose itself through the power of exclusion, that which would repress whatever threatens to explode it (which is just about everything outside itself). And the shrewd, self-deconstructing poem reminds us of this repression by its subtle, barely sensed, smuggling-in of the repressed.

It thus reveals what its cultural moment, its vision, its politics, admits or represses: the permissibilities of its words, what they see or are blind to. And it is of enormous historical import and gives the poet an indispensable role in allowing us to see what society's language hides as well as reveals— reveals by hiding as well as by saying. Here indeed is formalism moving—as Geoffrey Hartman has claimed—beyond formalism. But I can get to this "beyond" only by way of the paradoxical relations between closure and openness, identity and difference, such as my diagram was created to represent.

Lentricchia then has failed to grant your work the benefit of history, for instead of granting you a changing self-consciousness, he has saddled your recent work with the language and positions of earlier writings, as if time and various theoretical debates had not produced some sea-change in the problematic.

It is true that the realm of the theoretical dialogue has altered its character significantly during the course of my writings, and of course my own language and my framing of problems have continually altered to meet (or perhaps even to help create) the changing dialectic over the years. Yet Lentricchia does at times juxtapose quotations widely separated in time and intellectual content without always taking account of differing circumstances to which they are addressed—a lapse not to be expected from a theorist as careful as he is and as devoted as he is to historicity.

The major development, as I have said earlier, is a gradual change in my emphasis, moving from an existential-ist interest that acknowledges the realm of deadly fact—of facticity—beyond our words and their creations, to a neo-Kantian interest that allows nothing that is not constituted by language. I must confess that, even as late in my work as *Theory of Criticism*, I am at moments divided between being responsive to the sovereignty of death, the one deadly fact that licenses all others and undoes the pretensions of our words, and being responsive to a universal domain of linguis-tic fictions that even subjugate our notion of death to a verbal invention. Death, as the ultimate problematic, from time to time unsettles from the outside my confidence in the creative world of language, though the latter invariably returns to have the final word by reminding me that I have not experi-enced death except as a verbal entity. Assigning dominance to one or another of these has great consequences for any decision to be made about the independent availability of a reality that precedes the shapings of human symbolic sys-tems. And the development of my own career, in being re-sponsive to the changing emphases in this historical dialectic has, I admit, revealed a certain unsteadiness as I succumbed to one or the other emphasis. But I like to think that, beneath the ontology of a temporality created by an awareness of the fact of death, I meant—even in my earlier writings—to sug-gest the projection of the human construct, so that the domi-nating element is, after all, an *awareness* of death rather than the (as yet) unreachable fact itself.

This admission about your present relation to your existen-tialist roots forces me to ask not only about your present relationship to your earlier texts, but also about your relation to such notions as "contextualism." Where do you stand to-day vis-à-vis earlier work and this early concept? For some believe, I imagine, that "contextualism" remains in your the-ory unchanged by the ravages of the theoretical debate.

*Would you still wish to associate yourself with it or other
notions like "the poetic object," "the unique and particular,"
or even an unqualified "organicism"? As I read your work
none of these notions are ahistorical, despite charges that
they are.*

All these notions achieve another sort of formulation since,
say, *Theory of Criticism* in 1976. Instead of what seemed to be
the unqualified closure and totalization of what I originally
termed "contextualism," I have come to emphasize the poem's
capacity—through the duplicity I described to you earlier—to
suggest the self-conscious fictionality of that closure and thus,
by negative implication, the still beckoning world to which it
secretly opens. (What I am saying, by the way, can be applied
as a corrective to the notion of "organicism" as well.) Further,
the apparent claim of an ontologically secure "poetic object"
has given way to the acknowledgement that we can speak only
of an intentional object, phenomenologically dependent on
the perceptual and aesthetic habits and codes of poet and audience. We are, I have come to stress, dependent on the functions and expectations which our culture imposes upon our
perceptual intentionalities, so that such phrases as "poetic
object" must be taken within the phenomenological qualifications that allow a culture to project what it then sees as its
"objects."

From the way I have described these correctives
through an enlargement of theoretical perspective, it is evident that I believe, not that my earlier claims—next to my
more recent ones—were ontologically naive, so much as that
they knew better than they seemed to say, but fell into the
language of an earlier idiom without being sufficiently sensitive to it or critical of it. After all, it was as far back as my
study of Shakespeare's *Sonnets* in the mid-sixties that I de-
fended the metaphor as miracle, but only by insisting that
our sense of it as miracle rests on our knowing that it is
impossible for it to occur. Thus I saw the metaphor affirming

its power of figurational closure only while denying that it is
more than a verbal illusion, subject to being undone by the
linguistic realm beyond its circular grasp. So historical
change certainly is telling in my use of these terms, and they
function now with a differing force of qualification as the
problematic urgency shifts; but I think—if one reads the work
generously and with care—there may be more of a change in
the delicacy and self-consciousness of my language than a
substantive change in my claims. Which suggests that perhaps there is something transhistorical in them as well. But I
don't believe they are—or even were—ahistorical, for the anthropological interest I've mentioned has always been central
to my work.

*But isn't "contextualism" still open and vulnerable to char-
ges of aesthetic isolationism and elitism?*

I do not believe that, as contextualism now functions in my
work, it is any longer (if it ever was) open to these antagonistic charges. Lentricchia seems, in these charges, to be giving
us his version of the common charge, made by radical critics
against formalist criticism (even in its most socially conscious varieties), that it is arrogantly elitist. The suggestion is
that there is something anti-democratic in the notion that the
best of our poems should be accorded a "privileged" status in
comparison to less specialized uses of language. But how can
we not so privilege them when we see them making their
case for privilege with their every word? It strikes me as a
strange, and unfortunate, political analogy (attested to by the
use of terms like "privilege" or "elite") for critics to treat
relationships among texts—or among artifacts in general—as
if they were comparable to relationships among citizens
within a political-economic order. The ground for privilege
in one is hardly like the ground for privilege in the other, and

surely the acknowledgement of the better made or more significantly made artifact hardly has anti-democratic, or for
that matter mandarin, implications.

*Would you accept the critique of your work that argues that
you are wrestling not with an inherited problematic but with
an inherited language of neo-Kantian aesthetics, a language
that is invested with a spatial terminology?*

I would think that all issues that are central to a particular
theory, present or past, turn out—upon analysis—to be, not
problems of substance, but problems created by the inherited
language of the theoretical tradition in which they function.
Still, no matter how linguistically trapped we end up being,
this is not to deny that our theoretical drive is set in motion
by a desire to solve what seems like a real problem, one that
we resent having reduced to a verbal one. So we wrestle
stubbornly, somehow affecting our experience in a world beyond our language even as we recognize the prison-house.
     This paradox hasn't really changed much since critical
philosophy first began its struggles with the egocentric predicament in the eighteenth century—though of course it must
be recognized that this way of putting the predicament is also
the necessary projection of *its* inherited language. Still, my
work is no more exempt from these circular frustrations than
any others, so that it need not shrink from the force of your
question. There is a choice to be made, certainly, from among
the inherited languages, and mine may well be neo-Kantian
in some respects; but I'm not sure that another theoretical
context escapes its language to come any closer to solving the
problem. I find the neo-Kantian terms more useful than
others because they permit a theory that is well suited to the
kinds of literary art (or, for that matter, the kinds of the arts
in general) which I am most concerned with accounting for.
For the major Western canon through the mid-twentieth cen-

tury seems responsive to that inherited verbal network of assumptions.

If I am trapped by a spatial terminology, which presumably creates a mystification about my subject, then there is the suggestion that a de-spatialized terminology (temporal?) would disabuse us. But terminology is inevitably spatial—even that which struggles to free itself for "pure" temporality. Time is no less a human category than space, as Kant reminds us. Perhaps the only freedom for a theorist comes from the desperate attempt to escape from language and its fixity by writing a word and then drawing a line through it to cancel it, in the manner of Heideggerian Post-Structuralists; it's their equivalent, I suppose, to my own annoying habit of the "even-as." In effect, then, I am imprisoned by the spatial and am matched by a twin theorist (shall I call him Paul de Man?) whose devotion to the temporal is not liberating but only fashions a companion cell to mine. Yet I must try to think through him as he must try to through me: so we both have to indulge the even-as, to self-deconstruct or, perhaps, self-destruct. But in so doing each anticipates—imaginatively becomes—the other.

Yet, as a final word, let me remind you that I see one way for us to press language to overcome its fixity, to flow around the contradictions of the spatial and the temporal: since my essay in 1967, I have seen it in the poetic manipulation of the "ekphrastic principle." And I feel confident that my attempt to trace the operation of this principle—which is growing into my next book—moves me beyond the spatial confines that concern you.

Throughout your career, one problematic remains constant, the distinction between poetry and other forms of language. Do you still understand this difference in language to be one of kind and not degree? Would you still argue for an essential difference as opposed to one, say, established by history, as a cultural classification or category?

In recent years I have tried in a number of places to clarify
the specially qualified sense in which I have intended a distinction between poems and other discourse. What is at stake
is the old Russian Formalist doctrine of poems as systems of
deviations from discursive norms. Now deviationist theory
seems to require the assumption that there *is* a normal discourse. But Post-Structuralist concern with the narratological
and figurational character of all writings has reminded us
that no discourse is normal or neutral but is already troped as
it is written. From this perspective any distinction between
poetry and nonpoetry would appear specious. Yet, given my
anthropological perspective, I retain an interest in the distinctions that our culture has made among its discursive
modes, even the apparently common sense distinction (based
largely on intention) between fiction and reference, even
though the Post-Structuralist critique would seem to preclude it. So I see the concept of a poetic mode of discourse as
one that is attendant on our learned response to—and our
resulting projection upon—a culturally imposed aesthetic occasion. Of course, the poet, similarly enculturated, supplies
the coded stimulus which arouses and cooperates with that
response. Some of these stimuli work far more effectively
than others, and critics try to tell us which they are, turning
them into exemplary poems.

So I am hardly claiming "an essential difference" (to
use your phrase) but see that difference as culture-bound—
though that's enough, I should think, since the books we read
are themselves totally culture-bound. This qualification
means that we are dealing only with differences in degree
rather than in kind in the uses of language. Nevertheless,
under the aegis of the aesthetic occasion, partly self-induced
(though with the help of the object), we treat the poem as if, as
a unique discourse, it represented a difference in kind. And as
for "normal discourse," it is a fiction invented by us in binary
opposition to our self-consciously developed illusion of a discourse to which we respond as aesthetic; for what we are
persuaded is poetic depends on the fiction that there is a nor-

mal discourse from which it deviates. In fact, we create the norms by inferring them out of the supposed deviations *from them*, reading backwards from the existing poem to what must have been the pre-poetic, neutral elements from which it arose. But these latter fictions, the norms of discourse, are only our postulates required by our respect for what seems so extraordinary in the poem we have helped to constitute. It is, then, only in this highly skeptical and hence qualified sense that I argue for the differentness of poems—and for that from which they differ.

Earlier you accounted for changes in theoretical tastes, but how would you account for the change in the taste for critical theory? How do you explain the boom in the theory market, if there is one?

I suppose there is a boom in theory, if I can judge from the popularity of the School of Criticism and Theory among young scholars who feel they'd *better* worry about theory as well as those who really do worry about it. And there is evidence too in the increasing number of literature departments offering theory and seeking to have some of its members engage in the theoretical debates. We have moved in the years since the School of Criticism and Theory had its first session (in 1976) from having only a small minority who were initiated into the mysteries of recent theory to having so many initiates, and so widely spread, that we are in danger of having the mystery dissolved. That's a boom with an enlarging supply of younger people and an increased retooling of older ones.

To account for this boom in theory I think I'd have to return to my answer to your first question and speak about the sense of excess left us by the New Critics. For years there was an endless number of increasingly refined explications of every member of the poetic canon: readings and reconsiderations and re-reconsiderations, often dwelling on smaller and smaller points of disagreement. Critics were just working too close to their objects (treating them "as objects" and hence as "essentially fixed and dead," in the words of Coleridge). So by reaction there was an inclination to back off and talk in larger, more abstract terms. That's probably one cause, and a major one. A second might be the growing imperialism of the recent science of linguistics. Yet a third might be the failure of the newer versions of the social sciences and of philosophy to engage many of those who would have been the constituency of an older social science or an older philosophy, so that many of these drifted into literary study without the intense literary sensibility and calling of the older literary scholar. And these would very likely be attracted by theory more than they would by the analysis of texts, before which they might well feel impatient. A fourth likely cause can be traced to the intellectual spirit of the times and the growing interest in theory across the academic board, with literature belatedly seeking a methodological self-respect parallel to what has swept from the sciences to the social sciences and has now caught up with history as well. The newly acquired theoretical habit, in its exaggerated form, may, perhaps, reflect a somewhat anti-humanistic impetus; but in the criticism of some theorists we still find soundly humanistic motives for the recent obsession with theorizing. (Guess whose work I would cite as an example.)

Regardless of the motive, this *is* a time for self-consciousness, for a critical review of our methods, in all the sciences and the arts; and the development of critical theory is our contribution to this tendency.

Is this move to embrace theory a healthy one for departments of literature? I mean, while various theories may not be healthy for certain notions of literature, is the trend toward theory a hope for a profession which is liable to be reduced, as some suggest, to either service departments or departments of classics?

Certainly I feel that the growth of theory in departments of literature was, some time back, a healthy development for a discipline that did not examine its varied enterprise with a sufficiently critical, self-conscious eye. The study of literature for generations had rested on assumptions and on the development and treatment of a canon based on those assumptions, none of which had ever been put in question. So insofar as it is good for the seeker of wisdom to question his manner of seeking, the awakening of theoretical awareness is of course healthy.

Now we must ask about the complaints we often hear around us about the excesses of this concern for theory and the harm it has done to the study of literature, at best by neglecting it and at worst by precluding it. But we must understand that the kind of theory in the ascendancy in recent years does not merely take a new position on the old canon but must undermine the canon since it radically reconceives the total operation of language in a way that must de-privilege literature. Therefore, it is no innocent theoretical claim like others before it, since it demands, if we take it seriously, nothing less than the disestablishment of our disciplinary institutions as we have known them. Not a course syllabus, not a program curriculum, and not a department limited by a sense of its discipline would be left standing. So your suggestion that the move to theory "may not be healthy for certain notions of literature" is an understatement, so long as by theory we mean recent theory of the sort we have been discussing. Consequently, to the extent that the departments of literature are going to have any devotion to and responsibility for transmitting our literary heritage—that is, to the extent that they are to remain departments of literature—it cannot be altogether healthy for them to nurture just the sort of theoretical interest that would undo them.

I must admit thinking back, not altogether with disapproval (though marveling at the naiveté), to the days when criticism assumed for itself the crucial role of mediating between literary works and the culture, and of ruling as the arbiter of taste. Unless one is ready to welcome a revolution in academic organizations that would remove the critical-scholarly mission from them (as I am not), we may still have to urge some such role, even if we are no longer so confident we can justify it in theory. My simple affection for our culture's most remarkable verbal accomplishments, and my need to attend to their mysteries, call forth from me a fealty which I cannot altogether yield up. Either we accept the logical consequences which some theories would urge upon us and remake our institutional structures and their objectives, or, perhaps not always consistently, we must at once allow theory to flourish in order to keep literary study honest *and* subject theory to the very academic structure (the department devoted to literary study) which it would subvert.

It may well be that we *will* have to take the more radical alternative and reconstruct (after having deconstructed) our institutional organizations if, as you see others suggesting, we are not to be transformed into service departments or classics departments. But, since I am addressing here questions of what practices I find preferable and not questions of practical academic salesmanship, I suggest we resist.

I understand the new rage for critical theory as a response to, as well as a symptom of, the crises in the profession, but does it go deeper than that?

In pre-theoretical days, the conventional scholarly procedures which were applied to literary study all assumed a theory of language as a direct and uncomplicated representational process. Today we have become accustomed to worrying about "the problematic of representation" in the study of language itself, and since the introduction of that awareness, we have had to concern ourselves with theoretical issues before we could begin to think about what—on these new semiotic grounds—it was now possible to say about the verbal arts. Our conception of the history of poetry and of criticism has, from this time, to be reformulated by what theory will permit.

But of course the questioning of the representational dimension of language—more precisely, of language as it functions within the poetic occasion—began well before the current mass break-out of such questions. Its revolutionary phase has been with us at least since Nietzsche and Bergson, and—thanks in part to the mediation of T. E. Hulme—it stimulated the early, theoretical efforts of the New Critics, for whom (as followers of I. A. Richards), poetic discourse begins with the intramural play of words that blocks normal reference.

Later, however, more general semiotic claims, deriving from a more self-conscious concern with verbal representation, have moved these questions well beyond the limited practical objective of the analysis of poems, such as we had in the New Criticism. Consequently, much of our theory that has recently been calling most attention to itself has ranged widely—beyond literature, narrowly conceived—throughout the realm of writing, pressing its doubts about the representational mission which we used to take for granted. It can now trace its case back through Descartes to Plato, and it boasts many modern heroes. So perhaps, in the spirit of someone like Richard Rorty (*Philosophy and the Mirror of Nature,* 1979), we can claim a prior need for theory simply to define what our subject is, or whether we have a subject. Such thinking, of course, would establish an absolute priority for theory before any criticism or interpretation could begin, hence calling for and justifying what you have referred to as "the new rage for critical theory."

But isn't this upheaval in theory affecting pedagogy? And couldn't the opposition to many of the new theories be seen as one rooted in the practice of the classroom? After all, New Criticism was always more a pedagogy than a theory.

Your claim about the New Criticism is correct. It may have disrupted the peace within departments of literature almost four decades ago but, whatever its unwelcome theoretical intrusions and the unease produced by them, it did produce healthy and unprecedented innovations in the teaching of literature. And that did turn out to be its value for those who finally welcomed it, whether expectantly or grudgingly. In the end it conquered departments because it conquered the classroom, from the freshman introduction to literature to the graduate seminar. Thus the contribution of the New Criticism is often viewed more in the realm of theory.

Perhaps it is this fact that has led literary scholars to expect from newer theories a similar immediacy of classroom application. To the extent that they do, they have been largely disappointed—mainly because these theories, for the most part, spring from assumptions that would preclude an older pedagogy characterized by the analysis of canonical literary texts. These theories and their new permissibilities come first, as already written, and as reconditioning readers about all that is already written in whatever they read, in whatever—that is—they have already interpreted. And the concept of literary texts, as out there waiting to be interpreted, is, as a result, dissolved in advance. Simultaneously dissolved with it is the conventional pedagogical situation, together with the mission that created it. This is why I suggested, in my previous answer, that the programmatic and institutional consequences of taking most recent theories seriously are profoundly destructive of most of what we have taken for granted.

As if to turn aside from these more apocalyptic projections of tendencies in recent theory, a number of American deconstructionists (one thinks especially of the Yale School) seeks to allow their theory to accommodate the classroom situation. In the hands of some of them, even the most extreme notions are applied to the analysis of literary texts, part of the same secure canon known in prestructuralist days. It may be that the American pedagogical tradition, brought to so intense a level by the New Criticism, has imposed itself upon such radical theorizing and has in these cases domesticated it. In them we can look at the newer theory as really not so subversive continuations of the New Criticism, even if under strenuously anti-New Critical theoretical guises. The one continuing difference would be the indulgence of wayward responses to "undecidables" and hence the greater laxity in prescribing interpretive rigor for the students. For, obviously, if the representational operation of language is seen as a myth fostered by logocentric assumptions, then the critic's language cannot be subjected to the transcendental authority of the poem as a privileged text. Thus liberated for its own free play, the work of interpretation becomes its own primary text, involved through intertextuality with others but free of the obligation of secondary reference to them. And this is hardly the critic-to-poem relationship that we, as proper pedagogues, used to urge upon student readers—which may be why many continental-style deconstructors are impatient, if not altogether unhappy, with what they feel to be infidelity on the part of some American theorists.

So, in what is radical and original about recent theory, the conventional pedagogical task would be violently transformed and, if we restrict that task to the exploration and glorification of the canon, subverted. On the other side, in what turns out, in recent theory, to be not so different after all in its application, we may wonder whether new theory is being faithfully served or is itself being subverted, thanks to unsubdued conservative instincts.

How about the teaching of the history of critical theory? How important do you think the history of theory is and what is its role in refining for us both the theoretical problematic and our capacity to delineate it?

I think it is unfortunate that, despite the greatly increased interest in critical theory these days, there may well be, on the part of many of our recent theorists, less interest than there used to be in the history of theory. This lack of interest leads, in younger theorists, to a lack of knowledge; and with some of them, alas, the ignorance is all too evident and has seriously unfortunate effects on their theorizing. So I would strongly urge the study of historical documents and perspectives, and the development of a historical consciousness, upon those who would theorize on their own and who would comment on the theories of their contemporaries. Yet I am aware of the pressure on young theorists these days by doctrines that, by their very nature, militate against any respectful study of the history of theory.

There are a couple of obvious advantages to the study of the history of theory, and a couple that are less obvious. It is hardly novel, or—I hope—debatable, to maintain that a knowledge of the efforts of our forebears may teach us how to avoid repeating some of their errors, and it should prevent us from presenting as our own new answers to problems those which have been tried previously—and perhaps refuted previously. There are standard positions and refutations which one is well off knowing, if only to avoid embarrassment, but also—if enough of one's fellows are ignorant—to avoid the waste of time and energies in seeking to advance a discipline that has already struggled through a number of noble and truly original attempts to solve its problems. It is surprising these days to see some theoretical proposals being set forth as if for the first time, when history is littered by the debates set off by these proposals long ago.

But there are more subtle advantages to be conferred by the knowledge of the history of criticism. Primarily I see us learning from it a capacity for self-criticism, for distancing ourselves from our own positions, as we witness the sequence of hard-won and hard-held positions, each finally collapsing as history's anti-provincialism went to work on them. But perhaps the most instructive lesson provided by our studying older texts comes from their introducing us to the self-contradictory character of their best examples. I have more than once commented on what I have called the "consistent inconsistency" of our most effective literary theory: the extent to which the critic-theorist allows his theoretical commitments to be undercut by the experience of the poem by the reading self. The conflict between developing theoretical construct and the ongoing literary experience, each of which seems to permit the other or to deny the other, creates a dialectic which the undogmatic and sensitive theorist encourages, even though it may lead him to those soft spots into which his structure seems to be slipping away. So perhaps the most instructive lesson taught us by the history of theory concerns the fragility of the very possibility of theory, so long as we limit theory to that which displays systematic consistency.

Is this notion similar to de Man's suggestion of "blindness and insight" as guides for our reading of key theoretical texts?

I see why you make the connection you do. We both deal with the self-undercutting tendency in the theoretical text, and we both seem to expend our analytical energies upon— and most appreciate—those moments in the text where such self-undercutting occurs. Both of us see what might otherwise pass for systematic weakness emerge as that which, while breaking open the system, brings to its text a far greater interest than a mere adherence to system might have earned.

But beneath these apparent similarities are differences which are highly significant and which, for me, point again to the special value of the study of historical texts. For the coincidence of blindness and insight which de Man probes for so perceptively is for him an inevitable accompaniment to writing as written. It is what happens to texts as they take on the consequences of textuality, the would-be construct unmaking itself in its very verbal formulation.

Unlike his, my own concern arises out of a systematic

interest, an interest in the possible coherence among terms and propositions, even though this coherence is overcome by the desire of the verbal system to find outside itself an object to which it can correspond with adequacy. The nature of the text may belie its ambition to find an outside object to which it can be true, an object over which it stumbles because it will not evade it. So while de Man's theorist struggles as he does as a consequence of the internal verbal maneuvers of his text, just by virtue of its being a text, mine has his difficulties as a consequence of his sporadic but recurrent referential obligation—his sense that the ongoing facts of literary creation and literary experiencing must somehow be accounted for in his own theorizing. It is the difference, in textual self-undoing, between an inescapable problem inherent in textuality itself, and a problem that arises in a text that tries, even if at times half-heartedly, to make itself a subservient accounting for another—an outside—text, perhaps another sort of text.

System is unsystematized for me, then, not through the unavoidable workings of the systematic language alone but through the challenge to that language by the individual historical acts for which theory is called into account. This difference in attitude, between de Man and me, toward the possibility of systematic constructs and the relation of these constructs to particular human experiences reveals profound differences in attitudes toward the theorist's obligations, and the critic's, as well as to the role of history in the thinking of both of them, whether they exist in two persons or in one.

Finally, what does the critic want?

I can try to tell you what *this* critic wants. This critic, as a dedicated, self-conscious reader, is obliged to want to be left alone by the theorist—and by the theorist in himself; but he can't be. He wants *not* to resist his own interiority; and he doesn't. Rather he wants to yield to it; and he must. So he wants theory to relax its hold and allow him to function as critic; yet he wants to comprehend its pressures so that, under its tutelage, he is made to question himself and his subject. For in recent years it is that questioning which has enlarged his subject and expanded it beyond literature, so that, as critic, he can treat a broader array of writings which share characteristics he used to think of as exclusively literary. This is one way the critic seeks to free himself from theory in order to confront his verbal object with an unimpeded directness and honesty, and yet subjects himself, if barely half-consciously, to its constraints.

But, really, shouldn't your question ask, what ought the critic to want? Or would not that way of putting it invite theory seriously to impinge upon his freedom, a freedom to pursue what he feels to be *his* primary discourse. Yet I want the critic to want to produce commentary on another, prior, and—yes—more significant text than his own, a text next to which his appears to be secondary, after all. Even so, the critic is aware, through epistemological skepticism, of the extent to which he is projecting—in response to his needs— the object he treats as primary. Thus I want the critic to be free to function within an ambiguous secondariness. Without at least this, I fear he forgoes his role as critic.

Finally, as critic I want—and I think I ought to want— my studies, no matter how close to their object I am working, to move from the metaphorical habit of words to the metaphorical habit of the culture that produced them. In speaking of metaphor before, I discussed—at its center—the illusion of inclusive totalization which it sponsored and we cherish; but the underside, turned away from us but implicitly there by negation, hides all that is excluded, though often pressing for admittance. And the critic should not resist looking for the meanings and the causes of these repressions as the inverse side of these cherishings—hidden causes lurking in the desires of private will or of social force. I suppose this is to confess that there is a life beyond language, full of dreams and drives that manipulate language *even as* (there it is again!) they are manipulated by language—indeed often seem to be created *by* the manipulations of language. And the critic, greedy as he is, wants it all, the world in language and the world beyond, finding them both finally there in what is written or hidden, repressed, though intruding a forbidden presence in the spaces of the written page.

All of which says little more than that the critic wants, and ought to want, to be trapped in language and to wallow in its play while responding with play of his own—so much so that he is not too keenly aware which language is which, the language within blurring into the language without. If this sounds too much like love play, we should remember that it's all still only words, after all. But the critic, aware of his weakness before words, should also remember this, should seek restlessly to break through to the world beyond *even as* (one last time) he wants to assure himself that really (!) the words are enough.

Speaking of enough, so is this.

12.

MURRAY KRIEGER
AT KONSTANZ

A Colloquy
Chaired by Wolfgang Iser

WOLFGANG ISER: On the occasion of his visiting appointment
at the University of Konstanz in summer 1982, Murray
Krieger was invited to the Fachbereichskolloquium, which is
an institutionalized forum in the Department of Literature
both for presenting work in progress from its members and
for discussing the work of prominent scholars in the field
coming from outside. The scholar invited is usually asked to
submit a paper which reflects the basic tenets of his or her
thinking so that the discussion can be entirely devoted to
further explorations of his or her ideas.

In Murray Krieger's case, his essay "An Apology for
Poetics," published in *American Criticism in the Poststruc-
turalist Age*, Ira Konigsberg, ed. (Ann Arbor: University of
Michigan Press, 1981), pp. 87–101, served as a point of departure, and all the arguments advanced in the discussion
started out from concepts put forward in this essay. This
holds equally true for the following introductory remarks
outlining Murray Krieger's position.

If literary theory is to be identified as a distinguishable

type of discourse within the realm of discourse, it is bound to have an object to which reference is made. Even if we were to collapse literary theory into a featureless continuum of ultra-textuality, we still would run into differences which mark off distinctive strands of discourse within the continuum, and thus involuntarily spotlight traces of distinctions. As literary theory has been a genre for more than three thousand years, history at least testifies to the existence of that special something which is conceptualized by that very discourse. Yet in these latter days of literary criticism, Murray Krieger maintains that a plea for literary theory can be made only in terms of an apology for poetics, reflecting the situation in which the state of the arts finds itself.

In order to substantiate this claim, past orientations for assessing the literary object have to be exceeded and current ones have to be brought under scrutiny. Hence Murray Krieger proposes a stance which is equidistant from both New Criticism and Post-Structuralism. New Criticism privileged the literary text and Post-Structuralism made it evaporate into textuality. In criticizing these two alternatives, Murray Krieger maps out his own position, which cuts across both of them.

New Criticism favored the idea of closure because the text most valorized reconciled all its apparent ambiguities and dichotomies, thus figuring perfection which, in turn, made the literary work congeal into an object. Instead, Murray Krieger argues, closure and openness pertain equally to the literary text, constituting its basic duplicity. Closure implies a retreat from the world, a status implicitly accorded to the art work by the New Critics. Yet closure results not so much in harmony, as the New Critics wanted to have it, but in exclusions which rebound on the art work, turning it into pure metaphor. This reconceptualization of closure signalizes that each presence represented by the work functions simultaneously as an indication of what it has displaced, the absence of which reinscribes itself into the represented presence. Consequently, the work is neither an object nor pure depiction of a given, but basically a metaphor meant to bridge an unbridgeable gap. Closure, then, ceases to be the ineluctable feature of harmony which the New Critics considered the be-all and end-all of the work, thereby revealing their unquestioned commitment to classical aesthetics. Instead, closure turns into a sign, highlighting a deep-rooted desire in the human make-up for the sense of an ending both in terms of space and time.

In this respect, Murray Krieger conceives of the text's duplicity as a means of charting anthropological dispositions of man, whose cultural activities arise out of a basic duality between closure and open-endedness. In so deviating from a New Critical position, Murray Krieger appears to swerve toward a Post-Structuralist one. Yet he intends to be equally discriminating regarding his own position by setting it off from what the Post-Structuralists had proposed.

First and foremost, he objects to having metaphor replaced by metonymy as the favored trope of those who advocate ultratextuality. Metaphor, he maintains, outstrips metonymy insofar as it is a form of "secular transubstantiation," implying, of course, that whatever representation displaces inevitably bounces back on it, showing it up for what it is: the illusion of presence. In contradistinction to this revelatory capacity of metaphor, metonymy is nothing but arbitrary sign-relationship. If, however, the difference between absence and presence is inscribed into metaphor itself, and metaphor is not only the constitutive feature of the text but also identical with. it, then this type of text can clearly be marked off from the continuum and be identified as literature.

In this respect, Murray Krieger applies the concept of deviation to textuality itself. This attempt carries an implicit irony, as deviation originally had to postulate a norm from which the literary text was meant to break away, whereas here, a concept which eliminated distinctions and made them shade into textuality has involuntarily provided a norm from which deviations can again be traced. This is the grandstand view adopted by Murray Krieger for his defense of the

specificity of the literary text and of poetics as a means of
theorizing both its structure and its function.

The endeavor to establish discontinuities in the continuum is bound to be critical to a great many conceptualiza-
tions of textuality which have emerged in the wake of Post-
Structuralism. If the literary text were conceived as a model
of communication, its basic duplicity would be resolved in
the code-governed transfer of its message. If it were considered as semiosis, a reduction of the technical operations of
its sign-relationships would occur. If it served as an index of
the *episteme*, it would be downgraded to an illustration of it.
As a structure of power or as an assembly of tropes, it would
be confined either to an indication of authorial intention or
to the pattern of rhetorical strategies. Whatever the frame of
reference in the approaches concerned, the literary text is
made to dissolve into something other than itself, and should
this be the truth of the matter, then, according to Murray
Krieger, poetics itself is destined to vanish as it no longer has
an object.

However, Murray Krieger sounds a note of hope, especially in view of the now rampant deconstructivist criticism.
What deconstruction promulgates has long since been a con-
spicuous feature of the literary text, Murray Krieger maintains, and he seems to be borne out by the constant return of
deconstructivist critics to the great works of literature for
tracing the "presence" of those principles in the text which
they advocate. Literature always discloses its fictionality and
thus brackets both the assertive and the predicative nature of
the sentence sequence out of which it arises. Furthermore,
literature as metaphor keeps acting out the game of presence
and absence since its inception, a procedure which almost
turns it into a paradigm for what deconstruction intends to
bring to a greater awareness. And finally, whenever deconstruction is brought to bear on other types of discourse, such
as philosophy and history, the exposure of the underlying
reifications does not result in total obliteration of their distinctive markers; one still can tell the one from the other. If

these distinctions were not to persist, how would it be possible to deconstruct historic discourse by means of resorting to literary categories, as Hayden White has attempted to do?

Yet, irrespective of Murray Krieger's own subversion of the deconstructivist argument regarding the uniqueness of the literary text, the basic reservation of the argument still stands: the literary text either symbolizes or represents a presence which appears to be self-referential, whereas each presence cannot help being a sign of an absence.

This fundamental charge against privileging the literary text is countered by Murray Krieger's having recourse to anthropological needs to which the text is supposed to respond. We seem to have a basic desire for closure, the frustration of which in our workaday reality spurs the imagination into action in order to provide what otherwise is denied us. Hence our preoccupation with endings and our constant fabrications of myths result from this ineradicable necessity. The literary text, Murray Krieger argues, relates to these cultural activities which are meant to compensate for our frustrations and deficiencies. He intends, however, to give it a different turn. The poetic medium signifies a presence which is self-referential though it allows the signifier to figure something else in addition. This very duality reflects the nature of language itself, which is both designation and figuration. The poetic discourse brings these two functions into co-existence, thus inscribing absence into presence and thereby making closure illusory.

Yet this illusion fulfills the nostalgic hankering after unity; it resuscitates the dream of an all-encompassing wholeness which was lost by entering the symbolic order, and which can only be recuperated within the symbolic order by poetry. This is the reason, for Murray Krieger, why poets manipulate the metonymic character of the signifier in order to turn it into a metaphoric entity. Consequently, each poem is part of textuality and a unique text at one and the same time. The metonymy of its signifiers makes it part of the continuum of textuality; the bridging of differences, however,

creates a metaphoric unity, the nature of which is the duplicity of closure and open-endedness.

MURRAY KRIEGER: In order to get things going let me expand
on what I say in my paper, "An Apology for Poetics," by
making three points. First, whatever I claim for the poem and
its privilege I do not claim objectively: I think everything
Professor Iser has said in his introductory statement acknowledges this qualification. I make these claims within the
provisional notion of the poem as an illusionary stimulus
constructed into an object only by a reader who, believing
himself to be following cues provided by the poem, seeks to
make that poem one by filling in the gaps and apprehending,
he thinks, patterns provided by the poem. The poem becomes
poem for us, then, only through an act of complicity made in
accordance with the aesthetic habit in our culture, after many
centuries that have fed that habit of turning sequence into
teleological structure.

The term *aesthetic* itself is literally derived from "aesthesis," whose meaning relates to how we perceive, and the
notion of illusion is, of course, embedded in the notion of
aesthesis, and of its German equivalent, *Schein*. In our tradition the author often creates in order to provide the reader
with what he is looking for, and will find if he tries hard
enough, whatever our skepticism leads us to deny about its
ontological status. And questions about its ontological status
I do not find interesting. In this, then, I mean to make common cause with Professor Iser as I read him. Like him and
like Ernst Gombrich, whose work has had an influence on
both of us, I am more interested in how we come to see and
project poems, and subsequently interpret the illusionary realities that come out of our seeing and our projecting, more
interested in those operations than I am in deconstructing
that projection in an attempt to discover what it is we really
have done to ourselves through this projection, and how de-
lusionary it may be. I want to account, that is, for the aesthetic from the inside, from inside a culture's perceptions
and activities. My interest, as phenomenological rather than

ontological, means to be in accord with Professor Iser's. I acknowledge a significant similarity in what the two of us are doing as we both attempt to demonstrate the difference between the functioning of "literature" and of non-literature, seeking out the apparently self-conscious fictionality of the literary in contrast to other discourse, however fictional that other discourse may often prove to be. I feel especially close to the work that Professor Iser is doing right now, and I very anxiously await the projection of some of these notions in the volume on fiction and the "imaginary" which he is working on now.

That is the first point. The second: despite what others claim about my work, I am anxious to find ways to get from the poem into history, whether it is private psychological history or public—social and political—history. My central concern with metaphor means to extend itself, means to focus, not merely upon metaphor as an all-enclosing and all-inclusive element, but also upon what the metaphor represses and excludes, what the poem seems to know is outside itself and in need of being repressed and excluded to preserve it as poem. I find that the enclosing, totalizing pretension of the poem as metaphor—or rather of our reading of the poem as metaphor—seeks to subject itself to the power of its own illusion, that which would repress whatever threatens to explode the metaphor and undo the poem—which is just about everything outside itself and its all-enclosing elements.

The shrewd, self-deconstructing poem reminds us of this repression by its subtle, barely sensed though self-conscious, smuggling in of the repressed. Now all this is enormously telling, it seems to me, about the private drives of the poet, but—even more—about the cultural moment: what its vision, its politics, admits or represses, what its words permit, what they see or are blind to, what their hearers are to hear or allow to be wasted on the air.

Such intimations are of great historical importance, allowing us to see what the poet's language hides as well as what it reveals, what role is played by the social as well as the psychological drive for power, a role revealed by the hiding as well as by the saying. They also tell us about the several successive societies of readers, each of which finds both its enclosing metaphors and what by implication it senses as the repressed. Each historical set of readers in its own way responds to the need to fill in the gaps, by means of which each constructs metaphorical wholes for its literary works. Our uncovering of such different totalizations is crucial in unlocking the critical procedure my sort of theory proposes, so that it may open outward into social history from what is too often thought of as a self-enclosed formalism.

One final point. I want to be candid about the overall objective which grounds and limits all my claims: they are, I remind you, based on the appeal to the anthropological, to the inside of culture. To put it another way, whatever system I have rests upon an agreed-upon indulgence of an aesthetic experience and our complicitous role in creating it. This objective, then, accepts the traditional canon as a given, a canon of works singled out as privileged (as "literary") because they seem to require our interpretation, as much interpretation as we can find for them and claim they deserve.

Now the members of the canon, of course, should shift about continually, for I hope we are not so locked into a particular group, so committed to any works, that we cannot permit some to be elevated into the canon and some to be dropped. But the requirements for membership reflect the claims of the theory, since these seek to justify such works. The claims allow the interpretations that seem adequate to the works in the canon, the very works that they seem to call for; and, in calling for each work, they remind us what to look for in it and, by the same act, have the work justify itself. Such is the curse of the inevitable circularity of theory.

Still, clearly such a theoretical structure does not preclude other kinds of theories which seek to satisfy other objectives outside this limited one created under the agreed-upon constraints of the aesthetic tradition of the West and the works that are there as we have made them there, that seem to have been composed in accordance with it. Perhaps, with too much candor, I should confess that the ultimate value of the theory is that it allows me to keep reading the things I want to read and enjoy, and to have good reasons for enjoying them.

So I return to my acceptance of the idea of a canon, with all that this idea implies about the historical assumptions of cultural acceptance under conditions imposed by patterns of power. Within our Western canon I find works that we see as self-privileging. That is, they internally seem to earn the privilege we bestow upon them. I say "seem to earn the privilege," because I must always remind myself that they earn it within their and our mutual complicity. It is, I say again, the complicity which I find the language of Professor Iser's *The Act of Reading* so useful to justify, as we find the clues we are looking for to satisfy the phenomenological search for pattern. For me this is the anthropological given, and I'd rather accept than deconstruct it. It is for me the enabling assumption for an aesthetic that our best poetic creations persuade us to invent. And they deserve nothing less than such an invention.

HANS ROBERT JAUSS: As central to the argument of your essay, "An Apology for Poetics," your critique of the false claims of Structuralist theory (esp. pp. 93–94) impressed me a great deal. Could one not intensify this critique with the following: 1) The premise of classic Structuralism is *de singularibus non est scientia*. Does it not follow from this at the very outset, that Structuralist theory is incapable of dealing with literary works in their singularity, or put another way, in their historical-aesthetic difference (*Alterität*)? 2) If Structuralist theory seeks to deconstruct the literary work as an "elite object," has it not also fallen victim to the fiction of a closed (and unrelated to the world) universe of signs, which it paradoxically denies poetry? 3) If Structuralist theory seeks to deconstruct the concept of literature into "écriture," doesn't it do this in circular fashion by admittedly deriving "écriture" itself from the teleological concept of the text in the paradigm of written literature? Isn't the world as "écriture" consequently just as much a literary fiction as the semiotic notion of "world as text"?

KRIEGER: I thoroughly agree with you, and especially with your suggestion that the teleological conception of text is in many ways the ground from which the Structuralists' notion of *écriture* arises. Hence my suggestion that what is happening is that, instead of literature being deconstructed into *écriture*, *écriture* is being constructed into literature. But your notion of "historical-aesthetic difference," or *Alterität*—as a kind of deviation from the norm—is beyond their consideration. In effect, all texts are seen by them as already troped, so that there is no neutral ground to serve as a discourse to be deviated from. On the other hand, our argument against their claim may itself appear to rest upon assumptions common to the deviationist aesthetic, and these appear to posit the properly disputed claim that there is something to be termed normal discourse. But, I must remind you, I am aware that for me the distinction between normal discourse and deviation is heuristic only, though I think very usefully heuristic. I posit normal discourses as a concept which I can use to describe supposed deviations in order to find the special ways in which poetry is working. So normal discourse is a nice negative reference for me in that it allows a standard which, by the way, does not exist for me any more than it does for those devoted to the notion of *écriture*. We could easily agree about that. The difficulty which deviationist theory presents is precisely that there can't be any deviations unless one acknowledges a normal discourse, and if one acknowledges, under the pressure of recent language theory, that all discourse has tropological and narratological elements, these prevent any version of it from being normal. How can we have a deviation, if we don't have a normal discourse to deviate from? Obviously what the deviationist critic has done, and I am one, is to create a necessary fiction of a normal discourse which exists only by extrapolation from what the finished poem seems to be. That is, one would have to extrapolate from the poem a supposedly pre-poetic discourse from which the poem is to be seen as deviating. As you suggest, this pre-deviated-from model is all that the Structuralists have come along and given us—perhaps the very model which the poet might start out with, but which the poem would never end up as being. So in that sense I like the notion of its being heuristic, though I think some of our Structuralist friends might like it less.

JAUSS: I see a difficulty with your notion of "aesthetic need," if you define this as "need for closure" (*AP*, 96). If it is maintained of a theory of perception that it accords with the need "to close the form we perceive" (*AP*, 96), then it seems to me on the other hand similarly the case of a theory of aesthetic perception, that it is able to invest the imaginary object with absolute perfection in order to make perceptions aesthetically meaningful.

And moreover, it is this reception of the imaginary object which enables closed meaning structures (*Sinnstrukturen*) to open onto horizons of new (or repressed) meaning. The "sense of an ending" seems to me much more of a "*structural apocalypse*" with which aesthetic experience can never be satisfied. Aesthetic experience ensues from the transgressive need to challenge the given, which is always grounded in the conventions and norms of a closed world. This transgressive need opens up new meaning possibilities (*Sinnmöglichkeiten*) within the interminable process of telling and retelling, interpreting and reinterpreting. I remind you of Paul Valéry's critique of the classical-organologic conception of the work of art, in which he proposed an alternative notion of poiesis, which suspends the organically closed form in the never-ending process of form-building (and thus too, of the plural and contingent forms of poetic structures). The closed form of a work on which you seem to insist would in this view derive from the illusion of a reader who has not seen through the classical prejudice of a work's autonomic status.

KRIEGER: I am not in disagreement with you in that I freely acknowledge, first, that for me the need for closure is consistent with a "theory of aesthetic perception," as you describe it, and, secondly, that the "imaginary" (my "illusionary") object does not rest in closure but, through reflexivity, opens itself outward through its implicit self-denials. So I have no trouble with the notion that we must reopen any aesthetic object that is threatening closure. It seems to me precisely the double movement that I have been trying to suggest. As we work with these poems and as we think they seek to have us work with them, they threaten closure at every moment, but in such a way as at the same moment acknowledging the deceiving character of that closure, the fact that theirs is a fictional closure which must be taken only as fiction, therefore leaving a world of unenclosed materials outside the walls, always banging on those walls and threatening to break them down.

At the most elementary level, every time any of us talks about a poem in class or picks up a poem at home and asks "why" about any of its words or any of its lines or characters or incidents or figures, we are making many assumptions of totalization or of closure, since we assume there is a satisfying answer to be found for the "why." Our habit of reading in a way that is perceiving aesthetically (and here I am betraying a leaning toward *Gestalt* such as Gombrich, Iser, and others have betrayed on other occasions) leads us, when reading poems, to want to make each of them fill in the gaps and come together to find itself a totality. Now that of course seems wholly in accord with the New Criticism. But what I have learned in the last fifteen or so years—and have become increasingly explicit about—is that in the poem and in our response to it there is a continual self-consciousness about the inadequacy of the games the poet is playing to force closure (and the poet plays all kinds of formal games to achieve it). This self-consciousness leads to the subversive element that you mention Valéry talks about, which I have always sensed as well: it is the duplicity that Professor Iser discussed, that which doubles every attempted closure back upon itself.

Generally it is, in effect, the dual, self-contradictory "reality" we sense as we contemplate the characters onstage as at once one of us living lives like ours and as utterly apart, in the unempirical realm of repeatable make-believe. And they somehow must be seen as partaking of both at once, enclosed in their own world that, showing itself to us as artifice, opens—by negative reference—to another projected "reality" outside which the inside can never enter, or rather is protected from entering.

Let me refer again to a favorite, because obvious, example I have used from "The Rape of the Lock." The assemblage is about to take their coffee, which is being heated. What is to transpire is nothing but an empty ceremony in this ceremonial world that excludes what we might think of as flesh-and-blood "reality." But the language which relates the ceremony to us reminds us, in its double meanings, of that other "reality" being repressed: " . . . the fiery spirits blaze. / From silver spouts the grateful liquors glide, / While china's earth receives the smoking tide." I take especially the phrase "China's earth," which is violently and brilliantly duplicitous in that it means at one and the same time the refined earthen artifact from China and the earthy peopling process of that populous country. And in the "silver spouts" and "grateful liquors" which become the "smoking tide" received by "China's earth" we have the ceramic equivalent of copulation, the exclusion of the biological by the ceremonial artifice which imitates the fleshly, even uses its language, though only to remind us of what it must not show and cannot permit. The prolific realm of peopling lies just beyond the frame of the poem, repressed and excluded, though by means of its language the poem manages with a wink to direct us to its outside, the hidden side of its glorious moon.

Nor is this trick an isolated one in the poem, since throughout its course its language plays similar games, all serving the very notion of the rape of the lock, the only rape possible in this decorous closet of a world which shuts out those acts which its words, from "rape" onward, remind us are *not* taking place. The excluded is constantly there, in the underside of the language, banging on the walls the poem seems to want us to construct around it, trying to get in. But, as we have seen, the poem is also acknowledging surreptitiously the impossibility of the exclusion it struggles toward.

Thus a poem that with so much care encloses a fragile world apparently maintained by its metaphors, subverts its enclosures and reveals their emptiness, by indirection opening our vision outward to that fully peopled world it so willfully would ignore. In doing so this poem exposes a new awareness that eighteenth-century poets (and others) too often dared not admit was there, and it is a brilliantly illuminating anthropological document for producing this exposure.

JAUSS: If I understand correctly, your theory calls for a new dialectical notion of "negative reference," according to which the poetic work, in its negative reference, does not simply suspend excluded reality, but preserves it as something negated (as the background to what has been excluded), which remains the condition of the work's being understood. It seems to me that Adorno anticipated this when he interpreted Goethe's famous poem "Uber allen Gipfeln ist Ruh" as a text which, although suggestive of a harmony with nature, at the same time evokes by negation the excluded, restless, and unpleasant reality of our world. If I correctly understand the premises of your theory, then would not your concept of fiction also have to be defined as "negative reference," which for example would make possible the narrating of events, thereby enabling us to reflect and gain knowledge of reality?

In your critique of Hayden White, however, it looks as if the use of poetic fiction always fails to deal adequately with the supposed objectivity of historical truth. White's categories of "emplotments" have more than demonstrated their work in understanding nineteenth-century historiography. I would argue against the view that White's categories reduce historical truth to the mere illusion of poetic fiction (we can for the moment set aside his claim about their origin in the rhetorical figures of metaphor, metonymy etc.). Fictional structures, to which the principles of the Aristotelian fable (beginning, middle, end) already belong, by no means transform history into a closed "other" world of fiction, but first make—comparable to Kant's regulative ideas—complex historical reality knowable in meaning contexts. Wolfgang Iser has himself also set out why poetic fiction must no longer be understood as a world opposed to reality, but as the basis for contact (*Mittelungsverhältnis*) with a communicaton of "reality." The fictive generates meaning as it opens the way for experience. If this should be the case, would one not also have to include poetic fiction in your catalog of metaphysical assumptions to be deconstructed, which already includes different assumptions of the classical ontology of literature (*AP*, 95–96)? That is, poetic fiction, like these assumptions, could no longer be understood as a totalized structure (a self-realized teleological closure). Would not the communicative function of fictions offer yet another possibility to your "Apology for Poetics?"

KRIEGER: Your suggestion rests on a series of epistemological expectations which Hayden White's extreme skepticism could not accept. It is he, not I, who sees only the fictional element in historical discourse, and who, consequently, would collapse any distinction between historical and poetic fictions. You would still retain a privileged, pre-discursive and extra-discursive "reality" which White has precluded (or pretroped). As a matter of fact, I find White's categories of "emplotments" even further from epistemological issues than I have so far suggested. I remember, when I first looked at the title of the crucial introductory essay to his *Tropics of Discourse* ("Tropology, Discourse, and the Modes of Human Consciousness"), I was startled by those final words, which turn us from any interest that could move outward toward possible historical constructs or "realities," to one that moves inward into consciousness. This is a troublesome overdetermining of White's structural categories, one that makes them substantive, so that as you read you discover he is talking, not about emplotments, but about existential projections of modes of consciousness. Consequently, he forgoes any heuristic advantage of the sort that you have proposed.

However, I think we could ignore any difference between us concerning our interpretation of Hayden White, and the force of your question remains to be dealt with. You seem to be suggesting that, by means of my notion of negative reference, poems can be related to reality after all—perhaps no less so than history, even if more obliquely so. If White identifies historical and poetic fictions by virtue of a common tropological autonomy that approaches discursive solipsism, you finally bring them together from the other side, through their common discursive capacity to disclose reality, to be instruments of historical cognition. How tempting I find this move as I seek with anthropological arguments to bolster my "Apology for Poetics." But I must resist.

In my recent writing I have become more and more anxious to show that the realm which the poetic metaphor seeks to exclude in its less self-conscious moments is also in the end just another realm of discourse rather than the realm of experience itself, so that it is also fictional. Next to the poetic enclosure, it may feel like reality, like raw existence itself, but the negative reference that—against the primary poetic thrust—points us toward it is still verbal only: it has us trade one illusionary semantic possibility for another, as in "China's earth," in which the flesh of a mythically conceived population of China is superimposed upon the ceramics of the mythic refinements of China's art. My constant return to the hobby horses of *Tristram Shandy* in recent essays stems from this notion of a multi-layered set of verbal and textual illusionary possibilities, with which I would replace your suggestion of the clean polarity between illusion and reality, of fictional enclosure and its negative reference to a privileged, if excluded, world of actual experience. I prefer to bracket them all as variations operating within the linguistic realm.

So, unlike you and White (in what I see as your opposed ways), I still seek to distinguish history from poetry, though hardly on grounds as secure as they were for Aristotle. In a rather obvious and common-sense way, I suggest that, in dealing with history, White and others deal with texts that apparently mean to be something other than fiction: they would hardly present themselves as self-conscious fictions, and most historians would hardly be flattered to be told that they were really fiction writers. Most of them would wish that they were somehow "truer" than historians who came before them (or than competing historians around them). To that extent, then, history and poetry cannot be treated similarly as fictions. Nor, I would argue as you would not, can they be joined by a similar function of referring, positively or negatively, to reality. I focus rather on the difference between them. The difference is that poetry seeks to justify its fictional status: it not only wants to be a fiction but wants to acknowledge itself as a fiction. Further, as a self-conscious fiction, it provides several sets of perspective glasses, and through them a collection of conflicting, mutually exclusive verbal realities whose coexistence it sustains. In this sense it remains for me a discourse apart, one which I prefer not to deconstruct. I cannot enclose it within a universal set of narratological emplotments because, as you have agreed in an earlier statement, to do so would be to turn poetry into a form of undifferentiated *écriture*, thereby giving up on it as something that deserves to have a poetics written about it.

GABRIELE SCHWAB: Professor Krieger's insistence on the distinctive character of the work of art, its microcosmic unity *and* its openness to the world, the indeterminacies in work and reception *and* the need for closure, leads to his conception of aesthetic duplicity, which makes him a leading mediator of conflicting ideas in the contemporary critical domain. The challenge of Professor Krieger's position lies in the fact that he sees this aesthetic duplicity to be grounded in the anthropological functions of literature. The questions I should like to raise concern the specific nature of this duplicity and its anthropological implications.

At first glance it seems that Professor Krieger's conception of aesthetic duplicity stems from a happy marriage of theoretical features normally belonging to rival theories. I should like to summarize four basic arguments which form the core of his new positive model. Two of these focus primarily on qualities of the aesthetic work while the other two deal more with the reception process:

1. The poetical work possesses a self-referential quality which operates as an inbuilt device delimiting it from a surrounding world to which it nevertheless relates. Such self-referentiality neither permits one to view a work of fiction as a self-contained cosmos nor as merging with an all-inclusive background.

2. The poetical work possesses the power to convert differences into identities (pp. 90f, 95f). This accounts for a constructive tendency in the work, its particular presence, manifested especially in that fusion of differences realized in metaphor (90). This identity is not total and not so much grounded in the object as in the process of reception.

3. In the reception process the reader actualizes the work's potential of identities according to his "need for closure" (96). This need, an anthropological fact rooted in imagination, is fundamental for aesthetic experience in general.

4. Another basic characteristic of the poetic work is its *deconstructive element*, which "keeps it open to the world, to language at large, and to the reader" (p. 97).

Obviously, the anthropological "need for closure" and the work's "power to convert differences into identities" have mainly constructuve functions. However, in what way may these be related to the deconstructive element? The "something" that keeps literature open to the world is attributed to the linguistic nature of the work, to the transient and empty character of its signifiers. Created by means of self-referentiality, it will hardly be overlooked by a reader familiar with Post-Structural theory. The moment of "presence" is thus reflexively broken. Closure and deconstruction may coexist, be it in the form of an act of reading and its reflexion, or in the form of an actual aesthetic experience in the context of a whole series. But it also seems to coexist in the poetic language—a coexistence, which results in "the paradoxical nature of language as aesthetic medium" (p. 97).

In all, these four basic qualities of a poetic work and its reception constitute the *fundamental duplicity* which helps to differentiate the work of art from other texts and which, in turn, forms the basis of Professor Krieger's dual aesthetic theory.

However, such an aesthetics of duplicity seems to be somewhat unequally balanced. Granted that there is a "need for closure," is there a corresponding "need for deconstruction" which could claim an equal aesthetic status? And, even more importantly, where may the roots of the anthropological need for closure be found? Professor Krieger relates it to the "dream of unity" suggesting "the secret life-without-language or life-before-language . . . the very life which the language of difference precludes. . . . In poetry we grasp at the momentary possibility that this can be a life-in-language" (*AP*, 100). If Professor Krieger describes the "miracle" of closure (*AP*, 91) in such a way, does he not also need a more embracing anthropological model, once he has taken the first step toward anthropology?

I carry this argument even further: doesn't the power to experience prelinguistic unity as "life-in-language" presuppose a "deconstruction" of "ordinary" language experience? The duplicity of the work would then have to be based on an anthropological model which conceives of two different modes of imagination mediated by the work's double and yet unifying "*Gestalt.*" Yet, Professor Krieger insists on not relating his duplicity to two different modes of imagination. But to give coherence to his model, he is still obliged to account for a deconstructive power not rooted in language alone, but—like the need for closure—in anthropology.

One solution would be to follow the historical line of Kantian and romantic aesthetic theory and appeal to reflexivity as an anthropological power when pressed to specify the motivational force behind the deconstructive elements. If he pursued this line of thought, Professor Krieger would have given up a view of the work of art as a self-contained object, but would still remain tied to the old dualism of sensitive and reflexive capacities. Reflexivity, however, as far as its independence and its motivating forces are concerned, has come under heavy attack in our century, especially from deconstructivism. Thus, the self-reflexive deconstructive power Professor Krieger refers to is not identical with the deconstructivist's deconstructive power, which is turned mainly against the closures stemming from reflexivity.

This problem has even further corollaries. If Professor Krieger wants to avoid grounding duplicity in art on a duplicity of imagination, does that not implicitly lead to a rather Kantian relation of closure, imagination and synthesis, whereas the deconstructive quality of the work would be an additional, but not a basically aesthetic value? Drawing the consequences immanent in Professor Krieger's dual poetics, it seems to me that he reproduces the very conceptual dichotomies of the divisions which he tries to overcome. He has identity, closure, presence, fullness, microcosmos on one side and difference, openness, absence, emptiness on the other. Yet, his general sympathy with deviationist aesthetics should also acknowledge that deconstructive qualities may themselves have a dual aspect: they deconstruct ordinary identities in order to construct new aesthetic "identity," which might indeed evoke or merge with pre-linguistic modes of experience. Wouldn't this invite one to connect the "dream of unity" with a poetic language mediating between a primary mode of imagination and a secondary mode of imagination which has its origin in the acquisition of language? Then the "miracle" would lie in the merging of two areas which in everyday life exclude each other.

KRIEGER: I find these comments intensely probing, and as troubling as you meant them to be. I see two related issues as the major ones you raise. First, you ask how I would relate (and must I not relate?) my notion of duplicity to the anthropological and perceptual appeal I make in my attempt to account for our habitual search for closure. This question implicitly requires me to confront a second, one more intimately tied to the practice of criticism, which asks where the locus is of the duplicity that turns closure upon itself, in spite of itself, and, through negation, finds an opening after all.

Let me turn to the second question first. Am I claiming—as I think I am—that both sides of the paradoxical combination of elements, those forcing closure and those undoing it, can be seen as originating in the literary work, or am I claiming rather that the closure alone orginates in the work, while the counter-movement that opens it outward is the reader's deconstructive reaction? I believe you suggest that it is the second (a judgment appropriate to the "reception aesthetic" associated with the University of Konstanz), though in this case I would disagree. But on the other hand I do agree with your observation that in my framework the two moves—toward and away from closure—do not occur in parallel ways, are not analogously related to the work and our response to it, so that there is an imbalance between them as I assign them their functions.

Thus you are concerned that, for me, only the closed totalization, as pre-deconstructive, is the work's responsibility, while it is language's special character, as it flows through us, that leads us in the opposite direction. But I mean to argue, instead, that it is not the skepticism of the reader's verbal awareness and its inclination toward demystification that turn the incipient closure duplicitous. These (the skepticism and the inclination) may exist in us and are perhaps easily stimulated, but both opposed stimulating tendencies can be traced to the work in its workings. For it is the very nature of the aesthetic medium, as we have instituted it, to look both ways, so that the very act of aesthetic closure provides its own denial that becomes our opening. So I claim that the duplicity results, not from our need to demystify the would-be totalized closure by opening it to our own realities, but from the verbal intricacies of the work's self-conscious fictionality that doubles its every move upon itself, thereby accompanying aesthetic affirmation with denial, simultaneously a construct and a self-deconstruction.

Yet, if I may return to the first question, it is true that I find a difference in the origins of these doubled (and yet opposed) moves—as these relate to the culturally imposed habits of human response—and this difference, with good reason, disturbs you. I claim that the closure we find, or attempt to find, is related to our perceptual habits as these have been culturally conditioned. So our tendency is to pursue closure, not duplicity. But if the challenge that closure imposes upon itself which, in self-denial, returns us to openness does not—like closure itself—derive from our habitual need, then whence comes it? And is it then less firmly (which is only to say less anthropologically) grounded than is the closure?

I am proposing that this counter-movement derives from the language itself as it has—again in accordance with Western tradition in the arts—been tortured into functioning as an aesthetic medium. I am not claiming, as some Post-Structuralists would, that it derives from the dynamics of language itself, but—I repeat—from language as transformed into aesthetic medium. Duplicity is, as you have suggested I would say, the consequence of a mediation. And whence comes the mediation? Why, from the medium, of course.

Our habit of seeking closure is an aesthetic habit, one cultivated within the Western tradition since Aristotle posited closure as the response to a teleological need not normally satisfied outside the aesthetic realm. It finds a fulfillment for a world of experience and of language normally left unfulfilled. But most of our experience, as non-aesthetic, would evade the tightening restrictiveness of language that has been subjected to poetic pressure. Our usual reading habits, responding to such a language, are just those which the aesthetic must work on us to suspend, so that we can invoke those other habits we have been taught to carry at the ready when the occasion and the work which helps provoke it seem to summon them to a special response. The obstacles of our ordinary reading habits may thus be overcome by the culturally learned, extraordinary reading habits, but as we. respond to the self-conscious way in which the work suggests its own as-if-ness, its fictionality, we also sense the return of the emptiness of the words as non-aesthetic, which we associate with the casualties of everyday experience. Not that the sense of aesthetic closure is to be even momentarily abandoned, but it is sustained only in the teeth of its frailty, indeed its illusionary evasions.

Now there are, of course, some readers who will not be roused from their disposition to read the poem as if it was the morning newspaper, those who are not alive to the potential sacredness of the aesthetic occasion. And there are some who succumb so completely to it that they put to sleep the deconstructive awareness that permits the poem to remind us of the illusion we are fostering, and those less exclusive ones we are excluding or repressing. Even more, there are nominal poems that do not deserve to be treated as other than a newspaper, although the conventions of the occasion may themselves persuade some readers to argue in their behalf. Then critical debate about the virtues of the poem in question can ensue. Presumably we would be seeking to justify the outside stimulus for the suppressing of one set of reading and responding habits for another. One set may be just about always there for us as we carry on our business, at peace with the absences that empty our words. But the other set is conventionally authorized for us within a culture that has sought to reserve special occasions for exploring what the unattainable dominion of verbal presence and identity would be like, in spite of our persistent involvement—in temporal experience as institutionalized in an arbitrary and metonymic language—with openness and difference, with the consequent emptiness of signification.

In claiming that our aesthetic pursuit of closure is culturally conditioned, I am suggesting that it is a habit that is at once anthropological and perceptual. How both? For the perceptual claim would rather suggest the realms of technical psychology, or at least epistemology. Obviously, however, I am following the lead of Ernst Gombrich in claiming that what we see and how we see it are the results of perceptual habits both created and served by the culture's visual tradition as embodied in its arts. So, for all practical purposes, the perceptual habit *is* the anthropologically induced habit. And within the Western aesthetic this habit looks for—and thus makes, and thinks it finds—closure as its aesthetic objective, although it is also prepared to respond to what Rosalie Colie used to call the unmetaphoring (or deconstructive) recoil action also provided by the literary work.

The latter may seem to be a contrary accompaniment to the pressure for closure, a counter-aesthetic thrust always challenging the aesthetic pressure. Yet the anti-aesthetic must be taken as necessary to the validation of the aesthetic so that it becomes, paradoxically, the integral part of the aesthetic that guarantees it, but only by guaranteeing its irreducible duplicity. This is the argument that leads me to see the poem as a metaphor that has known metonymy but tries to appear as metaphor anyway, without denying the metonymic state of language beyond its moment. Thus that part of the aesthetic which is anti-aesthetic allows us to frame the object while threatening to break through the frame that holds it within; persuaded by the picture, we look, with it, just beyond its own carefully wrought edges, much as we do, for example, in Velasquez' *Las Meniñas*, about which we have had so much comment in recent years.

Yet the anthropological-perceptual pressure to find (by making) closures persistently returns as a way of keeping us in touch with a magical manner of signifying, of having words that can touch or even become our most internalized visions, which are otherwise not available to us as linguistic creatures. I would propose that we readers reach for a pre-linguistic or pre-symbolic level of response which is immediate, unmediated; that is, we feel immediacies of response, though we cannot know them because our knowledge is linguistic and symbolic, and our consciousness of knowledge is linguistic and symbolic. In that sense there is no pre-linguistic or pre-symbolic level, except that we have this feeling that there are pure responses which come, as it were, before—before mediation. Yet everything in language *is* mediation, and with a special kind of mediation—that which is related to its peculiar medium—in poems.

My assumption, like the Structuralists', is that where language is, there already reigns difference. And any notion of identity is lost with the loss of language as metaphor, succeeded by the awareness of language as a differential—which is to say, a metonymic—instrument. We have had in the old days the romantic anthropologist who used to talk about the primitive possibility of our having a monistic language that precedes "difference," with the natives eating their gods. It is the sort of thing you still get in a historian of religion like Eliade, for whom there is the possibility of linguistic identity, the miraculous collapsing of difference. This kind of anthropology has been exploded, of course, by what Structuralists, as linguists, have taught us about the way signs work.

What I am saying is that poetic language, having like all language known metonymy, is not an innocent working for the mystifications of identity; rather, it is already in the realm of metonymy and cannot get out. Is it an act of nostalgia still to cherish identity—an attempt by the aesthetic to recover a lost past? That possibility is not what interests me so much as the attempt by poems to discover a way of speaking, or by us to discover a way of reading, which will allow language to have a primal force. We who deal with those poems, indeed with the best of them, have—I think—an obligation to discover how their language is working, working by virtue of words that are doing just what words are not supposed to be able to do: somehow to find a way of capturing the gods. Poets seem to have been aware that language is empty until someone manages to force it beyond its incapacities, and poets seem to have appointed themselves to try for this break-through. I am trying to suggest a theory that will help us to trace and justify what they do.

ANSELM HAVERKAMP: Professor Krieger, your own "Apology," as it were, deals with an issue whose tradition is characterized by critical treatment in an apologetic mode, and whose identity over and above the inconsistencies of this tradition could, in fact, only be maintained apologetically. Must the first aim and anxiety of a new poetics continue this tradition of the old, and implicate the realm of literary productions within the rhetorical domain of everyday speech? The rhetorical character of the question is perhaps all too obvious. It surely may be heuristically useful "to distinguish poetic from other discourse (by means of a deviationist aesthetic)." But this distinction still presupposes the very rhetorical continuum of speech (that is, of discourse, as an all too hasty totalization of the rhetorical field might suggest), which the poeticalness of literary texts is said to have always already interrupted. What then ought the aim (if not the anxiety) of a new poetics be which takes its point of departure no longer from the rhetorical primacy of speech, but from the hermeneutic difference between the discursiveness of speaking (*Diskursivität*) and the textual qualities of written texts (*Textualität*)?

The hermeneutical discontinuity of texts within the field of discourse, that is, textuality as a discontinuous sphere of written texts within the domain of spoken language, functions as an open structure (as open systems are open to surrounding environments). This structure, if I follow your argument adequately, under the influence of a deep seated anthropological "need," awaits closure, and in the case of literary texts provokes their calculated closings. Poetic texts, in your view, somehow await though resist their own closure. Between the rhetorical structure (*Appellstruktur*) of semantic ambiguity which provokes closure, and the linguistic potential of a semantic undecidability which precludes closure, you propose a duplicity which enables the possibility of closure and openness simultaneously closing off and opening up. This duplicity is based on what you call "the primacy of the operation of the aesthetic in us all," or more generally, "the aesthetic need," which is the foundation of an apparently unproblematic complicity between author and reader. You don't subscribe to the naive New Critical faith in the unifying power of metaphor which satisfies this common need; neither do you propagate the Structuralist disillusionment brought about by the metonymic arbitrariness which effectively undermines the epistemological claims of any "organicism." Mediating the conflicting tendencies, you speak of "poetic identity despite language's normal incapacities," and conjure a duplicitous notion of metaphor which metaphorically (if not metonymically) combines metaphor and metonymy, "a metaphor that has known metonymy."

Reducing metonymy to mere arbitrariness, the fashionable predilection for metonymy effaces the seminal distinction of a Structuralist poetics, though the very success of it rests largely on, and is in fact the result of the metonymic reduction. The original distinction, however, as developed from Jakobson to Lacan, comes closer to your own intentions than the reductive account of your summary allows. The Saussurean metaphor of projection which Jakobson appropriates, and the Freudian metaphor of condensation which Lacan favors and develops into the metaphor of superimposition, provide models for "a metaphor that has known metonymy." The reduction of the structuralist problematic aligns your own notion of duplicity more closely with formalist concepts of metaphor than is necessary and desirable. Duplicity, as you have it, seems rather an argument for a kind of double closure, or alternative closure which anyway ends up in closing off.

It is difficult to see to what extent this duplicity can ever surpass the impasses of a semantics of tenor and vehicle which was intended, though not successfully, as an interactive model as well. Richards' interaction-theory, however, leads beyond the inherent limitations of the formalist position, limitations which seem to be maintained in your apology for a formalist dualism. Being attentive to the duplicity within the interaction of metaphor may be a progress beyond New Critical varieties of so-called fusion, but it is not enough to account for what is going on in the activity of reading metaphors. The metaphorical illusion of poetic identity (an illusion of presence, as you admit) is the result of a substitution of signifiers whose insisting force (*Drängen*) originates within, and remains efficacious despite its repression (*Verdrängung*). Where there is metaphor there is presence within absence, to bring Lacan back to Sartre, a dialectics of presence and absence which qualifies the imaginary impact of reading.

However one would like to elaborate these models of metaphor, they could certainly provide for what you call "the poem's differentness from other discourse," but in a different way. This differentness would not be grounded in semantic closure or hermeneutic totalization, as you suggest, but in an aesthetic resistance to the structural coercion (*Strukturzwang*) of the interpretive process, ironically "resisting our constructive tendency," and thereby setting free the aesthetic as functional pleasure (*Funktionslust*). The extent to which even deconstruction, which you use as a counter, can account for this remains to be seen.

KRIEGER: First I should like to pursue for a moment your discussion of the relation of my notion of duplicity to New-Critical ambiguity on the one side and to Post-Structuralist undecidability or instability on the other. What is at stake, of course, is my argument for the distinction—if there is one—between poems and other discourse. The term *ambiguity*, I would say, operates within the New-Critical poetic exclusively under the blanket of closure. That is to say, the claim is made that the total poem is enclosed only by virtue of the several disparate, if not opposed, meanings that are working together. It is essentially the Hegelian model in which all oppositions unite, so that it is no accident that again and again these critics use Coleridge's passage from chapter 14 of the *Biographia Literaria* in which the imagination "reveals itself in the balance or reconcilement of opposite or discordant qualities."

So the balancing and the reconciling control the direction of the ambiguities as they intermingle in spite of their polar tendencies. Opposition fuses into a system that is marked exclusively by closure (exclusively despite the inclusive representation of the several-sided ambiguities). Any threatened opening is a threat to the system that would empty it of its poetic character. On the other side, the Post-Structuralist notion of undecidability or instability suggests that there is no limit to the ever-opening concept of textuality. There is no limit to the mobility of the signifiers which seem to chase themselves across the vast network of language stretching before and after.

My notion of duplicity is differentiated from the Post-Structuralist in that it treats a single verbal sequence as if it could, *pour l'occasion*, be treated as a discontinuous text which appears to us, under the aegis of the aesthetic moment, to have certain determinate sets of internal relations. This duplicity would differ, however, from New-Critical ambiguity because it does not represent a synthesis in the Hegelian model; there is no balancing or reconciling of opposite or discordant qualities. Instead, it puts us on the razor's edge, and yet we seem to fall off both sides, at once into and outside the text as metaphor. It is at once contained within the work's domain and yet subverts that very possibility by entering the language system beyond, which it also finds sanctioned—however indirectly—within the work. And I return to my old maxim that seeks to clarify what the poem asks us to believe—tentatively and illusionarily—when it asks us to believe its metaphor: it asks us to believe in a verbal miracle, in which words are seen overrunning their bounds, their distinctions of property, only while reminding us that we can indulge a miracle only so long as we know it cannot have happened. For if we believe it did really happen, then it's a miracle for us no longer.

But now to your objections. I do not feel the force of your complaints as I do some others, because I think they arise in large part from a verbal misunderstanding that can be traced to the ways our different languages use the term *dis-course*—or at least to the way you seem to translate my use of that word. You assume that my interest, as I distinguish poems from other discourse, is to begin with "everyday speech" and then to deal with deviations from it. And your concerns spring from your sense of the inadequacy of the realm of speech for grounding a poetics. Consequently, you ask that I turn from the limiting conception of discourse as speech (your *Diskursivität*) to the different framework produced by the conception of written texts (your *Textualität*).

Not surprisingly, you are suggesting a correction that would lead toward the hermeneutics of reader response, although I believe that I have, in effect, adopted it in advance. For *discourse* is not restricted to speech in English, but can refer to written texts as well, and in my work usually does. "Normal" discourse is not, for me, "everyday speech" at all. In fact, in my essay "Poetic Presence and Illusion II" (in *PPI*) I have explicitly, and with some care, distinguished between the realms of *parole* and *écriture* and dealt with the differing considerations imposed by each of them and with the special problems of textual interpretation arising from the collision between them as we read. So, to the extent that your concerns derive from the restriction of my term *discourse* to speech, they are ill-founded. My work, I believe, is as much riveted to the problems of textuality as any reception-aesthetician should require.

Perhaps it is this (mis)reading that leads you to view my notion of aesthetic response as resulting from a "complicity between author and reader." But this is to make the aesthetic interaction a speech act, as I would not, since for me the complicitous relation exists not between reader and author but between the reader and the poem as a written text. Further, the role of the aesthetic, for me, goes beyond the linguistic distinctions of Jakobson to which you seek to reduce my position. For I cannot permit it to rest in generic grammatical notions. I am sufficiently responsive to phenomenology to recognize the role played by our disposition in permitting language to work

for us in special ways, and this disposition is not derived from
the operations of language itself. What converts grammatical
functions into functions that serve as an aesthetic medium
(Michael Riffaterre would call them "ungrammaticalities") is
the self-conscious fictionality which we are prepared as aesthetic readers to entertain and which the work seems to us to
be soliciting us to entertain.

It is under the aegis of this conventional receptivity
that those deviations occur which enable us to respond to
linguistic forms as aesthetic. It is in accordance with this
disposition that we can entertain the illusion of the closed
metaphorical construct, though as "a metaphor that has
known metonymy," it helps sustain our consciousness of its
illusionary, self-created limitations.

Consequently, my argument springs from claims about
intentionality rather than claims about a universal grammar or
semiotic. I would derive my hermeneutic from—in your
words—"what is going on in the activity of reading metaphors" and hence, within an interactive model such as you
seem to prefer, for I have more in common with reception
theorists than I do with Jakobson. It is the aesthetic intentionality that leads me to the deviations that create the aesthetic
medium, that lead me—in other words—to the manipulations
of our fictional, our imaginary, stage-space in our self-conscious response to the aesthetic occasion and to the specially
made stimulus that sets it off, provided we are willing and
knowledgable enough to be complicitous. And, in speaking of
the work as metaphor, I would go on, as I have elsewhere, to
discuss the strange commingling of pressure and repression
(Drängen and Verdrängen), much as you have. So, much as I
distrust an answer to an objector that concludes by insisting
that, at bottom, there is little disagreement, I like to believe
that such may well be the case in this instance.

ULRICH GAIER: If one sees, as you do, the poetic as the enticement for the reader to deviate from the continuum of the text,
shouldn't one, then, take into account other possibilities of
enticement beyond the structure of the text? For instance,

such a text as a newspaper article has nothing poetic in itself
to entice the reader to deviation; if published, however (as
has been done by Peter Handke), in a collection of poems, a
newspaper article seems to obtain this "poetic" quality.
Shouldn't one, therefore, not only account for the mere structure of the text, but also for the entire communicative situation, including the specific conditions of author and reader
(and the variations in these conditions), the mutual presuppositions of the partners, and the media as these are conditioned in and by their historical change?

KRIEGER: You properly remind us, once again, of the governing role of the reader's perspective and the dependence of
that perspective upon the context of what you call "the entire
communicative situation." And you go on to suggest that,
under the proper "communicative situation," just about any
text might be seen as displaying what you term " 'poetic'
quality." No argument there.

For us to see the poem as aesthetic object, it and we
must share several different sets of mutual presuppositions
(or rather we must have them and read them into the object
as sharing them), thereby leading to our sets of expectations
for which we seek satisfaction in the work at hand. When we
argue with one another about whether or not a particular
poem adequately fulfills them, we may be able to come to
certain agreements, at least about the grounds for deciding. If
we think our expectations are being met, we tend to project
the appropriate stimulating features onto the object. But the
critic in us wants to decide between what feels like a power
built into the poem by the maker to control our response and
a power we might be projecting onto undeserving newspaper
language. Yet it is true that the habitual occasion prepares us
to read as if we can find the power in the poem, so that we
may make a poem out of whatever we are reading—even
broken-up lines which are indeed from the newspaper.

Whether our projections are or are not justified by
what seems to be on display before us is what critics argue
about. But that is not at all to deny that we can be fooled by

deceptive devices, such as you suggest, which impose upon our habits of reception. Still I think it *is* accurate in such cases to say we are being "fooled," which suggests that the claims being made about the constructed forms, sponsored only by our response to the conventions of the occasion, are indeed our unjustified projections in that they are utterly arbitrary, without any anchoring in the stimulating object. So while I freely concede your point as it applies to our actual reading habits as aesthetic or would-be aesthetic respondents, for me the question of *ought*—how we ought to respond if we seek an appropriate response to the stimulating features of the work at hand—remains one which any critic still anxious to perform must be honest enough (and pragmatic enough) to acknowledge.

What I have been doing is to install a series of cultural supports—what you call "the entire communicative situation"—as enclosures around our capacity to see. This cultural context constitutes an anthropological ground for what we see, thus replacing the ontological ground our philosophy has been forced to give up, though (I must confess) giving up as little critical ground as possible. We discover or project out of a cultural commonness of language and expectation and history and tradition, and these of course differ enormously with time and place. But still there remains the habit we have, as readers of valued aesthetic objects in our culture and its traditions, of sitting down and opening to a page and reading, and trying to read in a special way; and we get very disappointed if something on the page does not startle and disrupt our make-believe-normal-but-really-not-at-all-normal reading, and send us moving back and forth in the text, trying to watch all sorts of things going on at once. And if spots of text here and there do not start to light up, first singly and then in patterns, we may well begin to wonder whether we are reading a poem or the morning newspaper.

I repeat, nothing I have said is meant to deny that we may well be the sole creators of those flashing lights in our habitual anxiety to find them and respond to them, and that, whatever the case, our attribution of poetic quality will confidently follow. But I cannot believe that this act, when it is especially high in the scale of the arbitrary, is not at times corrigible by reference to the text. Further, I must acknowledge that the kinds of patterns that readers find or create will vary as their expectations do, vary with their language and their language of expectation. Again I refer to the help given us by investigations like those of Professor Jauss, because it is precisely the study of the history of the interpretation of individual texts that helps tell us how to read now by illuminating the kinds of language we have at our disposal. In conclusion, then, I do not see that the fact that we project, sometimes more in complicity with the poem than at other times, should bother us so long as we still agree to make great demands of the poem and to cultivate the fiction that we can discover what the extent of *its* powers over our response ought to be.

JURGEN SCHLAEGER: I wonder what "price" you have had to pay for your ingenious reconciliation between two diametrically opposed concepts of the structure and function of "successful literary works." I think that this price can be best measured in terms of historical applicability. It is true, you try to base your concept on the anthropological make-up of the human psyche, thereby implying a methodological shift from an ontological to a reader-response point of view; but, to my mind, this does not make your notion of "the paradoxical simultaneity of closure and utter openness" less normative.

Considering the immense variety of "successful literary objects" the conclusion is conceivable, if not unavoidable, that this variety could be understood and classified in terms of differing relations between closure and openness. There may be literary works the achievement of which consists in the minimalization of that basic tension between openness and closure. There may be others which created and still create aesthetic pleasure by playing upon our need for closure; and again, there may be works whose success lies in the continual subversion of our attempt "to close" them. A strict exclusion of gradation from your concept of literary discourse seems to me to sacrifice too much on the altar of harmony between modern poetological schools.

KRIEGER: Your question assumes that I view all poems as partly closed, partly open, some more one way, some more the other, in a continuous gradation from one extreme to the other, an entire spectrum, leading from almost total closure to almost total openness. It is a tempting notion in its friend-liness, for it is attractively reassuring in its catholic accep-tance—and pleasantly easy, too easy. But it is one I must reject, for it strikes me as a flight from theory with all of any theory's necessary repressions.

Instead, mine is a quite different model: according to it, in reading (as in watching a play) we seek a form that produces total closure, except that as we find each form clos-ing, we find it also—through its apparent consciousness of its own fictionality—opening itself totally toward that which its closure would exclude. So every act is an act of unqualified closing that must in the very process reverse, and thus open, itself. The model is built on an all-or-none, changing into an all-*and*-none arrangement, quite different indeed from the continual eclectic compromising between the ratios that share partial openness and closure.

Still, you must ask, what about those obvious differ-ences among works along that spectrum you observe, running from those that seem most referential to those most wrapped in their own artifice? The question really is, are there poems about whose value we might agree—within broader agree-ments about our common expectations and so on—which do not persuade us to read them my way in order to earn that evaluation? (Of course, the circularity of this procedure is obvious enough.) What of poems, you may ask, which are largely open on the one hand or, on the other hand, poems which seek closure without betraying a fictional self-refer-ence? (By self-reference I do not mean the obvious operation in which some parts of the poem are referred to by other parts, but rather the poem's referring to its own artiface, to its character as an unreality, as a merely illusionary fiction.)

In order to collapse the differences along the suggested spectrum and so find among them a common tendency to fictional self-consciousness, I recall the perspective given me by Ernst Gombrich, who teaches us to argue for the self-referential character of those art works which at first appear most explicitly mimetic and hence the least artful. He reminds us that even the *trompe l'oeil* painting, which seeks altogether to lose its artfulness by merging into the reality it would imitate, calls not less attention to its unreality, but more. Representative of the most "realistic" possibilities of art, it paradoxically reminds us of the fictional nature of the mimetic claim of all art. I believe this line of argument answers your attempt to hold out many poems from my attempt to find in them the subversion of the closure they seek to impose.

But of course my every word here confirms your stated fear that my notion cannot be saved from being a normative one. Clearly I restrict my claims to what you quote me as calling "successful literary works," and I discover these as I find them satisfying the criteria I use to define them—just the circular procedure I acknowledged earlier. But surely I would not include all the texts that you and others might want me to in a would-be descriptive method that seeks to evade the normative. In this and my other answers, clearly I do not fear being normative; indeed, I would not dream of seeking *not* to be. I confess I could not feel any theoretical power in a poetics that does not accept its normative fate, even if I admit the theoretical difficulties inevitably courted by bringing questions of value to the surface of our awareness and allowing them to dominate our argument, as they probably would in any case.

WOLFGANG ISER (concluding remarks): As I reflect upon the exchange of arguments, two issues figured prominently in the discussion: what exactly is duplicity and how do we conceive of mediation? There seemed to be basic agreement on duplicity as a conspicious feature of what we have come to call the literary text. Thus, the concept of duplicity as delineated by Murray Krieger was not in dispute; on the contrary, it became the pivot of the discussion around which the interchange revolved. What emerged, however, as contentious was the way in which mediation is to be understood.

Murray Krieger indicated that the idea of mediation loomed large in his argument, for which it provided a basic underpinning. Yet it seemed what he intended to mediate concerned primarily a fundamental dichotomy, yawning between two diametrically opposed theories regarding the literary object: New Criticism and Post-Structuralism. His theory reshuffles the New-Critical perception of closure just as much as it intends to recast the Post-Structuralist conception of presence as illusion. His aim in doing so was to establish duplicity as the hallmark of the literary text, in consequence of which mediation was conceived as a reorganization of the relationship between two mutually exclusive theories, epitomized in the concept of duplicity as mediation between closure and openness. And as the distinctive quality of the literary text appeared to be in question, mediation according to Murray Krieger comes to full fruition when the blending of opposite notions in regard to the literary text serves to pinpoint the disputed singularity.

This was the juncture from which disagreement began to spread, which nevertheless was pervaded by the uncontested idea that duplicity and mediation are crucial to the literary text, though their interrelation could not exhaustively be dealt with as long as language was the overriding issue for its investigation. Murray Krieger had to make language his prime concern, as he wanted to separate the literary text from other types of text in view of the currently overpowering impact écriture exercises on the theory of literature. Yet to ground the specificity of the literary text in language primarily is bound to lead to a feature analysis which turns out to be a last resort whenever the language model is paramount.

This apparent restriction imposed on duplicity resulted from the intertwining of two theories, whose main preoccupation is the poeticity of language in the one case and the textuality of discourse in the other. Duplicity, then—so the discussion showed—should no longer be confined to the "prison-house of language" and instead be linked to other frames of reference, if its claim to being the distinctive mark of literature is to be upheld. And as Murray Krieger himself has opened the gate leading to a realm outside language by tying closure to a human need, the confines of language were exceeded in the discussion.

The concept of closure itself came under scrutiny. Supposing it originated from an anthropological desire which seeks expression in the literary work, what makes it different then from that kind of closure which governs our perceptual activities? A pure percept resulting from these activities is not as yet endowed with aesthetic qualities which rather arise out of a gestalt-breaking effort. Now, if the duplicitous nature of the text were to fulfill this very function, duplicity itself had to be traced back to anthropological dispositions. Murray Krieger, however, did not seem to be inclined to conceive of duplicity in this way; for him it is to be brought about by the verbal intricacies of the work's self-conscious fictionality.

Should closure and duplicity really have different roots, the anthropological issue raised will be headed off into an unpremeditated direction. Closure, then, as reflected in the text, tends to appear as an anthropological constant, which is either exposed or manipulated by linguistic operations whenever it is pushed over the threshold of the unconscious into the symbolic order. By unfolding this implication inherent in Murray Krieger's theory, a vital problem of literature's relation to cultural anthropology moved into focus. Is literature merely a mirror of the anthropological givens, or is it perhaps a divining rod for finding out something of our make-up? Instead of being an illustration of such assumed givens, the literary medium might serve as a field of exploration for the workings of the human imagination and promise insight as to why the imaginary potential has been fed back into human reality for the last 2,500 years since its documented inception.

Cultural anthropology, then, could turn out to be less a frame of reference for determining what literature is, but emerge itself as an area of investigation for providing answers to questions such as: why do we stand in need of literature and its fictions? In case there is such a revelatory capacity inherent in literature, its specificity should be conceived more in terms of functions than in terms of structure. Structures and features would then become subservient to the functions the text is meant to fulfill, which simultaneously would account for the kaleidoscopically changing forms of literature as responses to existing challenges.

Thus the differences between Murray Krieger's position and that held by the participants in the discussion came into the open. Murray Krieger made a case for duplicity as the hallmark of the literary text in order to prove that literature becomes literature by virtue of this very feature; if there is literature it must have a specificity of its own which can never be derived from anything other than itself. In defending his position Murray Krieger orchestrated his idea of duplicity, which in the end turned out to be an embodiment of mediation itself.

The participants, on the other hand, gave a tilt to this idea of mediation by asserting in different ways that literature has to be mediated with either the human make-up or with the historical situation out of which it arose, or with the modes of communication in order to bring out the specificity in question. Thus, duplicity, though agreed upon as an important concept, can only be taken as a heuristic notion for finding out what remains hidden in the workings of the human mind, what is revealed by the responses to a situational challenge, and what allows for the communication of an experience which has never been in the orbit of its potential recipient.

Although there was no basic disagreement about the

issues under consideration, the mode of tackling them brought out different intellectual temperaments marked by opposing points of departure: a linguistically and structurally oriented approach on the one hand and a hermeneutically and anthropologically oriented one on the other. Each of them is trying to rescue the text, though on different grounds, either by its self-produced singularity or by the multifarious-ness of its function.

A CHECKLIST OF WRITINGS BY MURRAY KRIEGER

Eddie Yeghiayan

1949

Review of *The Post of Honor*, by David Dortort. *Christian Science Monitor*, May 13, 1949, p. 20.

Review of *The Sphere*, by Ramon Jose Sender. *Christian Science Monitor*, May 24, 1949, p. 18.

Review of *The Track of the Cat*, by Walter Van Tilburg Clark. *Christian Science Monitor*, June 11, 1949, p. 22.

Review of *Alfred Tennyson*, by Charles Tennyson. *Christian Science Monitor*, June 30, 1949, p. 11.

Review of *The Witness*, by Jean Bloch-Michel. *Christian Science Monitor*, October 6, 1949, p. 15.

1950

"Creative Criticism: A Broader View of Symbolism." *Sewanee Review* (Winter 1950), 58(1):36–51.

"The Unliterary Criticism of Determinism." Review of *The Novel and Our Time*, by Alex Comfort. *Western Review* (Summer 1950), 14(4):311–314.

1951

"*Measure for Measure* and Elizabethan Comedy." *PMLA* (June 1951), 66(4):775–784.

1952

"Toward a Contemporary Apology for Poetry." Ohio State University, Ph.D. dissertation, 1952. (Abstract in *Dissertation Abstracts* [June 1958], 18[6]:2142–2144.)
"Critics at Work." Review of *The Kenyon Critics*, John Crowe Ransom, ed. *Western Review* (Summer 1952), 16(4):325–328.

1953

Editor (with Eliseo Vivas). *The Problems of Aesthetics: A Book of Readings.* New York: Rinehart, 1953.
"The Ambiguous Anti-Romanticism of T. E. Hulme." *Journal of English Literary History (ELH)* (March 1953), 20(1):300–314.

1955

"Benedetto Croce and the Recent Poetics of Organicism." *Comparative Literature* (Summer 1955), 7(3):252–258.

1956

The New Apologists for Poetry. Minneapolis: University of Minnesota Press, 1956; London: Oxford University Press, 1956.
   Translation into Spanish published by Centro Editores de America Latina, Buenos Aires.
" 'Dover Beach' and the Tragic Sense of Eternal Recurrence." *University of Kansas City Review* (Autumn 1956), 23(1):73–79.

1957

"Critical Theory, History and Sensibility." Review of *The History of Criticism, 1750–1950. Vol. 1: The Later Eighteenth Century, Vol. 2: The Romantic Age,* by René Wellek. *Western Review* (Winter 1957), 21(2):153–159.
Review of *Theories of Convention in Contemporary American Criticism,* by Robert M. Browne. *Modern Language Notes (MLN)* (November 1957), 72(7):551–553.

1958

"Tragedy and the Tragic Vision." *Kenyon Review* (Spring 1958), 20(2):281–299.
"Critical Dogma and the New Critical Historians." Review of *Literary Criticism,* by William K. Wimsatt, Jr. and Cleanth Brooks. *Sewanee Review* (January–March 1958), 66(1):161–177.

1959

"Conrad's *Youth:* A Naive Opening to Art and Life." *College English* (March 1959), 20(6):275–280.
"The Dark Generations of *Richard III.*" *Criticism* (Winter 1959), 1(1):32–48.

1960

The Tragic Vision: Variations on a Theme in Literary Interpretation. New York: Holt, Rinehart and Winston, 1960.
"Recent Criticism, 'Thematics,' and the Existential Dilemma." *Centennial Review of Arts and Sciences* (Winter 1960), 4(1):32–50.
   A condensed version of the final chapter of *The Tragic Vision* (1960).

1961

"Afterword." *Lord Jim,* by Joseph Conrad. New York: New American Library, 1961.

"Afterword." *The Marble Faun; or, The Romance of Monte Beni*, by Nathaniel Hawthorne. New York: New American Library, 1961.

"Contemporary Literary Criticism: Opening Remarks," by Murray Krieger; and "General Discussion on Contemporary Literary Criticism". In Hazard Adams, Bernard Duffey, et al., eds., *Approaches to the Study of Twentieth-Century Literature*, pp. 107–113, 144–122. (Proceedings of the Conference on the Study of Twentieth-Century Literature, First Session, May 2–4, 1961, Michigan State University.) East Lansing: Michigan State University Press, 1961.

"The 'Frail China Jar' and the Rude Hand of Chaos." *Centennial Review of Arts and Science*, (Spring 1961), 5(2):176–194.

Review of *The Epic Strain in the English Novel*, by E. M. W. Tillyard. *Journal of English and Germanic Philology* [JEGP] (April 1961), 60(2):311–314.

Review of *Irony in the Drama: An Essay on Impersonation, Shock, and Catharsis*, by Robert Boies Sharpe. *Journal of English and Germanic Philology* [JEGP] (July 1961), 60(3):550–552.

1962

"After the New Criticism." *Massachusetts Review* (Autumn 1962), 4(1):183–205.

"Contextualism Was Ambitious." *Journal of Aesthetics and Art Criticism* (Fall 1962), 21(1):81–88.

"Conrad's *Youth*: A Naive Opening to Art and Life." In Lee Steinmetz, ed., *Analyzing Literary Works: A Guide for College Students*, pp. 106–112. Evanston, Ill.: Row, Peterson, 1962.
    See above: "Conrad's *Youth*" (1959).

"Dostoevsky's *Idiot*: The Curse of Saintliness." In René Wellek, ed., *Dostoevsky: A Collection of Critical Essays*, pp. 39–52. Englewood Cliffs, N.J.: Prentice-Hall, 1962.
    See above: *The Tragic Vision* (1960), pp. 209–227.

Review of *Obsessive Images: Symbolism in Poetry of the 1930's and 1940's*, by Joseph Warren Beach. *Journal of English and Germanic Philology* (JEGP), (April 1962), 61(2):448–451.

Review of *The New Romantics: A Reappraisal of the New Criticism*, by Richard Foster. *Criticism* (Fall 1962), 4(4):369–372.

1963

The New Apologists for Poetry. Bloomington: Indiana University Press, 1963.
A paperback reprint of the edition published by the University of Minnesota Press in 1956. Includes a new preface.

"Every Critic His Own Platonist." *CEA Chap Book* (Supplement to the *CEA Critic* [December 1963], 26[3]:25–28).

"Tragedy and the Tragic Vision." In Laurence Anthony Michel and Richard Benson Sewall, eds., *Tragedy: Modern Essays in Criticism,* pp. 130–146. Englewood Cliffs, N.J.: Prentice-Hall, 1963.
See above: "Tragedy and the Tragic Vision" (1958), and *The Tragic Vision* (1960).

1964

A Window to Criticism: Shakespeare's "Sonnets" and Modern Poetics. Princeton, N.J.: Princeton University Press; London: Oxford University Press, 1964.

"Critical Historicism: The Poetic Context and the Existential Context." In Leon Edel, ed., *Literary History and Literary Criticism,* pp. 280–282. [Acta of the Ninth Congress, International Federation for Modern Languages & Literatures (FILLM), August 25–31, 1963, New York University]. New York: New York University Press, 1964.)

"The Poet and His Work—and the Role of Criticism." *College English,* (March 1964), 25(6):405–412.

1965

"Belief, Problem of," and "Meaning, Problem of." In Alex Preminger, ed., *Encyclopedia of Poetry and Poetics,* pp. 74–76, and 475–479. Princeton, N.J.: Princeton University Press, 1965.

"Contextualism and the Relegation of Rhetoric." In Donald Cross Bryant, ed., *Papers in Rhetoric and Poetic,* pp. 46–58. (Conference on Rhetoric and Poetic, November 12–13, 1964, University of Iowa.) Iowa City: University of Iowa Press, 1965.

"The Discipline of Literary Criticism." In John C. Gerber, ed., *The College Teaching of English*, pp. 178–197. New York: Appleton-Century-Crofts, 1965.

"Tragedy and the Tragic Vision." In Robert W. Corrigan, ed., *Tragedy: Vision and Form*, pp. 19–33. San Francisco: Chandler, 1965.

See above: "Tragedy and the Tragic Vision" (1958), and *The Tragic Vision* (1960).

1966

The Tragic Vision: Variations on a Theme in Literary Interpretation. Chicago & London: University of Chicago Press, 1966.

A paperback reprint of the edition published in New York by Holt, Rinehart and Winston in 1960.

Editor. *Northrop Frye in Modern Criticism.* (Selected papers from the English Institute, September 7–10, 1965.) New York & London: Columbia University Press, 1966.

Includes an introductory essay by Krieger, "Northrop Frye and Contemporary Criticism: Ariel and the Spirit of Gravity."

"Critical Historicism: The Poetic Context and the Existential Context." *Orbis Litterarum* (1966), 21(1):49–60.

A revised and expanded version of paper delivered at the 9th Congress of FIILM at New York University in August 1963.

See above: "Critical Historicism" (1964).

"The Existential Basis of Contextual Criticism." *Criticism* (Fall 1966), 8(4):305–317.

"*Measure for Measure* and Elizabethan Comedy." In Rolf Soellner and Samuel Bertsche, eds., *Measure for Measure: Text, Source, and Criticism*, pp. 91–99. Boston: Houghton Mifflin, 1966.

See above: "*Measure for Measure*" (1951).

"Tragedy and the Tragic Vision." *Midway*, No. 27 (Summer 1966), pp. 2–25.

See above: "Tragedy and the Tragic Vision" (1958), and *The Tragic Vision* (1960).

1967

The Play and Place of Criticism. Baltimore: John Hopkins University Press; London: Oxford University Press, 1967.

A volume of collected essays reprinted—occasionally in original form, sometimes slightly revised, sometimes considerably rewritten or supplemented. The essay "The Innocent Insinuations of Wit: The Strategy of Language in Shakespeare's *Sonnets*" appears here for the first time.

Contents:
1. The Play and Place of Criticism.
2. The Innocent Insinuations of Wit: The Strategy of Language in Shakespeare's *Sonnets*.
3. The Dark Generations of *Richard III*.
4. The "Frail China Jar" and the Rude Hand of Chaos.
5. "Dover Beach" and the Tragic Sense of Eternal Recurrence.
6. *The Marble Faun* and the International Theme.
7. From *Youth* to *Lord Jim*: The Formal-Thematic Use of Marlow.
8. The Ekphrastic Principle and the Still Movement of Poetry; or, *Laokoön* Revisited.
9. The Disciplines of Literary Criticism.
10. Joseph Warren Beach's Modest Appraisal.
11. Contextualism Was Ambitious.
12. Contextualism and the Religion of Rhetoric.
13. Criticial Dogma and the New Critical Historians.
14. Platonism, Manichaeism, and the Resolution of Tension: A Dialogue.
15. Northrop Frye and Contemporary Criticism: Ariel and the Spirit of Gravity.
16. The Existential Basis of Contextual Criticism.

"*Ekphrasis* and the Still Movement of Poetry; or, *Laokoön* Revisited." In Frederick P.W. McDowell, ed., *The Poet as Critic*, pp. 3–26. (Conference on Poet as Critic, October 28–30, 1965, Iowa Center for Modern Letters, University of Iowa.) Evanston, Ill.: Northwestern University Press, 1967.

1968

"*Bleak House* and *The Trial*." In Jacob Korg, ed., *Twentieth Century Interpretations of Bleak House: A Collection of Critical Essays*, pp. 103–5. Englewood Cliffs, N.J.: Prentice-Hall, 1968.
    See above: *The Tragic Vision* (1960), pp. 138–140.

"Conrad's *Youth:* A Naive Opening to Art and Life." In Michael
Timko and Clinton F. Oliver, eds., *38 Short Stories: An Introductory Anthology,* pp. 49–57. New York: Knopf, 1968.
    See above: "Conrad's *Youth*" (1959).
"The Continuing Need for Criticism." *Concerning Poetry* (Spring
1968), 1(1):7–21.
"*Ekphrasis* and the Still Movement of Poetry; or, *Laokoön* Revisited." In James Calderwood and Harold E. Toliver, eds., *Perspectives on Poetry,* pp. 323–348. New York: Oxford University Press,
1968.
    See above: "*Ekphrasis* and the Still Movement of Poetry"
(1967), and *The Play and Place of Criticism* (1967), no. 8.
"The 'Frail China Jar' and the Rude Hand of Chaos." In Maynard
Mack, ed., *Essential Articles for the Study of Alexander Pope,* pp.
301–319. Revised and enlarged edition. Hamden, Conn.: Archon
Books; London: Macmillan, 1968.
    See above: "The 'Frail China Jar' " (1961), and *The Play and
Place of Criticism* (1967), no. 4.
"Jacopo Mazzoni, Repository of Divine Criticial Traditions or
Source of a New One?" In Rosario P. Armato and John M. Spalek,
eds., *Medieval Epic to the "Epic Theater" of Brecht: Essays in
Comparative Literature,* pp. 97–107. (First Comparative Litera-
ture Conference, July 6–7, 1967, University of Southern Califor-
nia.) Los Angeles: University of Southern California Press, 1968.
"Literary Analysis and Evaluation—and the Ambidextrous Critic."
Contemporary Literature (Summer 1968), 9(3):290–310.
    Revised version of this essay appears in L. S. Dembo, ed., *Criti-
cism: Speculative and Analytical Essays,* pp. 16–36. Madison:
University of Wisconsin Press, 1968.
"The Varieties of Extremity: *Lord Jim.*" In Norman Sherry and
Thomas C. Moser, eds., *"Lord Jim": An Authoritative Text,* pp.
437–447. New York: Norton, 1968.

1969

"The Critical Legacy of Matthew Arnold; or, the Strange Brotherhood of T. S. Eliot, I. A. Richards, and Northrop Frye." *Southern
Review,* N.S. (Spring 1969), 5(2):457–474.

"*Eloisa to Abelard:* The Escape from Body or the Embrace of Body." *Eighteenth-Century Studies* (Fall 1969), 3(1):28–47.
"Mediation, Language, and Vision in the Reading of Literature." In Charles S. Singleton, ed., *Interpretation: Theory and Practice*, pp. 211–242. Baltimore: Johns Hopkins University Press, 1969.

1970

(With Allen Tate). "American Criticism, Recent." In Joseph T. Shipley, ed., *Dictionary of World Literary Terms*, pp. 371–374. Revised and enlarged edition. Boston: Writer, 1970.
"The Dark Generations of *Richard III*." In Melvyn D. Faber, ed., *The Design Within: Psychoanalytic Approaches to Shakespeare*, pp. 347–366. New York: Science House, 1970.
  See above: "The Dark Generations of *Richard III*" (1959), and *The Play and Place of Criticism* (1967), no. 3.
" 'Dover Beach' and the Tragic Sense of Eternal Recurrence." In Jonathan Middlebrook, ed., *Matthew Arnold: "Dover Beach,"* pp. 15–23. Columbus, Ohio: Merrill, 1970.
  See above: " 'Dover Beach' " (1956), and *The Play and Place of Criticism* (1967), no. 5.
"The 'Frail China Jar' and the Rude Hand of Chaos." In John Dixon Hunt, ed., *Pope: "The Rape of the Lock,"* A Casebook, pp. 201–219. Nashville: Aurora Publishers, 1970.
  See above: "The 'Frail China Jar' " (1961), and *The Play and Place of Criticism* (1967), no. 4.
"The Innocent Insinuations of Wit: The Strategy of Language in Shakespeare's *Sonnets*." In James L. Calderwood and Harold E. Toliver, eds., *Essays in Shakesperean Criticism*, pp. 101–117. Englewood Cliffs, N.J.: Prentice-Hall, 1970.
  See above: *The Play and Place of Criticism* (1967), no. 2.
"The Meaning of Ishmael's Survival." In Herschel Parker and Harrison Hayford, eds., *Moby-Dick as Doubloon: Essays and Extracts, 1851–1970*, pp. 270–271. New York: Norton, 1970.
"*Measure for Measure* and Elizabethan Comedy." In George L. Geckle, ed., *Twentieth Century Interpretations of Measure for Measure: A Collection of Critical Essays*, pp. 104–106. Englewood Cliffs, N.J.: Prentice-Hall, 1970.
  See above: "*Measure for Measure*" (1951).

"Murder in the Cathedral: The Limits of Drama and the Freedom of Vision." In Melvin J. Friedman and John B. Vickery, eds., *The Shaken Realist: Essays in Modern Literature in Honor of Frederick J. Hoffman*, pp. 72–79. Baton Rouge: Louisiana State University Press, 1970.

"The State and Future of Criticism: The Continuing Need for Criticism." In Brom Weber, ed., *Sense and Sensibility in Twentieth-Century Writing: A Gathering in Memory of William Van O'Connor*, pp. 1–15. Carbondale & Edwardsville: Southern Illinois University Press; London: Feffer & Simons, 1970.

Revised version of "The Continuing Need for Criticism" (1968).

1971

The Classic Vision: The Retreat from Extremity in Modern Literature. Baltimore & London: Johns Hopkins University Press, 1971.

"The Existential Basis of Contextual Criticism." In Hazard Adams, ed., *Critical Theory Since Plato*, pp. 1224–1231. New York: Harcourt Brace Jovanovich, 1971.

See above: "The Existential Basis of Contextual Criticism" (1966), and *The Play and Place of Criticism* (1967), no. 16.

"Fiction, Nature, and Literary Kinds in Johnson's Criticism of Shakespeare." *Eighteenth-Century Studies* (Winter 1971), 4(2):184–198.

"Mediation, Language, and Vision in the Reading of Literature." In Hazard Adams, ed., *Critical Theory Since Plato*, pp. 1231–1249. New York: Harcourt Brace Jovanovich, 1971.

See above: "Mediation, Language, and Vision" (1969).

"Reply to Robert Kalmey." *Eighteenth-Century Studies* (Winter 1971–1972), 5(2):318–320.

Reply to Robert Kalmey's "Rhetoric, Language, and Structure in *Eloisa to Abelard*," *Eighteenth-Century Studies* (Winter 1971–1972), 5(2):315–318, which comments on Krieger's "*Eloisa to Abelard*: The Escape from Body or the Embrace of Body" (1969).

"Tragedy and the Tragic Vision." In Robert W. Corrigan, ed., *Tragedy: A Critical Anthology*, pp. 762–775. New York: Houghton Mifflin, 1971.

See above: "Tragedy and the Tragic Vision" (1958), and *The Tragic Vision* (1960).

"Die Tragodie und die Tragische Sehweise." In Volkmar Sander, ed., *Tragik und Tragodie*, pp. 279–302. Darmstadt: Wissenchaftliche Buchgesellschaft, 1971.
German translation of "Tragedy and the Tragic Vision" (1958).

1972

Review of *The Possibility of Criticism*, by Monroe C. Beardsley. *English Language Notes* (September 1972), 10(1):75–77.

1973

Visions of Extremity in Modern Literature. Vol. 1, *The Tragic Vision: The Confrontation of Extremity;* vol. 2, *The Classic Vision: The Retreat from Extremity*. Baltimore & London: Johns Hopkins University Press, 1973.
Paperback reprints of *The Tragic Vision: Variations on a Theme in Literary Interpretation* published in New York by Holt, Rinehart and Winston in 1960, and *The Classic Vision: The Retreat from Extremity in Modern Literature* published in New York and London by the Johns Hopkins University Press in 1971.
Includes a new "Preface" by Krieger (vol. 1, pp. vii–xvi).
"The Critic as Person and Persona." In Joseph P. Strelka, ed., *The Personality of the Critic*, pp. 70–92. (*Yearbook of Comparative Criticism*, vol. 3.) University Park: Pennsylvania State University Press, 1973.
" 'Dover Beach' and the Tragic Sense of Eternal Recurrence." In Jacqueline E. M. Latham, ed., *Critics on Matthew Arnold: Readings in Literary Criticism*, pp. 40–47. London: George Allen and Unwin, 1973.
See above: " 'Dover Beach' " (1956), and *The Play and Place of Criticism* (1967), no. 5.
"Introduction." *The Editor as Critic and the Critic as Editor*, pp. iii–vi. (Papers read by J. Max Patrick and Alan Roper at a Clark Library Seminar, November 13, 1971.) Los Angeles: William Andrews Clark Memorial Library, UCLA, 1973.
"Mediation, Language, and Vision in the Reading of Literature." In Gregory T. Polletta, ed., *Issues in Contemporary Literary Criticism*, pp. 585–613. Boston: Little, Brown, 1973.
See above: "Mediation, Language, and Vision" (1969).

1974

"Contextualism." In Alex Preminger, ed., *Princeton Encyclopedia of Poetry and Poetics,* pp. 929–930. Revised and enlarged edition. Princeton, N.J.: Princeton University Press, 1974.

"Fiction and Historical Reality: The Hourglass and the Sands of Time." In *Literature and History,* pp. 43–77. (Paper read at a Clark Library Seminar, March 3, 1973.) Los Angeles: William Andrews Clark Memorial Library, UCLA, 1974.

"Fiction, History, and Empirical Reality." *Critical Inquiry* (December 1974), 1(2):335–360.

A quite different version of this paper was delivered at the Clark Library Seminar on Literature and History, March 3, 1973, with the title "Fiction and Historical Reality."

"Geoffrey Hartman." Review of *Beyond Formalism: Literary Essays, 1958–1970,* by Geoffrey H. Hartman. *Contemporary Literature* (Winter 1974), 15(1):141–144.

" 'Humanist Misgivings about the Theory of Rational Choice': Comments on David Braybrooke," "Literature, Vision, and the Dilemmas of Practical Choice," "Preliminary Remarks to the Discussion of My Paper," and "A During-the-Colloquium Playful Postscript; or, a Satisfaction." In Max Black, ed., *Problems of Choice and Decision,* pp. 53–67, 398–431, 441–448, and 575–586. (Proceedings of a Colloquium co-sponsored by Cornell University Program on Science, Technology, and Society, and Aspen Institute for Humanistic Studies, June 24–26, 1974, Aspen Colorado.) Ithaca, N.Y.: Cornell University Program on Science, Technology and Society, 1975.

1976

Theory of Criticism: A Tradition and Its System. Baltimore & London: Johns Hopkins University Press, 1976.

"Introduction: A Scorecard for the Critics." *Contemporary Literature* (Summer 1976), 17(3):297–326.

"Poetics Reconstructed: The Presence vs. the Absence of the Word." *New Literary History* (Winter 1976), 7(2):347–375. A considerably reduced version of the final chapters of *Theory of Criticism* (1976).

"Reconsideration—The New Critics." *The New Republic* (October 2, 1976), 175(14):32–34.
"Shakespeare and the Critic's Idolatry of the Word." In G. Blakemore Evans, ed., *Shakespeare: Aspects of Influence*, pp. 193–210. (*Harvard English Studies*, vol. 7.) Cambridge, Mass. & London: Harvard University Press, 1976.
"The Theoretical Contributions of Eliseo Vivas." In Henry Regnery, ed., *Viva Vivas! Essays in Honor of Eliseo Vivas, on the Occasion of his Seventy-Fifth Birthday, July 13, 1976*, pp. 37–63. Indianapolis: Liberty Press, 1976.

1977

The New Apologists for Poetry. Westport, Conn.: Greenwood Press, 1977.
    Reprint of the 1956 edition published by the University of Minnesota Press.
Theory of Criticism: A Tradition and Its System. Baltimore: Johns Hopkins University Press, 1977.
    A paperback reprint of the edition published by the Johns Hopkins University Press in 1976.
Editor (with L. S. Dembo). *Directions for Criticism: Structuralism and Its Alternatives*. Madison: University of Wisconsin Press, 1977.
    Murray Krieger's opening essay "Introduction: A Scorecard for the Critics" (pp. 3–32), with the other articles in this volume, appeared originally in *Contemporary Literature*, vol. 17, no. 3 (Summer 1976).
    See above: "Introduction: A Scorecard for the Critics" (1976).

1978

"Literature as Illusion, as Metaphor, as Vision." In Paul Hernadi, ed., *What Is Literature?* pp. 178–189. Bloomington: Indiana University Press, 1978.
"Theories about Theories about *Theory of Criticism*." *Bulletin of the Midwest Modern Language Association* (Spring 1978), 11(1):30–42.

"Truth and Troth, Fact and Faith: Accuracy to the World and Fidelity to Vision." *Journal of Comparative Literature and Aesthetics* (Vishvanatha Kaviraja Inst., Orissa, India) (1978), 1(2):51–58.

"Truth and Troth, Fact and Faith: Accuracy to the World and Fidelity to Vision." *Literary Magazine* (Irvine), December 1978, pp. 3–5.

1979

Poetic Presence and Illusion: Essays in Critical History and Theory. Baltimore & London: Johns Hopkins University Press, 1979.

Contents:
1. Poetic Presence and Illusion I: Renaissance Theory and the Duplicity of Metaphor.
2. Jacopo Mazzoni, Repository of Diverse Critical Traditions or Source of a New One?
3. Shakespeare and the Critic's Idolatry of the Word.
4. Fiction, Nature, and Literary Kinds in Johnson's Criticism of Shakespeare.
5. "Trying Experiments upon Our Sensibility": The Art of Dogma and Doubt in Eighteenth-Century Literature.
6. The Critical Legacy of Matthew Arnold; or, The Strange Brotherhood of T. S. Eliot, I. A. Richards, and Northrop Frye.
7. Reconsideration—The New Critics.
8. The Theoretical Contributions of Eliseo Vivas.
9. *The Tragic Vision* Twenty Years After.
10. Poetic Presence and Illusion II: Formalist Theory and the Duplicity of Metaphor.
11. Literature vs. *Ecriture*: Constructions and Deconstructions in Recent Critical Theory.
12. Literature as Illusion, as Metaphor, as Vision.
13. Theories about Theories about *Theory of Criticism*.
14. A Scorecard for the Critics.
15. Literature, Criticism, and Decision Theory.
16. Mediation, Language, and Vision in the Reading of Literature.
17. Literary Analysis and Evaluation—and the Ambidextrous Critic.

Nos. 5 and 9 appear here for the first time.

"Literature vs. *Ecriture:* Constructions and Deconstructions in Recent Critical Theory." *Studies in the Literary Imagination* (Spring 1979), 12(1):1–17.

"Poetic Presence and Illusion I: Renaissance Theory and the Duplicity of Metaphor." *Critical Inquiry* (Summer 1979), 5(4):597–619.

"Poetic Presence and Illusion II: Formalist Theory and the Duplicity of Metaphor." *Boundary 2* (Fall 1979), 8(1):95–121.

   For diagrams inadvertently excluded from this article see "Errata," *Boundary 2* (Winter 1980), 8(2):367–368, and *Poetic Presence and Illusion* (1979), no. 10.

"The Recent Revolution in Theory and the Survival of the Literary Disciplines." In *The State of the Discipline, 1970s–1980s,* pp. 27–34. New York: Association of Departments of English, 1979.

   A special issue of the *ADE* (Association of Departments of English) *Bulletin,* No. 62 (September–November 1979).

"Reply to Norman Friedman." *Comparative Literature Studies* (September 1979), 16(3):262–264.

   See review by Norman Friedman of *Theory of Criticism* (1976) in *Comparative Literature Studies* (June 1979), 16(2):165–167.

1981

Arts on the Level: The Fall of the Elite Object. Knoxville: University of Tennessee Press, 1981.

   Contents:
   1. The Precious Object: Fetish as Aesthetic.
   2. Literary Criticism: A Primary or Secondary Art?
   3. Art and Artifact in a Commodity Society.

"An Apology for Poetics." In Ira Konigsberg, ed., *American Criticism in the Post-Structuralist Age,* pp. 87–101. (*Michigan Studies in the Humanities,* vol. 4. Papers presented as part of a Symposium in Critical Theory, 1979–1980, University of Michigan.) Ann Arbor: University of Michigan Press, 1981.

"Criticism as a Secondary Art." In Paul Hernadi, ed., *What Is Criticism?* pp. 280–295. Bloomington: Indiana University Press, 1981.

   A condensed version of *Arts on the Level* (1981), no. 2.

"Tragedy and the Tragic Vision," and "The Tragic Vision Twenty

Years After." In Robert W. Corrigan, ed., *Tragedy: Vision and Form*, pp. 30–41, 42–46. New York: Harper & Row, 1981.

See above: "Tragedy and the Tragic Vision" (1958), *The Tragic Vision* (1960), and *Poetic Presence and Illusion* (1979), no. 9.

" 'A Waking Dream': The Symbolic Alternative to Allegory." In Morton W. Bloomfield, ed., *Allegory, Myth, and Symbol*, pp. 1–22. (*Harvard English Studies*, vol. 9.) Cambridge, Mass. & London: Harvard University Press, 1981.

1982

"The Arts and the Idea of Progress." In Gabriel A. Almond, Marvin Chodorow, and Roy Harvey Pearce, eds., *Progress and Its Discontents*, pp. 449–469. (Papers based on a conference sponsored by the Western Center of the American Academy of Arts and Sciences, February 1979, Palo Alto, Calif.) Berkeley, Los Angeles & London: University of California Press, 1982.

"Feodor Mikhailovich Dostoevski." In Laurie Lanzen Harries, ed., *Nineteenth-Century Literature Criticism*, 2:199. Detroit, Mich.: Gale Research, 1982.

See above: *The Tragic Vision* (1960).

"Poetic Presence and Illusion II: Formalist Theory and the Duplicity of Metaphor." In William V. Spanos, Paul A. Bove, and Daniel O'Hara, eds., *The Question of Textuality: Strategies in Reading Contemporary American Criticism*, pp. 95–121. Bloomington: Indiana University Press, 1982.

See above: "Poetic Presence and Illusion II" (1979), and *Poetic Presence and Illusion* (1979), no. 10.

"Presentation and Representation in the Renaissance Lyric: The Net of Words and the Escape of the Gods." In John D. Lyons and Stephen G. Nichols, eds., *Mimesis: From Mirror to Method, Augustine to Descartes*, pp. 110–131. Hanover, New Hampshire: University Press of New England, 1982.

"Theories about Theories about *Theory of Criticism*." In Paul Hernadi, ed., *The Horizon of Literature*, pp. 319–336. Lincoln: University of Nebraska Press, 1982.

See above: "Theories about Theories about *Theory of Criticism*" (1978), and *Poetic Presence and Illusion* (1979), no. 13.

Teoria Criticii: Traditie si sistem. Translation and preface by Radu

Surdulescu. Bucharest: Editura Univers, 1982. Romanian translation of *Theory of Criticism* (see above: *Theory of Criticism*, 1976).
Teorija Kritike. Preface by Nikola Koljevic, Svetozar M., Ignjacevic,
tr. Belgrade: Nolit, 1982. Serbo-Croatian translation of *Theory of
Criticism* (see above: *Theory of Criticism*, 1976).

1983

"A Matter of Distinction: An Interview." *New Orleans Review*
(Spring 1983), 10(1):48–62.
"Both Sides Now." *New Orleans Review* (Spring 1983), 10(1):18–
23.
"I. A. Richards." In Sharon R. Gunton, ed., *Contemporary Literary
Criticism*, vol. 24, pp. 391–392. Detroit, Michigan: Gale Research,
1983.
    See above: *The New Apologists for Poetry* (1956).
"In the Wake of Morality: The Thematic Underside of Recent The-
ory." *New Literary History* (Autumn 1983), 15(1):119–136.
"Literary Theory in the University: A Survey." *New Literary His-
tory* (Winter 1983), 14(2):432–433.
"Northrop Frye." In Sharon R. Gunton, ed., *Contemporary Literary
Criticism*, vol. 24, pp. 223–225. Detroit, Michigan: Gale Research,
1983.
    See above: "Northrop Frye and Contemporary Criticism"
(1966), and *The Play and Place of Criticism* (1967), no. 15.
"Orpheus *mit Gluck:* The Deceiving Gratifications of Presence."
Theatre Journal (October 1983), 35(3):295–305.
*Words about Words about Words: The "What" and "Why" of Liter-
ary Theory*. Irvine: University of California, Irvine, 1983. Distinguished Faculty Lecture presented February 24, 1983.

1984

"The Ambiguities of Representation and Illusion: An E. H. Gombrich Retrospective." *Critical Inquiry* (December 1984),
11(2):181–194.
"A Humanity within the Humanities: Literature Among the Discourses." *Journal of Literary Criticism* (Allahabad, India), vol. 1,
no. 1 (Summer 1984).

"The Literary Privilege of Evaluation." In Joseph P. Strelka, ed., *Literary Theory and Criticism in Honor of René Wellek*. New York: Peter Lang, 1984.

"Post-New-Critical Fashions in Theory." *Indian Journal of American Studies* (ASRC, Hyderabad, India) (July 1984), 14(2):189–206.

This is a revised version of remarks delivered at the American Studies Research Centre in Hyderabad, India on January 31, 1984.

"Words about Words about Words: Theory, Criticism, and the Literary Text." *Academe: Bulletin of AAUP*, (March–April 1984), 70(1):17–24.

The article is adapted from the Distinguished Faculty Lecture delivered at the University of California, Irvine on 24 February 1983.

See above: *Words about Words about Words* (1983).

To Be Published

Translation of "Literary Analysis and Evaluation—and the Ambidextrous Critic" (1968) into German to appear in Jurgen Schlaeger, ed., *Kritik in der Krise? Zur Funktion Literaturwissenchaft in der Moderne*.

See above: *Poetic Presence and Illusion* (1979), no. 17.

"Literature vs. Ecriture: Constructions and Deconstruction in Recent Criticism." In Victor A. Kramer, ed., *American Critics at Work: Examinations of Contemporary Literary Theory*, pp. 27–48. Troy, N.Y.: Whitston.

See above: *Poetic Presence and Illusion* (1979), no. 10.

"Optics and Aesthetic Perception: A Rebuttal." *Critical Inquiry*.

"Poetry as Art, Language as Aesthetic Medium." Douglas Bolling, ed., *Literature and the Arts*. (*Art and Philosophy*, vol. 2) New York: Haven Publications.

" 'Trying Experiments upon Our Sensibility': The Art of Dogma and Doubt in Eighteenth-Century Literature." In Alan Roper, ed., *Augustan Myths and Modern Readers*. Berkeley & Los Angeles: University of California Press.

See above: *Poetic Presence and Illusion* (1979), no. 5.

SELECTED STUDIES
OF MURRAY KRIEGER'S WORK

Free, William J. "Murray Krieger and the Place of Poetry," *Georgia Review* (Summer 1968), 22(2):236–46.

Graff, Gerald. *Poetic Statement and Critical Dogma*, pp. 15 n.28, 16, 19, 21–23, 75–76, 78, 90, 91 n.8, 103, 106–9, 139 n.4, 146, 180, 182. Evanston: Northwestern University Press, 1970.

Graff, Gerald. "Tongue-in-Cheek Humanism: A Response to Murray Krieger." *ADE Bulletin* (Fall 1981), 69:18–21.

Joseph, Terri B. "Murray Krieger as Pre- and Post-Deconstructionist." *New Orleans Review*, vol. 12, no. 4, forthcoming.

Kartiganer, Donald M. "The Criticism of Murray Krieger: The Expansions of Contextualism," *Boundary 2* (Spring 1974), 2(2):584–607.

Lentricchia, Frank. *After the New Criticism*, pp. xii–xiii, 16, 19, 29–30, 44, 64, 70, 158–59, 163, 169, 171, 184–85, 213–54, 268–69, 294, 336, 349–50. Chicago and London: University of Chicago Press, 1980.

Miller, David M. *The Net of Hephaestus: A Study of Modern Criticism and Metaphysical Metaphor*, pp. 16 n.10, 114–21, 155–57. The Hague and Paris: Mouton, 1971.

Morris, Wesley. "The Critic's Responsibility 'To' and 'For.' " *Western Humanities Review* (Summer 1977), 31(3):265–72.

Morris, Wesley. *Toward a New Historicism*, pp. 24, 50n, 116–18, 137, 150, 172, 187–209, 211, 215. Princeton: Princeton University Press, 1972.

Raaberg, Gwen. "Ekphrasis and the Temporal/Spatial Metaphor in Murray Krieger's Critical Theory." *New Orleans Review*, vol. 12, no. 4, forthcoming.

Webster, Grant. *The Republic of Letters: A History of Postwar American Literary Opinion*, pp. 24–25, 34–35, 37, 42, 64, 82, 118–119, 176–77,

190–20, 315 n.66, 325 n.3, 328 n.41, 354–55. Baltimore and London: Johns Hopkins University Press, 1979.

Weinsheimer, Joel. "On Going Home Again: New Criticism Revisited." *PTL: A Journal of Descriptive Poetics and Theory of Literature* (1977), 3:563–77.

Wimsatt, William K. *Day of the Leopards*, pp. xii, 183, 188–95, 203. London and New Haven: Yale University Press, 1976.

NOTES

1. Criticism As Quest: Murray Krieger and the Pursuit of Presence

1. "Criticism as a Secondary Art," in Paul Hernadi, ed., *What Is Criticism?* (Bloomington: Indiana University Press, 1981), p. 293.

2. Saving Poetry: Murray Krieger's Faith in Formalism

1. Krieger's first full consideration of deconstruction occurs in his *TC,* esp. part. 3. See my review in *Clio* (Spring 1978), 1(7):463–66.

2. Frank Lentricchia argues that Krieger fails to incorporate deconstruction and thus "he is swallowed by the theoreticians of deliberate triviality" (*ANC,* 242). See also Grant Webster, "Murray Krieger: The Unrevolutionized Critic," *The Republic of Letters: A History of Postwar American Literary Opinion* (Baltimore: Johns Hopkins University Press, 1979), pp. 190–202.

3. For a compact version of this article of faith about the "proper place" of criticism, see Krieger's "Criticism as a Secondary Art," in Paul Hernadi, ed., *What Is Criticism?* (Bloomington: Indiana University Press, 1981), pp. 280–95.

3. Both Sides Now

1. Even as I originally wrote these opening words for my oral performance upon the occasion of the MLA meeting, I anticipated how they would mock me when I read them (as you are now) as already written some time ago. For that very moment, during which, when speaking them myself, I was asserting my presence in them, is now well past, with only their ghostly reminder of their now absent author and his belated occasion left to contradict this cocky assertion of his presence. What

more impressive testimony could I muster of the illusionary nature of the assurances given us by *parole* as it fades into *écriture*? But illusion, after all, is what my poetics is all about.

2. I must seize this opportunity to remark, with special pleasure, Rose's perceptive observation about my use of "planet" rather than "sun" for the critic-satellite to revolve around. In searching my original composition notes, I find the word "sun" written but crossed out, and the word "planet" written over it and used. Next to it I find my scribbled comment to myself, "remember—this is no heliocentric theory!" So Rose's claim is utterly sensitive to my point. One cannot often expect so shrewdly sympathetic a commentator and must be grateful when he happens along.

4. Rereading Contextualism

1. Plato, Republic, book 10, in *The Dialogues of Plato*, Benjamin Jowett, tr., 4th ed. (Oxford: Clarendon Press, 1953), 2:468; hereafter abbreviated R and cited in parentheses.

2. Immanuel Kant, *Critique of Judgment*, J. H. Bernard, tr. (London: Macmillan, 1914), p. 69.

3. William K. Wimsatt, Jr. and Cleanth Brooks, *Literary Criticism: A Short History* (New York: Random House, 1957), p. 486.

4. Sigurd Burckhardt, "The Poet as Fool and Priest," ELH (1956), 23:279–98.

5. Paul de Man, "Sign and Symbol in Hegel's *Aesthetics*," *Critical Inquiry*, (1982), 8:761.

6. See Kenneth Burke, "Terministic Screens," in Burke, *Language as Symbolic Action: Essays in Literature, Life, and Method* (Berkeley: University of California Press, 1966), pp. 44–62.

7. Joel Weinsheimer, "On Going Home Again: New Criticism Revisited," *PTL: A Journal for Descriptive Poetics and Theory of Literature* (1977), 3:577.

8. Wayne Booth, "*The Rhetoric of Fiction*" (Chicago: University of Chicago Press, 1961), p. 75.

9. Krieger tells us that he has "been underlining the *ifs* to accentuate the hypothetical nature of the propositions I have been suggesting" (TC, 20).

10. Murray Krieger, ed., *Northrop Frye in Modern Criticism: Selected Papers from the English Institute* (New York: Columbia University Press, 1966), p. 5.

11. See Rosalie Colie, *The Resources of Kind: Genre-Theory in the Renaissance*, Barbara K. Lewalski, ed. (Berkeley: University of California Press, 1966); also E. H. Gombrich, *Art and Illusion: A Study in the Psychology of Pictorial Representation* (Princeton: Princeton University Press, 1960), 99; hereafter abbr. AI.

12. Cleanth Brooks, *The Well Wrought Urn: Studies in the Structure of Poetry* (New York: Harcourt, Brace & World, 1947), p. 10. Distorted bowls were introduced into the game in the sixteenth century. The protrusion on one side, called the "bias," analogizes with the enabling imperfection of the representational medium. While the green, which analogizes with the representational ground, was itself not free from distortions, called *rubs* by the players, Shakespeare and Brooks alike are alluding to distortion not in the ground but in the instrument of play.

13. Murray Krieger, "Contextualism," in Alex Preminger, ed., *Princeton Encyclopedia of Poetry and Poetics* (Princeton: Princeton University Press, 1974), p. 930; hereafter abbreviated "C" and cited in parentheses.

14. For one among many examples of such "coercion" see J. Hillis Miller, "Theory and Practice: Response to Vincent Leitch," *Critical Inquiry* (1980), 6:611: "the readings of deconstructive criticism are not the willful imposition by a subjectivity of theory on the texts but are coerced by the texts themselves."

15. Stanley Fish, *Is There a Text in This Class?: The Authority of Interpretive Communities* (Cambridge, Mass: Harvard University Press, 1980), pp. 269–92.

16. See Hans Vaihinger, *The Philosophy of "As If": A System of Theoretical, Practical and Religious Fictions of Mankind*, C. K. Ogden, tr. (London: Routledge & Kegan Paul, 1924), p. 99; hereafter abbreviated P and cited in parentheses.

17. See Krieger's analysis of the difference between his use of opposites and Hegel's in *CV*, 24–27.

18. Sir Philip Sidney, "An Apologie for Poetry," in Hazard Adams, ed., *Critical Theory Since Plato* (New York: Harcourt Brace Jovanovich, 1971), p. 168.

19. For a thoroughgoing analysis of the ocular theory of knowledge see Richard Rorty, *Philosophy and the Mirror of Nature* (Princeton: Princeton University Press, 1979). See also Paul de Man, "The Epistemology of Metaphor," *Criticial Inquiry* (1978), 5:13–30.

20. See Aristotle, *Poetics*, in Adams, *Critical Theory Since Plato*, p. 54. For an argument connecting teleological plot and moral value see Hayden White, "The Value of Narrativity in the Representation of Reality," *Critical Inquiry* (1980), 7:5–27. Krieger's "theoretical" statements are typically elaborated by their "practice," but for one example of "theoretical practice" see *A Window to Criticism*. Krieger takes as his primary premise the "mirror-window metaphor," using it "to perform for the *Sonnets* the sort of service William Butler Yeats performed for his poems in writing *A Vision*" (*WC*, 73).

21. Percy Bysshe Shelley, "A Defense of Poetry," in Adams, *Critical Theory Since Plato*, p. 503.

22. Stephen Booth, *An Essay on Shakespeare's Sonnets* (New Haven: Yale University Press, 1969), p. 1.

23. Samuel Taylor Coleridge, "On the Principles of Genial Criticism," in J. Shawcross, ed., *Biographia Literaria* (Oxford: Oxford University Press, 1973), 2:239. For Krieger's radical reading of Coleridge, in many ways analogous to my reading of Krieger, see "The Existential Basis of Contextual Criticism," *Criticism: A Quarterly for Literature and the Arts* (1966), 8:305–17; rpt. in Adams, *Critical Theory Since Plato*, pp. 1224–31.

5. Murray Krieger and the Impasse in Contextualist Poetics

1. René Wellek, "The Main Trends of Twentieth-Century Criticism," Stephen G. Nichols, Jr., ed., *Concepts of Criticism* (New Haven: Yale University Press, 1963), pp. 359, 364.

2. Grant Webster, *The Republic of Letters: A History of Postwar American Literary Opinion* (Baltimore: Johns Hopkins University Press, 1979), pp. 24, 190; hereafter abbreviated *TRL* and cited in parentheses.

3. Ernest Nagel and James R. Newman, *Goedel's Proof* (New York: New York University Press, 1958); also "Goedel's Proof, " in James R. Newman, ed. *The World of Mathematics* (New York: Simon & Schuster, 1956), vol. 3, 1668–95; hereafter abbreviated *TWM* and cited in parentheses.

4. Jacques Derrida, "Structure, Sign, and Play in the Discourse of the Human Sciences," in Richard Macksey and Eugenio Donato, eds., *The Structuralist Controversy: The Languages of Criticism and the Sciences of Man* (Baltimore: Johns Hopkins University Press, 1972), pp. 260–65. I am not suggesting a naive empiricism, but rather that philosophy and empiricism need not be in opposition. Cf. Jacques Derrida, *Of Grammatology*, Gayatri Spivak, tr. (Baltimore: Johns Hopkins University Press, 1976), p. 162. Theory, metaphor, and language itself are hypothetical views of the world, though we try to "rectify" them with the world insofar as possible. See also Derrida's "White Mythology" in *Margins of Philosophy*, Alan Bass, tr. (Chicago: University of Chicago Press, 1982), pp. 207–72.

5. See Murray Krieger, "Literary Analysis and Evaluation—and the Ambidextrous Critic" in *PPI*, pp. 303–22. See also *NAP*, pp. 150–53.

6. H. H. Price, "Clarity Is Not Enough," in Y. H. Krikorian and Abraham Edel, eds., *Contemporary Philosophical Problems: Selected Readings* (New York: Macmillan, 1959), pp. 268–81.

7. J. H. Van Vleck, "Quantum Mechanics," *Encyclopedia Britannica*, 1968 ed.; A. O. Williams, Jr., "Quantum Theory," *Encyclopedia Americana*, 1969 ed.; see Alistair I. M. Rae, *Quantum Mechanics* (New York: John Wiley & Sons, 1981) and Friedrich Hund, *The History of Quantum Theory*, Gordon Reece, tr. (New York: Harper & Row, 1974).

8. The kind of revolution needed is seen clearly by Derrida. In "White Mythology" he questions the use of philosophical language in its entirety and sees metaphysics as a white mythology which assembles and reflects Western culture alone. In short, he argues, a displacement and a rewriting of the meaning of science, of knowledge, and of truth is essential.

9. Harold H. Joachim, *The Nature of Truth* (Oxford: Clarendon Press, 1906), pp. 66–84.

10. P. F. Strawson, "Construction and Analysis," A. J. Ayer, et al., *The Revolution in Philosophy* (London: Macmillan, 1956), pp. 97–110.

11. See A. Heyting, *Intuitionism: An Introduction* (Amsterdam: North-Holland Publishing, 1956), p. 6; S. Koerner, *The Philosophy of Mathematics: An Introduction* (New York: Harper & Brothers, 1962), p. 128; Gilbert Ryle, *Dilemmas* (Cambridge: Cambridge University Press, 1954), pp. 111–20.

12. See the use of finite and infinite in Derrida, "Structure, Sign and Play," pp. 256–60. Derrida seems to see part of the danger of negative conceptual words such as ab-solute and in-finite in "White Mythology," and avoids the paradox of completed infinities in his concept of the supplement that never attains the status of a complement. At times, though, both Derrida and Aristotle seem to fall into the trap of thinking that "infinite" and "unlimited" mean the same thing, although something may unfold in an unlimited way without ever becoming a completed infinity in space/time. Sometimes Derrida sees supplements, substitutive significations, moving "to infinity"; other times he more correctly describes them as "indefinitely multiplied," as in *Of Grammatology*, pp. 159–63.

13. Andrew Parker, " 'Taking Sides' (On History): Derrida Re-Marx," *Diacritics* (Fall, 1981), 11:72–73.

14. Fredric Jameson, "Reflections in Conclusion," in Ernst Bloch, et al., *Aesthetics and Politics* (London: NLB, 1977), p. 213; quoted in "Taking Sides," 72–73.

6. Murray Krieger: A Departure Into Diachrony

1. I do not mean by this what Krieger usually terms the poem's "self-critical" structure; at least I do not intend only this. My point is not simply that the poem contains contradictions but that the contradictions are representations of social forces.

2. Krieger is aware of this new *Weltanschauung*, calling it a "skeptical" "post-Romantic" vision that demands an "arrogant humanism" (*TC*, 190).

3. See Herbert Marcuse on "Sartre's Existentialism" in *Studies in Criticial Philosophy*, Joris De Bres, tr. (London: NLB, 1972), particularly p. 188; abbr. *SCP*.

4. I have used the phrase "bourgeois society" in this essay even though Krieger does not, partly because I find it difficult to avoid reading Krieger's existentialism outside the context of Sartre's. Krieger here is talking about what we would call bad faith, but it is so generally distributed throughout society, as Krieger describes it, that a broader and more political term seemed called for. Krieger might resist politicizing his theory this way, but with due acknowledgment of this resistance, I am taking a different approach.

5. Eliseo Vivas, *Creation and Discovery* (New York: Gateway edition, 1965), p. 87.

6. Edward Said, *Beginnings: Intention and Method* (New York: Basic Books, 1975), p. 84.

7. Murray Krieger and the Question of History

1. See Wesley Morris' discusson of these versions of history in essay 6. Of course the notion of two conceptions of history is a simplification for present purposes. For a fuller discussion of the "economy" between writing and history in current theory, see Gregory S. Jay, "America the Scrivener: Economy and Literary History," *Diacritics* (Spring 1984), pp. 36–51.

2. Paul Ricoeur, *Freud and Philosophy: An Essay on Interpretation*, Denis Savage, tr. (New Haven and London: Yale University Press, 1970), pp. 28–36.

3. Murray Krieger, "In the Wake of Morality: The Thematic Underside of Recent Theory," *New Literary History* (1983–84) 15:133–34.

4. Murray Krieger, "Post-New-Critical Fashions in Theory," *Indian Journal of American Studies* (July 1984), 14(2):205. The accuracy of this characterization of suspicious reading might be considered in relation to Fredric Jameson's discussion of Kenneth Burke, a sophisticated analysis which shows that the "subtext" to which the literary work seems to respond is, for Burke, produced by the work itself. I have suggested that this is how "history" is produced for Krieger. See Fredric Jameson,

"The Symbolic Inference; or, Kenneth Burke and Ideological Analysis," *Critical Inquiry* (Spring 1978), 4(3):507–23.

5. Fredric Jameson, *The Political Unconscious* (Ithaca: Cornell University Press, 1981), p. 267.

6. It is tempting to think of these two Kriegers as having something like the uneasy relationship of the two prisoners in the Prisoner's Dilemma game that Krieger discusses in "Both Sides Now" in this volume and in "Literature, Criticism, and Decision Theory" in *PPI*, pp. 238–69.

7. Often to Krieger metaphor is itself a metaphor for the relationship between poem and world. Just as metaphor achieves its form only with the repression of the many differences between its two terms, so the poem achieves its form with the repression of the differences between it and the world of facticity to which it apparently refers. See the discussion of metaphoric duplicity in the Konstanz Colloquy.

8. Krieger uses the term "negative reference" in *AP*, 88ff. The concept of "negative reference" allows the critic to read the excluded text in a way not entirely unlike Jameson's reading of the subtext, and Krieger stresses his awareness of political and social exclusions in the Konstanz Colloquy. But the exclusions Krieger finds by negative reference seem always to harmonize with the inclusions—with the conscious text—according to a traditionally formalist aesthetic; they are not deconstructive as they are with more "suspicious" readers.

9. The mechanism of negative reference exists even more artfully in the description of the pouring of coffee, in which Krieger finds not only a repressed reference to the sex act, but also to the overpopulation of China. Here the simultaneous repression and ghostly echo of the real (a now-you-see-it-now-you-don't phenomenon) is a function of the structure of metaphor itself.

10. In the Konstanz Colloquy Krieger discusses history as textual discourse, revealing a newer Krieger than I have described. I have chosen to discuss moments of practical criticism which *enact* a stance toward history; Krieger's more recent statements have yet to inform a work of practical criticism.

11. Fredric Jameson, "Imaginary and Symbolic in Lacan: Marxism Psychoanalytic Criticism, and the Problem of the Subject," *Yale French Studies*, (1977), 55–56: 384.

12. Krieger's anticipations of other positions result from his continuing desire to exceed the limitations of a rigorous critical systematics—see James Huffman's analysis, essay 5. It is this continual exceeding that creates the effect of the "other" Krieger.

8. The Lure of the Text, or Uncle Toby's Revenge

1. In a review of *Theory of Criticism* (*MLN* [1976], 91:1634–38), Paul Miers said that "vestigal elements of New Criticism remain as excess baggage in Krieger's thought," and that "lacking concepts of intentionality and dialectic, he is constantly forced to pose his question in either/or terms" (1636). I believe these remarks are generally accurate, and I read Krieger's most recent works as an effort to overcome this problem. However, as I suggest below, it will take more than a theory of intentionality to reconcile Krieger's emphasis on the poem as *object* with the increasingly

phenomenological character of his poetics. Cf. Krieger's remarks on Miers' review in *PPI*, 201–2.

2. Cf. the "teasing elusiveness" of the poem (*TC*, 3), our "devotion" to works "which stand out there so nobly as objects to be admired" (*TC*, 16); our "idolatrous" attitude toward the poem (*TC*, 42) as a "beckoning entity" (*TC*, 46) and seductive "enrapturing" aesthetic object (*PPI*, 157; *TC*, 17), etc.

3. In "Literature versus Ecriture: Constructions and Deconstructions in Recent Criticial Theory," Krieger says that he is "wary of the grounds on which I dare claim verbal presence and fullness. And I am grateful for my recollection that the aesthetic domain—the domain of *aesthetics*, of *Schein*—has been, from Plato onward, acknowledged to be the world of appearance, of illusion, so that verbal power, under the conditions of the aesthetic, need not rely upon a metaphysical sanction to assert its moving presence" (*PPI*, 173; see also *AL*, 68–69). He adds in the same essay, "in the greatest literary works . . . those which, in other words, constitute the literary canon in the Western tradition, the illusion of an autonomous, self-generating reflexivity in language persists for those trained to read them appropriately (that is, in ways appropriate to our conventions for reading our elite literary works)" (*PPI*, 180).

4. The importance of Freud's discovery of the Oedipal struggle, Lacan says, is not that it revealed the truth of infantile sexuality or the existence of the unconscious, but that it "gives to the signifier/signified opposition the full extent of its implications: namely, that the signifier has an active function in determining certain effects in which the signifiable appears as submitting to its mark, by becoming through that passion the signified" (*E*, 284).

5. Jacques Lacan, "The Insistence of the Letter in the Unconscious," Jan Miel, tr. In Jacques Ehrmann, ed., *Structuralism*. (New York: Doubleday Anchor Books, 1970), p. 105; abbreviated as *IL*. Cf. the translation by Alan Sheridan in *Écrits*, "The Agency of the Letter . . ."

6. "The creative spark of the metaphor does not spring from the conjunction of two images, that is of two signifiers equally actualized. It springs from two signifiers one of which has taken the place of the other in the signifying chain, the hidden signifier then remaining present through its (metonymic) relation to the rest of the chain" (*IL*, 115).

7. See Anthony Wilden, *The Language of the Self* (Baltimore: The Johns Hopkins University Press, 1968), p. 168. Abbreviated as *LS*.

8. Lacan repeatedly associates death with the phallus, and frequently returns to Freud's *Beyond the Pleasure Principle* as a key text for the connection among death, language, and desire. He calls the phallus the third term in the binary Imaginary relation between self and other, and he also says that accession to the Symbolic is possible "only if a third term is supposed to be present in the Imaginary relationship itself: mortal reality, the death instinct" (*Ecrits*, 348; trans. *LS*, 146). So "when we wish to attain in the subject what was before the serial articulations of speech, and what is primordial to the birth of symbols, we find it in death" (*Ecrits*, 16). Compare the place of the phallus described by Jean Laplanche and Serge Leclaire in their Lacanian essay on the unconscious:

"The death-drive is that radical force, usually fixed and fixating, which surfaces in a catastrophic or ecstatic instant, at the point where the organic coherence of the subject in his body appears for what it is, unnamable or inexpressible, swoon or ecstasy, shouting its appeal for a word to veil and sustain it. Thus the death-drive surfaces without ever being seen. But we already perceive . . . that it constitutes the "bedrock," the foundation of the castration complex, . . . [and] it imperiously gives rise to the development and structuring of language."

("L'inconscient, une étude psychanalytique," in Laplanche and Leclaire, *L'inconscient,* VI Colloque de Bonneval (Paris: Desclée De Brouwer, 1966); Patrick Coleman, tr., *French Freud: Structural Studies in Psychoanalysis, YFS* (1972): 48:143–44.

    9. Anika Lemaire, *Jacques Lacan,* David Macey, tr. (Belgium, 1970; London: Routledge and Kegan Paul, 1977), p. 86. Cf. p. 246: "The absence of transcendence of the Oedipus places the subject under the regime of foreclosure or non-distinction between the symbol and the real."

    10. At the end of "Literature versus Ecriture: Constructions and Deconstructions in Recent Critical Theory" (1979; rpt. *PPI,* 169–87), Krieger mentions Geoffrey Hartman's effort to suggest a linguistic correlative for Lacan's specular image in the "specular name" that emerges through literature's unique "nominating" capacity (see Hartman, "Psychoanalysis: The French Connection," in G. Hartman, ed., *Psychoanalysis and the Question of the Text: Selected Essays from the English Institute, 1976–77* [Baltimore: The Johns Hopkins University Press, 1978]), and he associates it with the function of the mirror in Shakespeare's sonnets as described in *A Window to Criticism.* "The image of the mirror, as our double, seems to match our reality with its own, except that, as an illusion, it is without substance and not ourselves at all" (*PPI,* 186). But when in the next sentence he goes on to describe the necessary move from the mirror-stage of the poem to the "window" on the world that the poem must become, Krieger's theoretical language once again comes up short: "Further, I saw *the magical nature of glass* as permitting the unsubstantiality of the mirror image to open outward—through the mirror become window—onto a separate reality of its own" (*PPI,* 186, my italics).

    11. The note to this poem in M. H. Abrams, et al., eds., *The Norton Anthology of English Literature* (Fourth Edition [New York: W. W. Norton, 1979]) is instructive: "An adaptation of Petrarch, *Rime 190,* perhaps influenced by commentators on Petrarch, who said that *Noli me tangere quia Caesaris sum* ("Touch me not, for I am Caeser's") was inscribed on the collars of Caesar's hinds which were then set free and were presumably safe from hunters. Wyatt's sonnet is usually supposed to refer to Anne Boleyn, in whom Henry VIII became interested in 1526" (I, 466).

9. The Phenomenology of Spenserian Ekphrasis

    1. See Murray Krieger, " 'A Waking Dream': The Symbolic Alternative to Allegory." In *Allegory, Myth, and Symbol,* Morton W. Bloomfield, ed., Harvard English Studies, 9 (Cambridge: Harvard University Press, 1981), p. 22.

    2. Maurice Merleau-Ponty, *The Primacy of Perception and Other Essays on Phenomenological Psychology, the Philosophy of Art, History and Politics* (Evanston, Ill.: Northwestern University Press, 1964), p. 15.

    3. Edmund Spenser, *The Faerie Queene* (London: Oxford University Press, 1909), p. 365. See book 3, canto 2, stanza 17. (I have modernized the fonts.)

4. James Nohrnberg, *The Analogy of the Faerie Queene* (Princeton: Princeton University Press, 1976). "Besides the resemblances between Myrrha and Malecasta, there are resemblances between Myrrha and Britomart" (447). Earlier Nohrnberg brings in proximity the dependency upon the mirror and Glauce's speech to Britomart, "not so th' Arabian Myrrhe did set her mind" (442). Nohrnberg does not discuss the syllepsis on Mirrhour/Myrrha, and concentrates instead on the analogy of the female characters: Britomart, Malecasta, Florimell, in relation to Myrrha. Still, one has the impression Nohrnberg sees the connection, too, on page 442, since the rime of mirror/Myrrhe is so prominent.

5. See Roger Dorey, "La relation D'emprise" in *Nouvelle Revue de Psychanalyse* (Autumn 1981), no. 24.

6. See Jacques Lacan, "Le Stade du Miroir Comme Formateur de la Fonction du Je" in *Ecrits* (Paris: Seuil, 1966). The mirror stage mediates two narcissisms, that of the regressive self (ideal ego) which is at one with everything, experiencing what Freud called the "oceanic feeling" in *Civilization and Its Discontents*, and that of the ego ideal, that ideal self which we are not identical to but under whose scrutiny we measure ourselves and gain access to the superego. Lacan calls these relations part of the imaginary register, and it is here that Britomart plays out her role in book 3 of Spenser's *Faerie Queene*. This is not to say that the Law—the symbolic register—is foreclosed, however.

7. See Edmund Husserl, *Experience and Judgement* (Evanston, Ill.: Northwestern University Press, 1973):

"But actual givenness of the universal then requires that we pass beyond what is particular in the likenesses, eventually toward an open horizon of possible continuation. Whether the earlier cases are individually represented in addition does not matter. Thus it is evident that *the universal is not bound to any particular actuality*" (p. 329).

Also note Roman Ingarden, *The Literary Work of Art* (Evanston, Ill.: Northwestern University Press, 1973):

"What is in question here are not aspects that are experienced once and then lost for all time but certain *idealizations*, which are, so to speak, a *skeleton*, a *schema*, of concrete, flowing, transitory aspects. There are, in fact, no two concrete aspects of the same thing, perceived from the same side, experienced *successively* by one and the same conscious subject, which would be *completely similar in every respect*. Both their fully concrete contents and the manner in which they are experienced must always differ in varying degree. Meanwhile, when speaking of a regular affiliation of a given manifold of aspects to a given property of a thing, we assume the repeatability of the aspects in question. Thus it is clear that 1) if this regular affiliation is actually to exist, then what is at issue are not aspects taken in their full concreteness but only certain schemata, contained within them but still forming only a skeleton of them, which may remain as such despite the various differences that occur in the contents of the concrete aspects and in the manner of their experiencing; and 2) there really exists the idea of such schemata or schematized aspects" (pp. 262–63).

Ingarden's schematized aspects are, like Husserl's universal, always open to a "horizon of possible continuation." This does not mean that a work is open to infinite interpretations of all sorts, but that an interpretive structure or schematized aspect will limit the play of signification while at the same time making room for revisions and interpretive reconstructions.

8. André Gide, *Journal d'André Gide* 1889–1939 (Paris: Gallimard, 1948), p. 41.

9. Roland Barthes, *S/Z* (New York: Hill and Wang, 1974). The symbolic code is often a reflexive opposition which Barthes sometimes allies with the Lacanian law of the unconscious. Most interesting is Barthes' attempt to ally semiotics—much along Tartu School lines—with psychoanalysis, particularly in its specular or mirroring sense. The title *S/Z* and the ambiguous sexuality of La Zambinella make possible an investigation of a symbolic code in Balzac's *Sarrasine*—the work under analysis—which is reminiscent of a rather Gidean approach via *mise en abyme*.

10. Maurice Merleau-Ponty, *The Visible and the Invisible* (Evanston, Ill.: Northwestern University Press, 1968), p. 154.

11. Gilles Deleuze, *L'Image Mouvement* (Paris: Minuit, 1983), p. 13.

12. Murray Krieger, " 'A Waking Dream'," p. 21.

13. Murray Krieger, " 'A Waking Dream'," pp. 21–22.

14. See especially the German text in which Freud talks about Dora's subversion of the cure at that point when Freud is at the height of his powers:

"Es war ein unzweifelhafter Racheakt, dass sie in so unvermuteter Weise, als meine Erwartungen auf glückliche Beendigung der Kur den höchsten Stand einahmen, abbrach und diese Hoffnungen vernichtete. Auch ihre Tendenz zur Selbstschädigung fand ihre Rechnung bei diesem Vorgehen. Wer wie ich die bösesten Dämonen, die unvollkommen gebändigt in einer menschlichen Brust wohnen, aufweckt, um sie zu bekämpfen, muss darauf gefasst sein, dass er in diesem Ringen selbst nicht unbeschädigt belibe. Ob ich das Mädchen bei der Behandlung erhalten hätte, wenn ich mich selbst in eine Rolle gefunden, den Wert ihres Verbleibens für mich übertrieben und ihr ein warmes Interesse bezeigt hätte, das bei aller Milderung durch meine Stellung als Arzt doch wie ein Ersatz für die von ihr ersehnte Zärtlichkeit ausgefallen wäre? Ich weiss es nicht."

See Sigmund Freud, *Gesammelte Werke*, vol. 5 (London: Imago Publishing, 1942). The English translation in the *Standard Edition* loses the richness of what seems close to a rhetoric of knighthood in which the doctor as hero saves the lady in distress. He speaks of awakening the meanest or most evil demons which reside in the human breast, an awakening that forces the doctor to fight and to recognize that in this struggle the hero will not remain unharmed. But here Freud recognizes too that this "role" [*Rolle*] could have been played out in a much stronger way, and he wonders how therapeutic this game of knights and damsels might really be. "I don't know," he responds.

15. *Standard Edition of the Complete Psychological Works of Sigmund Freud*. 24 vols. James Strachey, tr. and ed. (London: Hogarth, 1953–1974), 7:120.

16. Luce Irigaray, *Speculum de l'autre femme* (Paris: Minuit, 1974). Irigaray sees hysteria as a way to deconstruct phallic mediations. She suggests Freud and Lacan can only represent woman in terms of the mirror that is male desire: phallogocentrism. It is in terms of this re-presentation of woman in the ambit of male desire that Irigaray posits a detotalizing notion of feminine desire or *jouissance* which refuses masculine and metaphysical closure. From a masculine or paternal order of mimetic conditions, woman is always already seen as Other, and Irigaray wishes to conduct her critique from this ex-centric margin of reflection. It is from this position that *mystère* leads to *hystère* as a critical tactic which disarticulates phallic relations between model/copy.

In Camille A. Paglio, "The Apollonian Androgyne and *The Faerie Queene*" in *English Literary Renaissance,* Winter 1979, 9(1):42–63, we find an approach somewhat similar to Irigaray's. Paglio argues that "Arthegall must be tempered from his extreme of brutish masculinity to become, in essence, more androgynous" (52). Again, "in *The Faerie Queene* the combatants are almost mathematical in their abstraction. The male body here is armored and invisible; it exists as a torpid, substantial instrument of force, without aesthetic dimension" (57). Paglio's analysis stresses the heterogeneous sexual aspects of Britomart, Belphoebe, and Malecasta, for example, stressing the idea of homoeroticism in books 3 and 4 which she believes facilitates an androgynous sexual balance which is aesthetically and morally just. "In Spenser, formlessness is amoral," she writes, "the boundaries of form must never be wantonly trespassed" (42). What has to be curbed in Paglio's estimation is the phallogocentric mentality of the male agencies in the narratives. As in Irigaray, Paglio wants to break with a mirror of representation that is predicated on a wholly male notion of desire. It is in this sense that she positively valorizes female homosexuality.

"Though in this scene Britomart, turning in bed to encounter an intruder, leaps to her feet enraged, Spenser does not deny her some small measure of Lesbianism, if that is not too strong a word, for she later customarily kisses and embraces Amoret and innocently sleeps with her (iv.i.49) and in loyally refusing to take the false Florimell as her paramour, she treats 'her owne Amoret' (i.v.v.20) as if she were actually Amoret's male champion." (51)

Lesbianism is not a perversion here, but rather a part of a feminine sexual economy which works against phallocentricism and thus achieves a heterogeneous sexual equilibrium whose bisexual valences are harmoniously or aesthetically balanced. Hence, Paglio refers to an androgynous Apollo.

Where I have difficulty with Paglio's account is in her early premise that "the armor worn by many of Spenser's virtuous characters in their testing and self-purgation is part of a system of imagery which conceives of personality as discrete and indissoluble, cohesive and luminous" (42). I think that rather than contribute to an aesthetically balanced notion of gender and sexuality, or to a "cohesive" notion of personality, the kind of heterogeneous female sexuality Paglio describes would be much closer to Irigaray's perception of an hysterical formation of consciousness which breaks with the logocentric kind of representational model Paglio finally allows her analysis to engage. I would say that our brief study of ekphrasis in Spenser would show that the system of imagery disarticulates personality as that which is discrete and indissoluble. That is, even here the fetish of the phallus is deconstituted.

17. See my "The Disarticulated Image: Gazing in Wonderland," *Enclitic,* vol. 6, no. 2, 1982.

10. After the Tragic Vision: Krieger and Lentricchia, Criticism and Crisis

1. Soon after the publication of *After the New Criticism,* Lentricchia accepted a chair in the Humanities at Rice University and has subsequently moved to Duke University.

2. See especially de Man's essay on Derrida, "The Rhetoric of Blindness," in

Blindness and Insight: Essays in the Rhetoric of Contemporary Criticism (New York: Oxford University Press, 1971.)

3. Krieger's essay appears in PPI.

4. These essays are collected in Stanley Fish, Is There A Text In This Class?: The Authority of Interpretive Communities (Cambridge: Harvard University Press, 1980). A battle against "essentialism" is pervasively (and persuasively) waged in these pages. There is, as Fish is fond of putting it, always an essence, a substantive core of truth, meaning, and value, but it is never the same one.

5. From his earliest essays on the romantic image and on the rhetoric of temporality to his final work, de Man's constant theme was the critical power of literature—of the texts that we have chosen to treat as cultural monuments.

6. Abrams says that "literary theory has been maneuvered into a defensive stance from which it has never entirely recovered. Alone among the major disciplines, the theory of literature has been mainly a branch of apologetics." See his Literature and Belief (New York: Columbia University Press, 1958), p. 2.

7. For example, Krieger writes that de Man rejects "the humanistic claim about poetry's unique power, seeing it as a mystification" (see PPI, 172–74).

8. Krieger may be regarded from this latter perspective as the last organicist, the only one who carries the organicist project to the end. But organicism, then, would have to retain the initial formulation Krieger gives it—as a refutation of formalism and as a way of making art responsive to the "phenomenological data of moral experience." In light of this position it is a telling irony that Lentricchia views Krieger as failing "to earn his ethical spurs."

9. Lentricchia's title is also discussed by Gregory S. Jay, "Going After New Critics: Literature, History, Deconstruction," New Orleans Review, (1981), 8:3 251–64.

INDEX